Initial Teacher Training and the Role of the School

V.J. Furlong, P.H. Hirst, K. Pocklington and S. Miles

with the assistance of M. Wilkin and S. Willcocks

Open University Press
Milton Keynes · Philadelphia

Open University Press
Open University Educational Enterprises Limited
12 Cofferidge Close
Stony Stratford
Milton Keynes MK11 1BY

and

242 Cherry Street
Philadelphia, PA 19106, USA

First Published 1988

British Library Cataloguing in Publication Data
Furlong, V.J. (V. John)
  Initial teacher training and the role of the school.
  1. Great Britain. Teachers. Professional education
  I. Title
  370′.7′10941
  ISBN 0–335–15618–5
  ISBN 0–335–15849–8 Pbk

131575

Library of Congress Cataloging-in-Publication Data
Initial teacher training and the role of the school / by V.J. Furlong
  . . . [et al.] with the assistance of M. Wilkin and S. Willcocks.
  p.   cm.
  1. Student teaching——England——Case studies. 2. Teachers——
  Training of——England——Case studies. I. Furlong, V.J.
  LB2157.G7155   1988
  370′.7′330942——dc19   88–12410 CIP
ISBN 0–335–15618–5
ISBN 0–335–15849–8 (pbk)

Typeset by Colset (Pte) Ltd, Singapore
Printed in Great Britain by St Edmundsbury Press, Bury St Edmunds

Contents

Initial Teacher Training
the Role of the School

Acknowledgements

The research on which this book is based derives from a Department of Education and Science funded project entitled *School-Based Training in the PGCE*. We would like to record our sincere thanks to the many teachers, students, lecturers and others associated with the Post Graduate Certificate of Education courses at the University of Leicester (Northampton Annexe), Leeds Polytechnic, University of Sussex and Roehampton Institute of Higher Education who so generously gave of their time during our research. Without their willing co-operation there would have been no project. We would also like to record our thanks to members of the research project Steering Committee and to colleagues in the Department of Education at Cambridge for their support and interest in all stages of the project. Finally, on behalf of the University of Cambridge Department of Education we gratefully acknowledge the financial support for the project provided by the Department of Education and Science.

1 Background to the Project

Introduction

Initial teacher training of all qualified teachers should include studies closely linked with practical experience in school, and involve the active participation of experienced practising school teachers. Satisfactory local arrangements to this end would have to be established. *The Department of Education and Science has recently commissioned a research project to monitor and evaluate four examples of such arrangements, so as to assist the development of good practice.* (Department of Education and Science 1983, emphasis added)

The Department of Education and Science has a long tradition of commissioning educational research, but until recently much of it has gone on quietly in university departments and colleges of education away from the public gaze. The history of the project which forms the basis of this book is rather different for it is based on the research so publicly announced in the Government White Paper quoted above. It concerns the training of teachers and the role that the teaching profession itself should take in that process. More precisely it focuses on what has come to be known as 'school-based' teacher training. As was mentioned in the White Paper, the vehicle for the research was an evaluation of four training courses, all of which were one-year Post Graduate Certificate of Education (PGCE) courses.

The development of 'partnership' between the training institutions and the teaching profession has increasingly become a central part of government teacher education policy throughout the 1980s. Any book which purports to report 'research' with its implied notions of independence and rigour but which is so closely allied with government policy initiatives must therefore begin by setting out its history and terms of reference; this is the purpose of this introductory chapter.

The changing context of teacher education

During the last twenty-five years there have been many significant changes in British teacher education; changes both in the number of teachers that we train as well as the means by which we train them. In 1963, for example, 26 261 students were admitted to training but by 1972 this number had nearly doubled to 50 623; by 1982, however, when this research began the number had dropped back again to 18 385. As Alexander (1984) points out, the primary reasons for these dramatic fluctuations were demographic – changes were forced on us by variations in the birth rate, something over which even the best organized administration has little control. Inevitable or not, the impact of these wild fluctuations on training institutions and those who worked in them was dramatic. A decade of expansion followed by a decade of contraction left few institutions looking the same as they did at the time of the Robbins Report in 1963; many disappeared altogether.

But if training institutions have gone through many metamorphoses during the last quarter of a century then so too have the courses by which we train our teachers. In 1963 the dominant route into teaching was via the three-year Teachers' Certificate course undertaken in a College of Education. At this stage the PGCE, the one-year course of training which students take after they have completed three years of undergraduate study, was very much the minority route. Moreover it was largely confined to the universities and directed to a specific group of teachers – those intending to be subject specialists in grammar and public schools. With the expansion during the mid 1960s and mid 1970s the numbers on three-year courses increased dramatically, and with this increase came the gradual move towards three- and four-year BEd courses (the Teachers' Certificate was phased out after 1979). However, the cutbacks of the mid to late 1970s were almost entirely directed at the three- and four-year courses – indeed the numbers on PGCE courses continued to expand up until 1980. By 1982, when this project was commissioned, the PGCE had been established as the majority route into teaching.

The changes in British teacher education from 1963 to 1982 are summarized in Figure 1.1. It clearly illustrates that the growing significance of the PGCE as a route into teaching came about in part by default – it was occasioned for the most part by the dramatic reduction in the alternative.[1] However, the PGCE itself has not gone without major changes. The numbers did increase considerably, especially between 1963 and 1973.[2] Perhaps more significantly, however, the dominant university/grammar school basis changed too. By 1980 the numbers on public sector PGCE courses equalled the numbers of those in the universities. A small but growing primary PGCE element had been added[3] and instead of most of the secondary students going into grammar or public schools, by 1982 the majority of them took up their first teaching posts within the comprehensive system.[4]

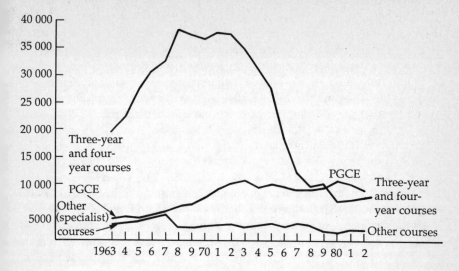

Figure 1.1 Students admitted to courses of initial teacher training in England and Wales 1963–82.
(Source: Alexander 1984:104.)

Given that the PGCE is now so significant in the training of the teaching force it is perhaps unsurprising that in recent years it has increasingly become the focus of enquiry and review. In 1979, the Universities Council for the Education of Teachers (1979) published a major consultative report on PGCE courses for training secondary school specialist teachers. They followed this with a further report on courses for primary and middle school teachers in 1982 (UCET 1982).[5] In 1980, 1981 and 1983, HMI issued a series of three pertinent discussion papers (DES 1980, 1981, 1983) dealing directly with issues of PGCE training in addition to making extensive comments on courses in *The New Teacher in School* published in 1982 (Department of Education and Science 1982). The Council for National Academic Awards (1982) contributed to the debate with policy statements in 1982 and 1983. Many others, including all the major professional associations for teachers, have added their voices. In addition, to provide much more detailed information as a basis for future developments, the DES commissioned a comprehensive statistical survey (SPITE Report 1982) of all university PGCEs during the year 1979/80 carried out by the University of Leicester School of Education.

Within the wide range of matters raised in these reviews, one cannot but note the almost universal agreement about the centrality of the role of school experience. This is no new situation. Throughout this period, as is well documented by

Alexander (1984), much redesign of courses had been taking place in order to strengthen the role of school experience. Moreover a number of experimental programmes had existed for some years, which sought not only to increase the element of school experience, but by giving it new forms, to link it more effectively to the theoretical and practical parts of the course. These approaches had, by 1982, become the focus of much greater interest. It was in order to explore further the possibilities of these more 'school-based' approaches to initial training, that the DES commissioned this research.

But why was there this increased interest in the early 1980s in 'school-based' teacher training? As has already been noted, a number of courses, the best known of which was at Sussex University (Lacey *et al.*, 1973), had advocated such an approach for many years. Perhaps even more significant is the fact that as long ago as 1944 the McNair Committee appointed by the then Board of Education to look into the 'supply, recruitment and training of teachers' concluded that the key to more effective training was to give the practical side greater weight. Specifically, McNair proposed that the staff of schools in which students were placed on teaching practice 'should be primarily responsible for directing and supervising [them]' (para. 261), although it was recognized that this would require training institutions 'to relinquish a measure of responsibility in the training of their students' (para. 270). Moreover, it was suggested that there should be greater *integration* of schools and colleges both in terms of personnel and in terms of student activity.

Given a forty-year history to such suggestions, a sudden burst of enthusiasm from the centre as well as from many training institutions does indeed need some explaining. We would suggest that in order to understand this initiative it is necessary to place it in context by looking in more detail at the changing pattern of objectives and curricula for teacher education in the post-war period. It was not until the focus of initial training came to be understood first and foremost as *specialized professional* preparation that initiatives to establish partnership with schools could take root on a wide scale.

Changing objectives, changing curricula

In summarizing the changes that have taken place in the aims and objectives of teacher education during the last thirty years we have drawn on the work of Bell (1981). Although his research presents a somewhat oversimplified picture it nevertheless captures the major trends of change over this period. Bell's study focuses on the changes that took place in the Teaching Certificate and BEd between the 1950s and late 1970s although close parallels can be drawn with the PGCE. He suggests that during this period teacher training institutions went through three broad phases indicated by their changing nomenclature: Teacher Training College; College of Education; Institute of Higher Education. At each stage and in each sort of institution he suggests that the structure, culture, organization of knowledge and typical modes of social interaction were different. Broadly he suggests that they corresponded with Weber's (1948) three ideal types of education: 'charismatic education'; 'education of the cultivated man or woman'; 'specialized expert training'.

Up until 1960 the two-year Certificate course in the Training College was the dominant mode of training. According to Bell, the primary concern of the course was to produce the 'good teacher' and he argues this was achieved through a form of 'charismatic education'. He suggests that at the heart of the training was the creation of a moral community, training being achieved by a process of socialization rather than functionally specific instruction. There was an emphasis on experimental knowledge rather than intellectual rigour with powerful personal loyalties being created between students and their lecturers. It was, suggests Bell, a 'person centred training' which resulted in a 'master/apprenticeship' relationship. Little wonder that the McNair proposals that training institutions should relinquish some of their power to teachers fell on deaf ears; a notion of partnership would have contradicted the underlying philosophy of the training process.

In the three-year Certificate course and early BEd which emerged in the renamed Colleges of Education from the early 1960s onwards the emphasis shifted. At this stage, according to Bell, the primary concern was the production of 'educated men and women' who happened to want to be teachers. Unlike the two-year Certificate, these courses were dominated by a differentiated curriculum with strong boundaries between different elements; education theory (with its own internal classification by 'disciplines'), professional courses in 'methods' of teaching and, most influential of all, 'main subject' – an academic discipline studied in its own right. A sustained and rigorous main subject study to the 'highest level that could be attained' throughout the full duration of the course was justified in terms of the personal education of the student. It was the *education* rather than the training of the student that was given primacy; professional or teaching 'methods' courses had a lower status. The model of what it was to be educated was, Bell argues, derived directly from the English university – courses were to be specialized and academically rigorous. Once again there was little room for talk of partnership with teachers in this process.

The final phase of development which Bell saw emerging at the time of his research was akin to Weber's 'specialized expert training'. The revised BEd degree course now taught alongside other degrees in an Institute of Higher Education, Polytechnic or University was of a very different character from its precursor in the Colleges of Education; following the James Report (1972) and Circular 7/73 (DES 1973) the curriculum as well as the institutional context of teacher training began to be rationalized. Bell argues that the changes brought about by this rationalization were three-fold. First, professional or teaching 'methods' courses grew considerably in status and became a formally assessed part of the degree. Secondly, the role of main subject study began to change; the rationale shifted from simply 'personal education' to include instrumentality as well. Instead of being legitimated purely as a means of securing the personal education of the student, main subject study also began to be presented in 'functional terms as background knowledge to inform a teacher's classroom performance' (18). Thirdly, the relationship between academic knowledge about education and the practice of teaching came under review with an increasing emphasis on establishing a rationally explicit connection between educational theory and practical teaching skills. As the James Report (1972) argued, the course should be 'unashamedly specialized and functional . . . sharply focused on objectives specified as precisely as possible'. The educational disciplines were only to be justified to the extent that they contributed to effective teaching.

Taken together these moves amounted to a greater concern with 'professionalism' in teacher education, but a professionalism of a particular sort.

> The notion of professionalism that was being advanced tended to emphasize an affectively neutral, trained expertise. The students were to be equipped with analytic, intellectual skills to enable them to improve, and evaluate, their classroom performance. The vision of teaching implied by this notion of professional training was more functionally specific than the diffuse, affectively loaded role portrayed by previous teacher trainers. (Bell 1981:17)[6]

As we have seen, Bell's analysis focuses only on the three- and four-year training courses whereas our concern is with the PGCE. Nevertheless some parallels could be drawn. Up until the mid 1970s the focus in the PGCE (or Diploma in Education as it was often known) was at least in part on the 'educated man or woman' model. Academic proficiency in 'main subject' was taken for granted. But like the BEd, the course was characterized by a strongly differentiated curriculum with strong boundaries between different subjects. Educational theory, which was legitimated as academic, abstract knowledge, was seen to have higher status than the more practically oriented 'methods' work. However, academic knowledge was not pursued as an end in itself; it was not justified in terms of the liberal education of the student. Rather it was believed that a thorough academic grounding in the educational disciplines was an essential prerequisite for effective teaching. It was believed that students could be 'prepared' in the training institution and they would then be in a position to 'apply' what they had learned in school on teaching practice. The academic study of psychology, philosophy and sociology was part of that preparation.

More recently the emphasis has shifted towards Bell's final stage. Courses have been redesigned and policy documents issued in order to promote the development of 'specialized expert training'. *It is in this debate that the issue of partnership with schools has been located.* The recommendations made by the McNair Report over forty years ago have at last found a context in which they have some resonance. Giving more emphasis to 'the practical', developing a closer integration between schools and training institutions could only make sense in a course which was devoted first and foremost to systematic professional development.

Clearly Bell's account of the development of training is highly schematic and oversimplified. Many of the changes he identifies took place concurrently rather than consecutively. Moreover, within different dimensions of any one course one can frequently find traces of a variety of different approaches (for example, in some contemporary secondary specialist curriculum studies or methods courses one can still identify traces of the charismatic approach even when the course as a whole is established on a different philosophy). To suggest a clear developmental approach as is implied by Bell is simply too neat. Nevertheless at a general level his model does seem to capture something of the major changes in the dominant *ideology* if not always the practice of teacher education during these years. Bell's account is therefore a useful description in helping us locate current initiatives. However, in trying to *explain* the current interest in 'school-based' teacher training it has two weaknesses. In the first place it does not explain why one model gave way to the next. Why is it that in the last ten years teacher training has increasingly been redefined as a form of specialized expert training rather than 'education'? (The 'march of progress' argument implicit in Bell's analysis would seem to be inadequate.) Secondly, why should a concern with increased professionalism be constructed as a need for closer partnership with schools? Surely professional rigour could have been interpreted in other ways? In trying to answer these questions it is apparent that we need to recognize a *professional* and a *political* context to the partnership debate.

The professional context of partnership

In the previous section we argued that attempts to establish a greater partnership between training institutions and the teaching profession could not take root on a wide scale until courses were seen first and foremost as a 'specialized expert training'. That philosophy has only recently gained broad acceptance. Yet it is also true that many professional groups within education have for a long time been urging such partnership. In a recent article Wilkin (1987) traces the changing debates in four professional spheres – the training institutions, the academic debate conducted mainly by philosophers of education, the CNAA and the teacher unions. In all of these groups she suggests there have been strong though not always dominant arguments in favour of partnership.

Within the training institutions themselves, as we have already noted, the trend to closer collaboration is one that has steadily gained momentum over the last 10 or so years.[7] Wilkin suggests that the motivations for such moves have been both negative and positive. On the one hand there has been the need to respond to demand from students and teachers that the educational theory in training courses must be clearly applicable to work in schools.[8] On the other hand, growing numbers of teacher educators, perhaps influenced by the academic debate on the nature of training or by the insistence of teachers, have urged the conceptual and professional advantages of a greater integration of theory and practice.

Philosophers of education – Dearden (1980), Hirst (1966, 1979, 1983), Peters (1976) and Wilson (1975) – who have been engaged in academic debate about what constitutes the 'best' form of teacher training, have also increasingly advocated closer forms of collaboration. Wilkin argues that at the time of the Robbins Report (1963), there was little doubt that the academic debate contributed substantially to the elevation of theory. Peters (1976) was particularly influential, stating that as education no longer had agreed aims, it was important for teachers to learn to think for themselves in a rigorous manner. More recently the debate has focused specifically on the nature of the relationship between theory and practice and there has been a progressive move away from early simplistic notions that theory 'shapes' or 'guides' practice. Hirst who has frequently been at the forefront of this debate will serve as an example. In 1966 he considered the proper role of educational theory derived from the academic disciplines of the philosophy, psychology, sociology and history of education to be to 'determine and guide' educational practice (Hirst 1966:40). However, by 1979 the idea that the academic disciplines of educational theory could alone act as the proper determinants of practice was being summarily dismissed: 'It is in principle quite impossible for the disciplines as such to provide us with all the knowledge and understanding we need to make rational practical judgements in the teaching context' (Hirst 1979:19). He goes on, 'the position is rather that in most practical situations we must act from a basis of common sense understanding acquired through experiences' (p. 19). But 'what the disciplines can do is progressively improve and refine our common sense, thereby making it more rational. They thus provide a continuous crucial critique of what we do' (p. 20). The problem with educational theory in terms of the disciplines alone, Hirst suggests, is that it fails to recognize the extensive theoretical powers that educational practitioners already possess. Teachers' common sense or practical theories are theoretical 'in the sense that they are subject to notions of cogency, rigour and disciplined reflection, and practical in that (they) respect and preserve the practical context in which educational problems emerge and any solutions have to be tested' (p. 68).

As the academic debate moves forward, the concept of teachers' practical theories becomes sharper. For Hirst (1983), the teacher's professional common sense refined both by practice and by the disciplines has now become the basis of 'practical principles' suggesting a logic and rationality that is missing from more mundane 'common sense'. The disciplines of education, although not exactly marginal, since their role is to refine practical principles, are nevertheless relegated to a secondary position.

As Wilkin (1987:34) notes, the implication of this line of argument is for closer forms of collaborative training

> Precedence is very clearly given to practical experience on the basis of which we develop a common sense understanding of our situation. But the disciplines of education must be kept in good repair as it were, since only then can they contribute to raising the quality of our common sense. Moreover, the teacher in school now shares the responsibility with the academic for being the student's mentor and the greater involvement of colleges in the schools is to be encouraged through the appointment of tutors who will hold joint school/training institution posts.

Hirst's current viewpoint has been heavily criticized by Hartnett and Naish (1986) and others for being 'narrowly practice focused' and having 'no adequate place for serious intellectual reflection' (p. 103); the academic debate continues. While some commentators (Mitchell 1985) see Hirst's work as having had a profound influence on the way we train teachers, Wilkin herself is more sceptical, suggesting that his views have often been used retrospectively to justify national and local policies adopted for other reasons. Whether or not the academic debate has *caused* any shift in practice is therefore open to question. Nevertheless it is clear that for some philosophers at least, closer forms of partnership have important justifications.

The role of the Council for National Academic Awards (CNAA) in forwarding or restraining the development of partnership in training is also difficult to define with precision, though in general terms it seems recently to have facilitated such a movement. Quoting Kerr (1985), Wilkin points out that the Council is a 'responsive' not an 'innovatory' body, its role being to approve courses, not to initiate them. In its early years the Council's primary concern would appear to have been to establish its credentials and it chose to do so through the rigorous maintenance of academic standards. At the same time, however, the interest of CNAA in the professional side of training has never been in doubt. It has an explicit commitment to innovation and to the integration of theory and practice[9] and since its inception (initially as the National Council for Technological Awards) an interest in the practice of skills. Furthermore there are serving teachers on the Board of Examiners for all courses containing an element of initial training. Wilkin therefore suggests that over the years the relationship between the CNAA and submitting colleges has eased. Institutions, having demonstrated their ability to establish intellectually rigorous yet professionally adequate degree courses in many fields, have been granted more autonomy. The result in teacher training has been a growing concern with professionalism, with the CNAA acting 'as a stabilizing yet facilitating force'.

The final professional group to be examined by Wilkin are the teachers themselves, for which she uses the National Union of Teachers (NUT) as an example. As far back as 1969, sections within the union were urging 'a substantial increase of structural relations between Colleges/Faculties of Education and the Schools' (NUT 1969:20). Specific proposals over the years have included the need to appoint 'Teacher Tutors' and 'General Tutors' with appropriate professional skills and personal qualities.[10] The importance of reformulating the theory/practice relationship has also been suggested. For example, in 1971 the union urged that the educational disciplines become more applied so that they could 'enable the students to examine practical problems theoretically' (NUT 1971:22). The objective of such proposals has been increased professional competence and this, together with the need to maintain high academic standards, has remained one of the central dimensions of teacher education policy within the union over the last twenty years. Wilkin suggests that the twin aims of professional competence and enhanced status through high standards have meant that the union's commitment to partnership has been real, even if at times it has brought its own contradictions.

Wilkin's work therefore clearly demonstrates that the proposals in the White Paper for more collaborative forms of training already commanded considerable professional support in the early 1980s. Yet despite such support, actual moves up until that time had been limited. The SPITE (1982) survey of university PGCE courses as well as the HMI (DES 1987) survey of public sector institutions revealed that at that time examples of joint responsibility and planning were rare. The 'specialist expert training' described by Bell as emerging in the late 1970s, in its early stages at least, did not necessarily bring in train closer partnership with schools. The innovations that did emerge could for the most part be characterized as 'school focused' rather than 'school based'. Despite the increased concern with professionalism, the direct involvement of schools other than in the traditional teaching practice remained limited.[11] In retrospect this does not seem surprising. As our own research has clearly demonstrated, there are significant resource, training and structural implications in the move to partnership. If real collaboration between the two sectors of education was to be achieved then more than logic or good will was needed; some external political intervention was probably essential.

The political context of partnership

Whatever the history of the professional interest in collaborative forms of teacher training, both the Department of Education and Science (DES) and the Government have recently taken a particular interest in training of this nature. What are the motivations behind current central initiatives in this area? One thing is clear – they differ in certain important respects from those articulated within the profession itself.[12]

In one sense the rise of 'professionalism' in contemporary teacher training described by Bell, with its growing emphasis on instrumentality and sharply focused objectives parallels many of the changes instituted in other sectors of the education system during the 1980s. It was the economic crisis of the early and mid 1970s that brought to the surface the underlying contradictions in many of the educational policies of the earlier decades. In *schools* during the 1950s and 1960s the emphasis of reform had been on increasing access so as to ensure the widest possible development of individual talent. It was simply assumed that fostering individual talent would be sufficient to ensure collective economic benefits through increased efficiency. However, as Jonathan (1986) points out

> When it became evident (as it did in the mid 1970s) that the second of these goals is not achieved as a by-product of pursuing the first, they are quickly conceived as conflicting alternatives. Once that is accepted it is a short step to claim that economic efficiency must take precedence. (p. 138)

It is certainly true that the economic crisis of the 1970s did indeed establish the opportunity for the DES and Government to institute a re-examination of objectives throughout the education system. Schools, it was argued, needed to be more closely harnessed to the needs of the economy; if that was the case then teacher education needed to come under review as well. The liberalism of the earlier period which focused on the 'educated man or woman' was challenged. No longer was it assumed that a well-educated teacher was by definition an efficient one and to the extent that these aims were seen as in conflict, then teaching efficiency had to take precedence. In both schools and teacher training greater control by the centre was seen as a prerequisite to change; the 'relative autonomy' of the education system had to be reduced. The attempt by the centre to take a more active role in determining the structure and content of teacher education might have been more easy to resist if it had not coincided with widely voiced dissatisfaction 'from below'. As we have already noted, the mid 1970s was also a period when both teachers and students were questioning what they saw as the lack of 'fit' between 'theory and practice'. The time was ripe for a reassessment of teacher education yet it is now clear that the *way* in which the centre has tried to construct an alternative has had in part a distinctive and explicitly 'ideological' character.

A major feature of the changes proposed in the curriculum of *schools* during this period is well known. Developing 'useful skills', acquiring 'relevant' knowledge, acquiring 'appropriate' social attitudes, becoming responsive to economic and social realities – these became important objectives for centrally initiated curriculum reforms in schools during the 1980s. And an important justification of these was 'market demand'; the school curriculum was explicitly evaluated in terms of the appropriateness of its 'products' for the 'consumer' and found lacking. Yet the major 'consumers' of education were not narrowly defined as parents or children – employers, it was argued, had equal rights. Nevertheless it was the Government that seized the right to interpret what the demands of employers and parents actually were – or ought to be. Despite the emphasis on 'democratic' market demand, the reality has been one of increased central control over the school curriculum.[13]

It may have been commented upon less frequently but it would seem that the way in which the 'centre' has attempted to reconstruct *teacher education* during this period has also been by opening initial training to the 'reality' of 'market demand'. However, here the 'consumers' (at least for the present) are less formidable – they are the teaching profession themselves. If we return to the White Paper, *Teaching Quality* (DES 1983), and to *Circular 3/84* (DES 1984) which followed, the then attempt to open up the curriculum of teacher education to 'market realities' is clear enough.

As the opening quotation to this chapter demonstrated, links between training institutions and schools in the planning and execution of their courses were to be strengthened.

> Experienced teachers from schools, sharing responsibility with the training institutions for the planning, supervision and support of students' school experience and teaching practice should be given an influential role in the assessment of students' practical performance. They should also be involved in the training of students within the institutions. (DES 1984, annex para. 3)

As we will see in the main body of our report, this is the stuff of school-based training. But several other important changes were also set in train so as to open up teacher education to the 'realities' of school. A minimum number of weeks which students should spend in school was defined for the first time;[14] tutors were to regularly update their practical teaching experience by returning period-ically to the classroom; and all courses were to be overseen by a local professional committee on which teachers, local education authorities and others were well represented. Courses which did not meet these and other criteria would not be validated by a newly formed body appointed directly by the Secretary of State – the Council for the Accreditation of Teacher Education (CATE). Perhaps most significantly of all from our point of view *Circular 3/84* (DES 1984) formally laid responsibility for initial teacher training on the Local Education Authorities as well as the training institutions.

Circular 3/84 contained a number of other proposals[15] for revisions to teacher training so as to establish 'Teaching Quality' but a central mechanism was to be the 'market demand' of the teaching profession itself. The reassessment of teacher education and the move to specialized expert training may have been in part a response to the economic crisis of the 1970s, but the way in which that reassessment has been orchestrated by the centre has clearly had a distinctive 'ideological' character. As in so many other areas of recent government policy, 'consumer demand' has been presented as the guarantor of quality, relevance and democracy. Yet as elsewhere the Government has at the same time taken it on itself to determine what that demand actually is; once again the democracy of the market place has been accompanied by the reality of greater central control.[16]

The motivations behind the political intervention to establish closer partnership between training institutions and schools were clearly very different from those of the profession itself; indeed it is not totally unreasonable to suggest that Government's interest in school-based training may have been in part an attempt to weaken the hold over training by the teacher training profession. Yet as we have already seen, to conclude that the current interest in closer partnership with schools was purely or even primarily the result of directives from the centre would be naive. The initiatives made by the centre, of which the commissioning of this research forms one small part, were in reality cautiously welcomed in many sections of the educational world. The four courses chosen for evaluation in our study readily volunteered to participate in the project and as we have seen, other courses were moving towards closer relationships with schools long before the intervention of *Circular 3/84*. Motivations may have varied and this has been highly significant in the way in which policy has developed in practice;[17] nevertheless many groups found enough common ground in government initiatives to give them their broad support.

Establishing the project

In order to establish the research project, in 1982 the DES invited four training institutions and four Local Education Authorities to co-operate in developing experimental 'school-based' PGCE courses. The precise nature of the school-based training to be established was not specified by the DES, each participating training institution being left to develop their existing course as they saw fit. It was therefore accepted from the start that what school-based training meant would vary significantly across the four institutions. In each case however, it was envisaged that in comparison with traditional courses, an increased proportion of the overall training would take place in school rather than in the training establishment and that practising teachers would be more centrally involved in both the planning and execution of the training.

Selecting the four courses

The four PGCE courses chosen to participate in the scheme were selected by the DES on the following principal criteria:

coverage of both primary and secondary training
public sector, university sector and geographical spread
strong LEA support with some additional funding
inclusion of courses already established as well as those being newly developed

The four courses selected were:

(i)   Northampton Annexe, University of Leicester, PGCE for primary and infant teachers (3–8 years)
(ii) Leeds Polytechnic PGCE for upper primary teachers
(iii) University of Sussex PGCE for secondary specialist teachers
(iv) Roehampton Institute of Higher Education (RIHE) PGCE for secondary specialist teachers.

The relationship of these four courses to the first two criteria is self-evident; the other criteria need elaboration.

LEA support was strong in each case, this support being manifest in the additional funding being made available. However, the degree of funding varied considerably. In Northampton, the LEA made available the equivalent of 0.015 teachers per student to be deployed in the participating schools plus one full time seconded teacher to assist with tutoring the scheme. At the other end of the scale was Leeds where the equivalent of 0.2 of a teacher per student was deployed in schools. In Sussex and RIHE, the figures were 0.03 and 0.07 respectively; in both cases the extra staffing was assigned to schools. (An additional budget of £5000 was also made available by the DES to each of the participating training institutions to cover extra costs associated with mounting the experimental course.)

The final criterion, the inclusion of new and existing courses, was met in that one of the institutions chosen to participate (the University of Sussex) had a school-based course of long standing. The other three institutions ran courses which, in the past, had included somewhat less involvement with schools and teachers. The participation of these latter three institutions in the experiment therefore necessitated their revising their courses to a greater or lesser extent. It should however be emphasized that what school-based training came to mean in the four courses varied considerably. In establishing their courses, institutions pursued different philosophies, established different priorities and worked within different constraints. Moreover, each of the courses had a history; even the three courses that underwent some degree of change were not fundamentally new in conception. Existing arrangements therefore also significantly influenced the nature of any innovations.

The research brief

Towards the end of 1982, the University of Cambridge Department of Education was invited by the DES to conduct an evaluation of these four experimental programmes using a 'case study' methodology. (Full details of the research design and methodology are set out in the Appendix.) The research brief specified that after an initial period for research design a programme of evaluation was to be established that would include two principal elements:

(i) during the academic year 1983–84 the experience of approximately 80 students participating in the four courses (15–20 from each) was to be monitored
(ii) those among this group (59 in all) who obtained teaching posts were to be followed up at various stages during their probationary year (1984–85).

The research, which was to run for 3¼ years, was to be carried out by a three-person research team (Senior Research Associate, Research Associate and Research Secretary) under the overall direction of two Joint Directors from the Cambridge Department of Education. The project was to be guided by a Steering Committee comprised of the project team, representatives from the four training institutions and their LEAs, representatives from the DES, six external participants chosen for their breadth of experience in teacher education, and a further two representatives of the Cambridge Department of Education. The teaching community was to be represented by three practising Headteachers.

The project formally commenced in January 1983 with the appointment of the Senior Research Associate. The Research Associate and the Research Secretary took up their posts in September 1983; the project formally concluded in March 1986.

Methodology

Full details of the research design and methodology used and their justifications are set out in the Appendix; at this point we therefore offer only a very brief summary.

In line with the principles of case study research, data was gathered by a variety of means including observations, semi-structured interviews as well as questionnaires, diaries and logs. In both parts of the project (the study of the courses and the probationary year study) the research design involved an indepth examination of the experiences of a sub-sample of students or probationers together with a more general survey of the whole cohort. In the first year 38 students were chosen to be followed in depth. They and the lecturers, teachers and LEA officials with whom they had contact were interviewed at regular intervals during the course of the year. These students were also repeatedly observed during their work in school and in their training institutions. In addition, in order to provide more general information, all students completed two major questionnaires at the beginning and the end of their training. Reports written by teachers and lecturers on each student were submitted to the research team on two occasions and all lecturers and teachers involved in the training kept a log of their training activities over a three-week period.

In the second year of the project 17 probationers were selected for detailed scrutiny and they, together with their headteachers, senior colleagues and LEA officials responsible for them, were interviewed on three occasions during the year. In addition, the whole cohort of 59 probationers completed two major questionnaires at the beginning and end of their probationary year and kept a diary covering the first four weeks of teaching. Finally, all employing LEAs were requested to submit copies of their end of year reports on the probationers to the research team.

Analysis – an overview of the book

The overall purpose of the research was to reach a judgement about the value of school-based training in the professional preparation of teachers. However, given that the four courses varied so much in the forms of training they had established, a straightforward comparison with the outcomes of more traditional courses was inappropriate.[18] The primary objective of the research therefore became to clarify the *principles* of school-based training. Once these principles had been established it would then be possible to use them as a basis for making evaluative judgements about these and other courses. Such principles could also serve course leaders and others as a basis for more rational course development and policy making.

The research project therefore involved four distinct steps which are reflected in the structure of the remainder of this book. (In reality, of course, to a significant degree these four steps took place concurrently rather than consecutively and influenced the data gathering as it proceeded.)

(i) Step one was to construct a detailed and in depth case study of each course and the experience of its graduates during their first year of teaching. The purpose of these case studies was to clarify the nature of the training offered and document such links as could be identified between particular training experiences and the performance of probationers. In line with the principles of this sort of research, the case studies explored the training from the point of view of the various participants – teachers, lecturers, LEA officials and students. In the probationary year, opinions about probationers' performance from heads, senior colleagues, and LEA officials were documented. In addition, probationers' own retrospective assessments of their training were recorded. The case studies therefore included many evaluative judgements about particular courses, but for the most part these were judgements of the participants themselves; the analysis was essentially internal. Given the restrictions of space in this present volume we reproduce here only two case studies in full: in Chapter 2 a case study of the University of Leicester (Northampton Annexe) PGCE for primary and infant teachers and in Chapter 3 the University of Sussex PGCE for secondary specialist teachers.[19]

(ii) The second step was to use our developing understanding of these particular courses in order to clarify the underlying principles of school-based training. By constantly comparing the four courses and by relating our findings to other theoretical work it has been possible to develop a model that helps elucidate the nature of professional training and the significance of school-based elements within it. This model is presented in Chapter 4.

(iii) In the light of this model it was then possible to return to the case study courses in order to make more explicitly analytical and evaluative judgements about the strengths and weaknesses of particular aspects of them. Again because of restrictions of space we reproduce in this volume only two examples of these more 'external', evaluative case studies. In Chapter 5 we present the analytical case studies relating to our remaining two courses – Leeds Polytechnic PGCE for upper primary teachers and the Roehampton Institute of Higher Education PGCE for secondary specialist teachers.

(iv) The final task was to use the model we had developed to explore some of the more general policy implications of school-based training for further course development, schools and training institutions. These policy implications are presented in Chapters 6 and 7.

In Chapter 8 we present a summary of the principal points from our study together with our main policy recommendations.

Notes

1. Presumably one of the reasons for the growth of the PGCE was that for planning purposes it is easier to use one-year courses to respond to demographic and other changes than four-year courses.
2. From 1963 to 1973 they rose by 280 per cent, i.e. from 3840 to 10 752 (Alexander 1984).
3. In 1982 the figure was 15 per cent of those graduating from PGCE courses (SPITE Report, 1982).
4. The SPITE Report (1982) shows that in 1982 70.8 per cent of graduates from university PGCE courses took up their first teaching posts in comprehensives, 3.8 per cent in grammar schools and 9.3 per cent in the independent sector.
5. See Department of Education and Science (1980), (1981), (1982) and (1983).
6. For useful discussions of both professionalism and 'technical rationality' in teacher education see Popkewitz (1987a); Ginsberg (1987); Densmore (1987).
7. See for example, Alexander and Wormald (1979) and Alexander and Whittaker (1980).
8. See for example, the James Report (1972), Crompton (1977), SPITE Report (1982).
9. See for example, University Grants Committee/Council for National Academic Awards (1973).
10. Teacher Tutors, it was suggested, should work closely with students in schools as well

as training institutions while General Tutors were to be appointed to oversee all of the students in one particular school.

11. See for example, Alexander and Wormald (1979), DES (1979), McCullock (1979), Alexander and Whittaker (1980), McNamara and Ross (1982), SPITE Report (1982), DES (1987).

12. For a fuller discussion of increasing central control in teacher education see Whitty, Barton and Pollard (1987).

13. As Jonathan (1986) points out, in Callaghan's 'Great Debate', the 'consumer' was differently constructed. Here it was pupils, parents and the wider public who were invited to appraise the products of the education service.

14. Not less than 15 weeks in the PGCE and 20 weeks in the four-year BEd.

15. Perhaps the most significant stipulation was that all students should have the equivalent of at least two years' full time subject studies 'at a level appropriate to higher education'.

16. It is an interesting irony of current policy that the reform of teacher education was to be achieved by opening up training institutions to the 'real world' of schools when at the same time schools themselves were thought to be so inadequate. Presumably if schools were bad they were nowhere near as bad as the training institutions!

17. See for example, Whitty, Barton and Pollard (1987).

18. See Appendix for a fuller discussion of this point.

19. Selecting two of the four case studies to report in full was a difficult task. After much consideration we chose those two courses that demonstrated the greatest degree of variation from more traditional patterns of training. The fact that these two courses presented a greater number of 'unusual' features is not *in itself* intended to be interpreted as evaluative. Details of the remaining two courses are presented in a more schematic form in Chapter 5.

2 Case Study: University of Leicester (Northampton Annexe) PGCE for Primary and Infant Teachers (3–8 years)

As was noted at the end of the last chapter, the first step in our research process was to produce a detailed case study of each of the four courses, describing the training offered and documenting such links as could be identified between particular training experiences and the performance of probationers. In this and the next chapter we reproduce two of these case studies in full; each is divided into three sections. In **A. Policy and intent** we summarize the main aims and organizational structure of the course. This is followed by **B. The implementation of the course**, where we describe in more detail how the course was realized in practice. In this section we also include evaluative comments on the main aspects of the course made by the principal participants – teachers, lecturers and students. Finally, in **C. The probationary year**, we present evidence from our study of the links between the aims of the course and the experience of its graduates during their first year of teaching.

A. Policy and intent

Introduction

Since 1972, the University Centre, Northampton,[1] an outpost of the University of Leicester, had mounted a postgraduate certificate course for teachers of the lower primary age range (3–8 years). In 1982/83 the course was redesigned with the intention of making it more school-based. Students were to spend a higher proportion of their training in carefully chosen schools where they would be tutored by selected teachers. The Project Team monitored the course during the following year (1983/84), after a number of modifications had been incorporated. The course reviewed here was therefore in its second year after a pilot run in 1982/83. In September 1983, 22 students commenced their primary training on this course.

At this time, the training offered in the College was unique in three respects. First, it was highly centralized in terms of both administration and the determination of content. It was a relatively small course and since its inception had been under the same Course Director who had strongly influenced its structure and organization. Peculiar to this course also was a very definite emphasis on practice. Proficiency in practical classroom skills was the foremost aim of the Course Director. A third unique feature was the IT-INSET[2] work undertaken by students in school and in collaboration with teachers. This investigation of some aspect of curriculum practice was regarded as a particularly crucial element in their training.

Course aims

This training course had four distinct aims. These were:

(i) that the student should evolve and develop a broad range of practical teaching skills
(ii) that appropriate personal qualities and professional attitudes should be fostered and developed
(iii) that on completion of the course the student should have progressed some way towards formulating a personal educational philosophy
(iv) that the student should engage in the systematic analysis of practice.

Each of these will now be considered in more detail.

Aim (i): The development of practical teaching skills

That students should evolve and develop a wide range of practical classroom skills is widely held to be a major function of teacher training at the primary level, and was strongly emphasized on this course. Promoting the learning of 3–8 year olds was considered to depend on the teacher having proficiency in four areas of professional competence, and the training was designed 'to promote these areas of professional competence in parallel and at progressive levels of rigour and skill'. The four areas were:

diagnosing children's stages of development and their individual differences and assessing the implications for their learning
selecting the content of the curriculum
providing learning experiences, tasks and activities which give the children the maximum opportunities for learning in all areas of the curriculum
organising and managing the (classroom) environment and the learning experiences of the whole class and continuously evaluating the progress and quality of that learning.

The main means of achieving this aim was the exposure of the student to a wide range of primary classroom practice. It was for this reason that students at Northampton were based in a serial practice school for two days per week for two out of the three terms and also undertook three block teaching practices, two of which were in other schools.[3]

Aim (ii): The personal qualities and professional attitudes of the student

A more general objective of the training concerned the development of certain personal qualities and professional attitudes in the trainee. The student should be helped to:

develop confidence and self-assurance
acquire attitudes considered appropriate for the 'good' educator (e.g. empathy, tolerance, compromise and flexibility)
accumulate the interpersonal skills necessary for sound working relationships with peers, teachers and other adults.

One means to realizing this aim was the careful initial selection of students. The Course Director, while acknowledging that she took the first degree attainment of candidates into account in selecting students, made it clear that she looked for other than simply academic qualifications. These could be experiential (e.g. recent close association or work with young children), but were more likely to be personal characteristics which were also latent professional qualities. The slightly older candidate was preferred, having been found in the past to be better able to withstand the pressures of a tightly programmed and demanding course. Candidates should also be articulate. Applicants who were expecting to be given knowledge were not favoured; preference was for those who would enter into a dialogue.

Fostering and encouraging interaction between members of the student body was a second means of developing the qualities mentioned above. Shared learning was a characteristic of several elements of the training. As mutually supportive and co-operative members of a close-knit group, students would be enabled to – indeed would need to – develop some of the interaction skills thought desirable in the 'good' educator. This shared learning was, however, considered essential for professional reasons as well. The major justification for structuring the course with this in mind was that it enabled students to participate in the collaborative, active and open approach to learning which as teachers it was advocated that they should practise. It was intended that the teaching methods on the course reflect those methods that students should be learning to employ in the classroom.

. . . It was deemed inappropriate to advise trainee teachers of the importance of the very real contribution which children can make to their own learning if little or no provision was being made for the same students to make a similar contribution in their . . . training. Thus the decision was made to move away from the formal lecture situation to the more challenging (format) . . . of seminar discussions. (Associate Tutor)

Aim (iii): *The development of a personal educational philosophy*

The third aim of the training was that students should have reached their own conclusions on educational issues and practices by the end of the course. It was felt that as trainee teachers they should be encouraged to challenge the current received wisdom and develop their own 'rationally' based educational principles. At the same time the Course Director and her associate tutors saw it as their task to nurture in the students 'a vision . . . of the sort of ideals that they should aim at'. Those ideals first and foremost were concerned with implementing an interdisciplinary approach to the curriculum.

The main means by which students were to arrive at their own personalized philosophy of education was by critically evaluating and assessing their own and others' educational practices. In sessions on 'Method', students would publicly account for their own teaching experiences, and these would be extensively debated – and even challenged – in order to generate alternative principles. As a consequence of having reflected extensively upon their own and others' practical experiences in this way, students should have acquired a personal theory of education by the end of their training.

This 'theory' essentially was a theory of classroom method. It was the product of the review by students of their own and others' teaching activities. As such it represented the students' personal variant of the interdisciplinary approach to the curriculum – a system of practical principles which students had come to recognize as justifiable educationally.

Aim (iv): *Experience of the systematic analysis of practice*

A fourth aim of the course was that students should develop a critical stance towards their classroom practice. The third aim above was concerned with the *product* of the constant review of their professional experience – a personal 'theory'. The focus of this fourth aim concerned the *process* of critical evaluation itself. It was hoped that on completion of their training students would have recognized the benefits of, and acquired the techniques for, the systematic analysis of practice. In other words they should have accepted the need constantly 'to reappraise the learning and teaching strategies employed and to view these as integral to the concept of teacher as learner and (of) education as a continually evolving process'.

The IT-INSET study was one important *means* by which students could gain these insights. This was undertaken in the student's serial experience school and in partnership with the Teacher Tutor. It entailed a close examination of a selected aspect of educational practice. The experience in itself together with the skills of scientific inquiry which should be acquired as part of the experience, were considered more important than any end product of the activity. The IT-INSET programme was further justified as 'a means of giving something back to the schools' and conceived of as a means of promoting a subsidiary course aim – to enhance the professional development of serving teachers. The choice of topic to be investigated was decided by the teachers rather than the college tutor or the students.

Course structure and content

Induction

Students accepted for the 1983/84 course were first brought together for a day in July. The main purposes this served were to familiarize them with the nature of the course which they would be following and its associated 'house style' and to provide them with a basic introduction to classroom observation techniques. In addition there was a presentation upon the IT-INSET work which they would be engaging in shortly and a practical group activity. At the end of the day students were given the opportunity to withdraw from the course. No one did.

Following this there was a compulsory two-week attachment to a primary school in the students' home vicinity. During this they operated as teachers' aides and undertook various observational tasks prescribed by the college (e.g. observe and prepare brief written commentaries upon teaching/learning activities in specified areas of the curriculum).

The main induction period signified the start of the course proper. It lasted for nine days, the first week being spent in college and the remaining four days in school. One of the main purposes behind the time in college was to commence the building of a group dynamic, which it was intended would be a significant feature of the training. It was also envisaged as a period in which to assign the students to one of five schools being utilized for purposes of serial experience during the Autumn and Spring terms. More generally this time was used, both in college and in the schools, to familiarize students with key personnel and routines.

The school-based component

Throughout the year two types of school attachment were alternated (see Figure 2.1). During *serial experience*, students spent two consecutive days each week in school. (The remaining three days were spent in the college.) The rationale for this form of attachment was that it allowed

> teachers and students to work *as a team* in planning and presenting the work at an appropriate level in order to promote maximum learning by the children. (Course Documentation – emphasis added)

Figure 2.1 The structure and content of the Northampton primary PGCE course

Term 1

Week 1	*Week 2*	*Weeks 3–5/7/ 10–12*	*Week 6*	*Weeks 8–9*	*Week 13*
College-based induction (5 days)	Intro. to serial school experience (4 days)	Serial school experience (2 days/ week) College programme (Curr. Studies) (Educ. Studies) (3 days/ week)	School half term. College programme extended	Block practice in serial experience school (10 days)	College programme

Term 2

Week 1	*Weeks 2–6*	*Weeks 7–12*
Preparation for teaching practice (including time at TP school)	Block teaching practice (5 days/week for 5 weeks)	Serial school experience (2 days/week) College programme (3 days/week)

Term 3

Weeks 1 and 6	*Weeks 2–3*	*Weeks 4–5/ 7–8*	*Week 9*	*Week 10*	*Week 11*
College programme (incl. 2-day workshop on RE and a 2-day environmental studies field trip, plus 5 days on special educational needs)	Preparation for final teaching practice	Final block teaching practice (5 days/ week for four weeks)	College programme (incl. coverage of multi-cultural education)	Preparation for 'Exchange of Roles' experiment (4 days)	'Exchange of Roles' experiment (5 days)

For their serial school experience, students were paired and allocated to the class of a carefully selected member of staff – their Teacher Tutor. The Teacher Tutors exercised a number of responsibilities on behalf of the students, an important one being that of deploying the students' time and energies in the classroom. This included gradually inducting them into teaching. Serial experience was regarded initially as a time for learning by observation. The students would then help out within the class, perhaps by working with individuals or small groups of pupils in accordance with the Teacher Tutor's direction. Gradually, they were given more responsibility and greater freedom to determine the structure and content of pupil learning. A proportion of the students' time during serial school experience – the Course Director envisaged about 25 per cent – was set aside each week for planning, researching, analysing and discussing their IT-INSET work.

Throughout the Autumn and Spring terms, students undertook serial school experience in a single school. In 1983/84, six students were placed in each of three schools and two in each of two further schools. The pattern of serial school experience was interrupted by three block teaching practices. During *block practice*, the students assumed responsibility for the work of a whole class within an age group different from that of the class to which they were attached for their serial school experience. Except for those wishing to teach in nursery education they were free to choose the age range they wished to teach on the second and third block practices. Nursery students were obliged to spend their final practice in a nursery class, unit or school. The first block practice lasted for two weeks. It fell in the middle of the Autumn term and took place in the serial experience school. For the second block practice at the beginning of the Spring term, which lasted for five weeks, the student was placed in a different school. Students then returned to their serial experience schools for the remainder of that term. The final block practice, which lasted for four weeks, was the main course item in the third term. For this the student was assigned to a third school. It was followed by the two week 'Exchange of Roles' experiment with which the course ended. In this the students as a body assumed responsibility for most aspects of staffing and running a first school. College tutors were on hand throughout, providing the necessary guidance or support. Students on the course thus had experience in three and in some cases four schools during their training.[4] The pattern of the school experience is shown in Figure 2.2

The college-based component

Throughout the first two terms students spent three days a week in college. Their college-based studies were designed to relate to and complement their experiences in school wherever possible. These studies comprised two components:

Curriculum Studies
Educational Theory (including 'Method')

The first of these aimed to promote *competence at teaching* across the primary curriculum. The purpose of the latter was to help students to develop *analytic insights* into the process of teaching and learning.

Curriculum Studies   According to course documentation, study related to different curriculum areas

> will concentrate on the principles underpinning organization of the constituent knowledge, skills and attitudes of each . . . area and will include specific work in schools to develop understanding of the practice.

The following areas of the curriculum were covered: Maths Education, Language and Literacy, Science Education, Environmental Studies, Dance/Drama, PE, Art/Craft, Music and Religious Education. Total coverage varied from 12 hours for subjects such as Religious Education and Physical Education to 24 hours for Maths Education and as much as 30 hours for Environmental Studies. Curriculum Studies were provided by lecturers from either the parent university or Nene College or by senior teachers from local schools.

Educational Theory   There were two strands to this. The first was 'Method', which was taken by the Course Director and ran twice weekly. It involved analysis of and debate upon students' experiences in school. The emphasis here was on forms of practice, although discussing practice-related issues and topics, such as the aims of primary education and the processes of teaching and learning, was woven into this work. Two practising headteachers known as Associate

Figure 2.2: The pattern of school experience.

	School A	*School B*	*School C*	*School D (or A)*
Autumn	16 days serial experience 10 days block teaching practice			
Spring	10 days serial experience	25 days block practice		
Summer			20 days block practice	5 days block practice ('Exchange of Roles')

Tutors contributed to this course element on a part-time basis. One of them had been involved on the pilot course and thus had some prior experience of teacher training. The other was the headteacher of one of the schools being used for serial experience.

The second strand in educational theory was Educational Studies of a fairly traditional nature. This component was staffed by lecturers from the parent university whose backgrounds were in psychology and sociology. The customary coverage of the philosophy and history of education was not included in the training. In part this reflected the Course Director's preference that student learning be grounded wherever possible in their school experience rather than deriving from the various educational disciplines. Educational Studies sessions typically were a mixture of lecture and seminar and were timetabled for after school so that Teacher Tutors could also attend. Towards the end of the course, sessions were also held on selected contemporary issues such as Special Educational Needs and Multi-cultural Education. These were led by outside presenters with the relevant experience and expertise.

Course personnel

Five sets of staff shared tutorial responsibilities on the course. These were:

in the *school*, the Teacher Tutors and the Supervising Teachers
in the *college*, the Course Director and two Associate Tutors, the Curriculum
   Tutors and the Education Studies tutors.

School Personnel

The Teacher Tutor

Each Teacher Tutor was allocated a pair of students for the duration of serial school experience. The responsibilities of the role, including the nature and extent of the Teacher Tutor's involvement, were broadly determined by the college and communicated to those concerned in meetings held both before and during the course, and in documentation. The meetings were convened and chaired by the Course Director.

The *professional* role responsibilities of the Teacher Tutor were:

serving as a role model, demonstrating 'good primary practice' and discussing
   what made it so with the students
providing information, guidance and advice in relation to the four areas of
   professional competence which it was intended the training should develop.
   Teacher Tutors were expected to discuss and analyse with their pairs of
   students the specifics of classroom practice: e.g. planning and implementing
   the curriculum on a daily, weekly and longer term basis; defining the

learning potential of a range of work in different areas of the curriculum; taking decisions concerning classroom environment, organization and the styles of teaching to be employed in order that objectives may be met

observing students teaching and providing a regular and appropriate critique of their practice. Once students were engaged in teaching, the Teacher Tutor was expected to monitor their performance and to provide constructive advice and suggestions as to how it might be improved and further developed

managing and participating in the investigation into a specific aspect of curriculum practice (the IT-INSET study).

The *administrative* responsibilities of the role of Teacher Tutor were:

determining how students' time in school was deployed, including making the necessary organizational arrangements. This entailed organizing students on a day-to-day basis as well as developing a progressively broader and deeper programme of classroom experience, in accordance with guidelines provided by the training institution

liaising with the training institution, most notably the tutor attached to the particular school and the Course Director

assessing student development over the period of serial practice. At the end of each term the Teacher Tutor would assess the student on a pro forma supplied by the college.

The Supervising Teacher

The college made a distinction between the class teachers in the serial practice schools, the Teacher Tutors, and their counterparts in the schools used for purposes of block teaching practice, the Supervising Teachers. Although the duties of the Supervising Teacher were not that dissimilar from those of the Teacher Tutor, they had a less intensive involvement with the student. It was hoped that they would: help determine the programme of teaching which the student would undertake; oversee the student's teaching, carrying out some classroom observation and providing constructive feedback; assess the student's development over the period of block practice. However, the college had very limited authority to enforce these demands – in contrast to the influence it could exert upon the Teacher Tutors.

College personnel

The Course Director and Associate Tutors

The position occupied by the Course Director may be unique in teacher training institutions. She had been in charge of the training since it was introduced and, as the only full-time member of staff on the course, had a brief which permitted her considerable autonomy. Over the years she had been able to determine its nature in accordance with her educational philosophy. Because it was such a small course, she alone was administratively and organizationally responsible for the training in its entirety, and her position attracted considerable authority as a consequence of its centrality and of the strength and charisma of her personality. Nevertheless, she remained accountable to the University (see Administrative Structure). She had a particularly critical teaching role in relation to the supervision and analysis of students' school experience. She also taught Curriculum Art as well as exercising general pastoral responsibility for all students.

The main *professional* components of the role of Course Director were:

teaching the Curriculum Art component and taking two sessions per week on Method
exercising general pastoral responsibility for all the students, and in addition functioning as a personal tutor for some of them
overseeing and monitoring all the IT-INSET curriculum investigations as well as exercising particular responsibility for this work in specific serial experience schools, including chairing the weekly review meeting
making supervisory visits to students in school, during both serial experience and block practice. Although the Course Director concentrated on those students for whom she had particular responsibility, nevertheless she also sought to visit all students periodically
assessing the students' professional development. This was done in conjunction with two Associate Tutors and took into account the views of Teacher Tutors and Supervising Teachers. As Course Director she exercised ultimate responsibility for the assessment of each student.

The important *administrative* components of the Course Director's role were:

organizing, managing and administering the course in its entirety
liaising with schools. This occurred at two levels. With respect to the overall administration and monitoring of practice, contact with headteachers needed to be maintained. For more specific information on the progress of individual students or whether teachers were encountering problems or were unsure of their tutoring role, more sustained contact with teachers was necessary.

The two Associate Tutors functioned as co-tutors as regards some part of the 'Method' work. In addition each liaised with a particular continuous experience school on behalf of the college and assumed pastoral responsibility for the students assigned to that school. Together with the Course Director these tutors formed a tight-knit group which determined the further development of the training, engaging in a great deal of analysis and discussion of current practice and identifying ways in which it might be further strengthened. One of the two

Associate Tutors made a contribution of particular note, helping to clarify and strengthen the philosophical elements underpinning the training. In doing so he drew upon personal beliefs developed in the course of his career in teaching (e.g. in an interdisciplinary and broadly-based approach to the curriculum, in promoting the autonomy of the child, preferably by employing a non-didactic approach to teaching).

The Curriculum Tutor

Curriculum Tutors contributed to the training in a teaching capacity only. Their task was to prepare students within a particular curriculum area. This included helping them to develop the necessary practical competences and to assemble appropriate teaching materials for use in the classroom. The curriculum input was distinctly practical in its orientation.

The Education Tutor

The Education Tutors, with a background in one of the foundation disciplines (Psychology, Sociology), were responsible for introducing students to selected educational issues as informed by that perspective. Their principal responsibility was to communicate the basic underlying theories associated with the processes of teaching and learning, and the social factors which influence school functioning and pupil achievement. At the same time it was intended that their coverage should enhance the professional development of Heads and Teacher Tutors from the schools used for serial experience who also attended these sessions.

Course assessment

Students were assessed both on their practical teaching competence and on three pieces of written work undertaken at different stages during the training. In all these elements students either passed or failed. No grades were given.

The three assessed assignments were:

a short child study based upon investigation undertaken during the first block practice (the child development component of the college-based studies related directly to this)

a study in depth of one curriculum area, to include relevant theoretical perspectives, critical reports of practical experience and examples of children's work. This was to be related to events which occurred within the Spring term block practice

a dissertation upon a topic of the students' choice, the account to incorporate a sound theoretical underpinning.

In addition to these items which were assessed, students were also required to submit two further pieces of work that were not formally assessed. They were:

an account of the IT-INSET work undertaken in school, this to include any
  relevant teaching and learning materials
short written or practical assignments relating to various aspects of the Curriculum Studies modules.

The procedure for assessing practical teaching competence was relatively complex. Teachers had a substantial advisory role in the process. Teacher Tutors in
the serial experience schools submitted formal reports on their students at the
end of each term; and Supervising Teachers submitted reports after each block
teaching practice. In both cases, however, these reports served to supplement
the decisions reached by the Course Director and the Associate Tutors. Each
member of this threesome assumed responsiblity for supervising a group of
students throughout the training. Every student was visited each week during
serial and block practice by his or her supervisor. These three tutors therefore
established a close familiarity with the development of their particular students
during the year. It was on the basis of this cumulative knowledge, and in the
light of reports submitted by teachers, that the final assessment was made.
However, in reaching the final decision, the Course Director had an important
moderating role. In addition to visiting regularly her own students, she tried to
see every student on the course at least once during one of the block teaching
practices.

Course administration

Since its inception, the training offered at Northampton had become increasingly independent of the parent university. The Course Director exercised sole
responsibility for determining the nature of the training and for administering
every aspect of the course. Over the years she had acquired a thorough knowledge of the schools in which her students were placed. This knowledge enabled
her to run the course with considerable expertise and authority. However,
despite her evident autonomy, she remained accountable to the Head of the
School of Education of the University, whom she kept fully informed of all
developments. This included forwarding all documentation in which changes to
the course were recorded. She also submitted a verbal report to colleagues at
termly meetings held for all those staffing the various teacher training courses
offered by the university. On these occasions the Head of the School of Education
was amongst those attending.

The selection of schools

The selection of suitable schools, most especially for the long period of serial
experience, was regarded by the Course Director as critical. There was an implicit
requirement that the schools chosen and the members of their staffs designated

as Teacher Tutors should serve as role models. The criteria upon which selection was based were as follows. First and foremost, the headteacher needed to be committed to the school-based training of teachers. He or she also needed to have sufficient authority to ensure that his or her staff took seriously their responsibilities as partners in the teacher training process. Also important was the climate of the school. It was felt that this should be sympathetic to the aims of the training as espoused by the college and actively supportive of the students. Additionally, the school needed to be a stable environment. Finally, school staff should be accustomed to working collaboratively and engaging in discussion of curriculum issues and practices.

All of these criteria were seen as essential if students were to derive the maximum benefit from the serial school experience. It was, however, acknowledged that the same degree of selectivity was not feasible when determining placements for the block teaching practices. The process itself would have been too time-consuming, while in all probability there would not have been sufficient schools to go round had the same criteria been applied. In consequence, the choice of schools for block teaching practice was 'a little bit hit and miss', it was admitted.

The schools having been chosen for serial experience, it was no less crucial to identify appropriate members of staff to serve as Teacher Tutors. This decision was left to the Head, the Course Director having indicated what, in her view, were the qualities ideally required. Broadly speaking, to be appointed as Teacher Tutors, teachers should:

have had at least five years' experience of teaching
by general acknowledgement be competent practitioners
be committed to the scheme and have an understanding of, and empathy with,
    the needs of students
have 'an open, receptive and imaginative mind'
recognise that 'a supervising responsibility holds within it the potential for
    personal development as well as the opportunity to facilitate the advancement
    of others'.

The ideal Teacher Tutor thus would be a good role model for the student as well as being an effective tutor, and every reasonable effort was made to find such teachers for the serial experience attachments. For the block practices this was accepted as less feasible and the college was obliged to compromise. It was, however, considered less critical in that students spent a greater proportion of their time in school engaged in actual teaching during block practice.

Resourcing

Negotiations between officials of the parent LEA, Northamptonshire, and the Course Director resulted in an increase in the staffing of those schools being used for serial experience. The Course Director had requested some 135 hours' supply teacher time in 1983/84, in order that Teacher Tutors might be released from their classes for half an hour each week to meet the students and a tutor from college. The Course Director fully recognized that this would not meet the actual investment of time demanded of the Teacher Tutors if they were properly to discharge their responsibilities to students, but was aware of the importance of not being seen to be asking for an amount which could be regarded as excessive. The Authority duly agreed to this request, which became effective in all five serial experience schools. There was no further enhancement to staffing in these schools. Those schools used for block teaching practice purposes did not receive any enhanced resourcing.

In view of the number of students accepted on the course in 1983/84, and the devolved nature of their training, it was apparent to the Course Director that, as the only full-time tutor, she would not be able to meet all the demands that would be made upon her. She therefore enlisted the assistance of two practising Headteachers on a part-time basis to act as Associate Tutors. One was a Head who had been awarded a year's secondment. Although pursuing a course of further study, he gave generously of his time to the PGCE course. His secondment constituted an additional cost to the Authority – although in practice this proved to be a relatively small amount since 75 per cent of the total sum was reclaimable from the National Inservice Training Pool. The second Headteacher was released from school for two days each week. No additional cost was in fact incurred by the Authority in this case as the parent university met the costs of supplying cover. The other personnel involved in the training – those contributing to Curriculum and Education Studies – were brought in on a sessional basis. Lack of time rather than insufficient resources was the main factor precluding an extensive involvement by these tutors. This was particularly so for those who covered Educational Theory.

B. The implementation of the course

As will be apparent from the above description the Northampton course was complex in terms of its structure, content and aims. In their school-based activities students worked closely with Teacher Tutors and to a lesser extent with their Supervising Lecturers, both groups of professionals being primarily responsible for the development of students' practical classroom competence. In addition, however, students' school-based work also included the IT-INSET project and participation in the 'Exchange of Roles' experiment. In college, students were involved in Curriculum Studies, Education Studies and the all-important 'Method' sessions led by the Course Director.

In this section we review how the many different components of the course were implemented in school and in the college. In so doing, we draw on our own observations as well as some of the evaluative comments made by those involved.

The school-based component

Key personnel: enactment of role

We examine in turn each group of personnel who functioned in a training capacity, focusing upon the areas of responsibility to which they attached emphasis.

The Teacher Tutor

Five Teacher Tutors in two schools were monitored by the Project Team, and were found to have a common approach to their tutoring in two important respects. These were:

that they exercised a high degree of control over the students' teaching programme in the school
that the classroom practice of the students remained their principal concern
  throughout.

Control over students' school experience by Teacher Tutors was manifest in two ways. Firstly, their concern to regulate and structure students' entry (i.e. the *rate*) into teaching. Secondly, the influence they were able to exercise over the *form* which the students' practice took.

Regarding the first of these, as students progressed through a series of pre-defined stages, so the role of the Teacher Tutor altered in relation to the student. Most Teacher Tutors devised a graduated programme which enabled their students to progress step by step toward taking charge of the whole class. Typically, initially students engaged in observation within the classroom and assisted wherever possible. At this stage the Teacher Tutor very much functioned as a role model – 'trying to show students good practice and encouraging them to do this', as one expressed it. The Teacher Tutor would explain and justify her practice and students would be questioned on what they had observed. Thereafter students would gradually assume some responsibility for teaching a particular topic or area of the curriculum to a small number of carefully chosen pupils. In doing so they were under the close direction and control of the Teacher Tutor, who took full responsibility for planning the work set, advising on learning materials, and giving students detailed instructions. The complexity of the task, the proportion of the class for whom it was intended, and the extent to which the student assumed responsibility, all increased over time.

As students exercised greater initiative for planning and executing their own ideas, the Teacher Tutors withdrew from directing them so explicitly, and assumed more of an advisory function. They would offer alternative suggestions and challenge students' proposals through judicious questioning – 'trying to get them thinking about what they proposed doing and why', as one put it. The overall responsibility of the Teacher Tutor was to ensure the continuous professional development of the trainee by guiding him/her through a hierarchical series of developmental phases – a method similar to that which was urged upon the students to practise with their pupils. This was accomplished by the gradual substitution of advice and monitoring for direction and intervention. At the end of each term the Teacher Tutor was required to submit a report on the student's performance to the college. Several teachers admitted to feeling uncomfortable with this aspect of their role and would have preferred the formal assessment of students to have been undertaken by college staff.

Teacher Tutors also shaped the school experience of the students in their charge by serving as role models in the initial stages, and subsequently exercising responsibility for planning and organizing students' teaching for them. Since the great majority of Teacher Tutors were recognized as competent practitioners, students were in a favourable position to witness and acquire these skills of 'good primary practice'.

The second common characteristic shared by Teacher Tutors was the belief that their principal function was to promote professional competency. Their work with trainees was firmly located in the context of their classrooms. When asked whether they had raised considerations of a more theoretical kind, for example, very few Teacher Tutors were able to cite any instances of having done so. They strongly believed that, above all else, the time spent by students in school was an invaluable opportunity for gaining practical experience: 'They do need all the practical work in school they can get.' There was in any case insufficient time to give much attention to theory. As one Teacher Tutor declared: 'Really and truly, when you've discussed what's gone wrong . . . once you've thrown in a few ideas . . . you haven't got the time to talk about anything else.' Teachers also maintained that as the extent of the practical experience increased, so theory would become more meaningful. In any case they perceived Educational Theory to be the province of the college.

A crucial factor in any consideration of what precisely Teacher Tutors undertook with their students concerns the time at their disposal. The only formal release time which Teacher Tutors received was employed, at the request of the college, in reviewing the progress of the IT-INSET investigation. Discussion between Teacher Tutor and students on the students' teaching, on problems encountered in the classroom, disruptive pupils and such like had to take place when it could be fitted in. This might be before or after school, or during the lunch hour. Usually such meetings were informal, ad hoc and frequently rushed, and for all these reasons were perceived as less than satisfactory.

The Supervising Lecturer

Although teachers were accorded considerable responsibilities in relation to the training of students, particularly so during serial experience, the supervision of students' practical school experience was not solely in the hands of teachers. The students' actions in both serial and block practice were also closely monitored and supported by the Course Director and Associate Tutors. These three tutors each took responsibility for a small group of students, visiting them briefly each week during serial practice and once a week during block practice. The Course Director additionally sought to maintain contact with all of the students and the serial and block practice schools in which they were placed, her school visits playing an important part in maintaining the integration of the course and consistency of student experience.

Where a student encountered substantial difficulties, a particularly intensive programme of visiting would be implemented by these tutors with the aim of turning the situation around in a relatively short space of time. In the ordinary run of events, during serial practice the purpose of these supervisory visits was to maintain contact with both student and Teacher Tutor. With the *student*, the lecturer would briefly observe any teaching taking place and advise on its improvement. Regular observation of students was necessary both for purposes of assessment (these lecturers had final responsibility for the assessment of students' practical classroom competence), and to serve as a basis for the all-important 'Method' sessions which took place in college. (As will be described below, 'Method' sessions were based upon the detailed and specific analysis of students' current classroom experience. It was therefore essential that the Course Director and her Associate Tutors maintained as close a knowledge as possible of students' current work in school.) With the *teachers*, regular contact was necessary also for purposes of assessment (lecturers wanted an 'early warning' of any difficulties students were encountering) and to enable teachers to establish an appropriate programme of work for their students. As the move to school-based working had given Teacher Tutors new and considerably extended responsiblities, the Course Director felt it important to support them until they became fully confident in their role. By regularly discussing student progress and the activities established for them, lecturers hoped in a sense to 'train' Teacher Tutors in how to work more effectively with students.

During the block teaching practices students were assigned individually to schools. Supervising lecturers visited as far as possible each week. During these visits they would observe the student teaching and conduct a brief discussion session afterwards, analysing difficulties and offering advice. In this way the 'training' was to some degree extended into the block practice. Observing students teach in a different context was also part of developing a rounded picture of their abilities for purposes of assessment. Finally, having observed the student teaching, the lecturer would discuss his/her progress with the Supervising Teacher.

The IT-INSET study (Initial Training and In-Service Education for Teachers)

IT-INSET is a programme of practice-based inquiry developed by Ashton and colleagues (1982). 'The overall goal of IT-INSET is to enhance skills for co-operatively evaluating the quality of pupils' curriculum experience and for making appropriate modifications' (Ashton 1983). Thus, the intention of those participating in an IT-INSET programme is to assess and perhaps modify some aspect of the school's curriculum, at the same time improving their analytic skills. As the initials imply, initial and in-service training are combined. A teacher, a college tutor and a student (or students) collaborate upon a practical investigation. IT-INSET 'takes classroom practice as central to development as a teacher, the three sets of participants working jointly on improving their skill in evaluating and developing the curriculum.' The curriculum is taken to encompass all of the experience of children in the classroom. The IT-INSET programme is concerned with promoting the following areas of skill: analysing classroom practice; applying theory; evaluating the curriculum; developing the curriculum; developing teamwork; and generating the process of co-operative curriculum review.

Ashton justifies the use of this approach in initial training in the following way:

> If students are to acquire the skills for co-operative curriculum review then there could be nowhere better than alongside teachers engaged in the same quest. The teachers are working for the specific benefit of their own pupils and can convey to the students the urgency of that demand together with something of their accumulated expertise. The students can aid the task and bring to it the thinking, ideas and materials they are in daily contact with in College. The Tutor can add his area of expertise and experience and, in addition, can revitalise his College-based teaching with current involvement in the work of children. (Ashton 1983)

IT-INSET in the context of the Northampton PGCE

The principles underpinning the IT-INSET procedures developed by Ashton and colleagues formed the basis of this element of the training at Northampton, although a number of modifications were introduced. The main differences were:

teachers had the freedom to choose a topic to work on for themselves or they could select a topic which was pursued in common within their school. (Actual practice across the five schools varied in this respect.)

although topics were curriculum-related, how they developed in practice was
   interpreted relatively liberally
while teachers were advised that approximately 25 per cent of the students' time
   in school should be devoted to IT-INSET, in fact they were given considerable
   autonomy to determine precisely how much time was set aside for this
because of pressure of other commitments the input from lecturers to this work
   was often less than ideal, being limited mainly to the weekly half-hour review
   session.

The significance of incorporating IT-INSET into a training course was
recognized by the core team of college tutors and was acknowledged as being a
most critical feature. It was spoken of as the one truly innovative element and the
single feature which most differentiated this from other PGCE courses. It was
also a key element which distinguished serial school experience from the block
teaching practice. An Associate Tutor noted of IT-INSET that 'these small
group projects help to introduce students and more experienced teachers to the
part which research and evaluation should play in their professional development'. The value of this, tutors maintained, was that it offered a means of
developing awareness and understanding of educational practice – which
should in turn lead to sounder practice in the classroom.

The specific advantages which tutors recognized for *students* in undertaking
IT-INSET were:

that they would enhance their insight into educational practice through having
   rigorously analysed a particular aspect of it
that they would learn specific relevant and useful skills (e.g. how to assess pupils'
   attainment, how to diagnose pupils' learning difficulties, development,
   programme evaluation)
that they would benefit from the experience of teamwork in a practical context.

For *teachers* the advantages which tutors espoused were:

that it provided the opportunity to investigate personal interests, perhaps
   exploring systematically a tentative theory
that in so doing the teacher could become more knowledgeable about that
   aspect of educational practice
that at the same time they might realize the potential contribution which
   evaluation and research can make to everyday classroom practice
that it would lead to teaching resources being developed
that individual pupils might receive more personal attention.

Choice of topic   In consultation with their respective Headteachers, Teacher
Tutors at three of the schools chose a school-wide focus for their IT-INSET
investigations. This was a departure from practice on the pilot run the previous
year, and reflected lessons learnt from that experience. One of the headteachers

summarized the main lessons learnt: that there was a need (a) to limit the scope of the inquiry by carefully defining the area of investigation; and (b) to choose a relevant and coherent topic. In the two remaining schools there was only one Teacher Tutor, and hence it was not possible to adopt a school-wide focus. The topics chosen in the various schools were: children's literature; religious education; aspects of language development; the marking of spelling in children's work; and classroom interruptions.

Evaluation of the IT-INSET study, including problems of implementation

The Teacher Tutors were aware of advantages deriving from having undertaken the IT-INSET study and the potential for professional enhancement which it offered. There was the opportunity to review in a systematic and reflective manner policies and practices which may have become routine and outdated. Several of those involved spoke positively of what, in general, had been accomplished. 'I feel that I have benefited from the chance to step back from an immediate involvement with my class. There are so many extra things which you can learn about individual children when you are on the outside looking in', was one teacher's assessment. For the students there was the excitement of engaging in a small piece of research, and the opportunity to influence the development of school policy. Teacher Tutors implied that students had become more systematic and evaluative in some areas of classroom practice as a consequence of having been required to focus their attention and reflect in this way. They had, moreover, become more knowledgeable through consulting the relevant literature.

What was achieved from the IT-INSET work varied from school to school. Most successful were the inquiries into children's language development and classroom interruptions. In the former specific topics were: the teacher's use of language and whether this facilitated understanding and enhanced retention in young children; ways of improving children's language performance; and the impact of educational games on language development. All three student/teacher pairings reached certain conclusions about their chosen topic and in the course of the inquiry developed some useful learning materials. The investigation into classroom interruptions, while perhaps less far-reaching, nevertheless was considered by the teacher concerned to have been amply justified by the drawing up of guidelines and the subsequent modifications to school practice.

Elsewhere the outcomes were more disappointing. The investigation into children's literature was considered by the teachers involved to have achieved limited ends. The students were thought to be better able to select stories in terms of their emotional content, whereas previously they had operated in accordance with what they assumed the children would find of interest. They were also better able to integrate stories into general classwork rather than their simply serving as 'fillers' at the end of the day. The teachers did not consider that they personally had benefited greatly. The investigation itself did not realize the aim of a school-wide policy on children's literature – hardly surprising perhaps given the time available. Elsewhere the inquiry which was intended to develop a religious education curriculum for the school unquestionably was the least successful of all. Various reasons were put forward for this. The choice of topic was contentious, some members of staff insisting that it was so very personal and hence likely to give rise to controversy. There was also a deal of uncertainty on the part of teachers as to how to proceed with the inquiry. The staff involved also felt that they had not always had the backing of their supervisors in instances of disagreement, nor received the support they had had need of at times. Finally, in the limited time available it was an ambitious project.

Our view is that the inclusion of the IT-INSET component in the course was an imaginative and challenging innovation. In the course of its implementation, however, a number of difficulties were encountered. When aggregated, these suggest that there are certain preconditions which are necessary if such curriculum inquiry is to have a good chance of succeeding. The first of these concerns the free flow of information between the relevant parties. If the best use is to be made of the skills, interests and commitment of teachers and students, they must be fully informed of the purposes and procedures of the exercise. Also, it is essential that students and in particular the teachers be acquainted with basic research techniques. Where this was not so, anxiety was generated amongst the teachers: 'We desperately needed guidance in the beginning, because none of us had ever done any research'. Thirdly, the interest of the participants in the chosen topic is also an important factor. There was some tension here between teachers collectively agreeing a school-wide topic for investigation and individual teachers selecting topics of their own choosing. It is less likely that all participants will be equally committed if a common theme is pursued. Indeed, one Headteacher of a school where this was the case reported towards the end of the course that the level of interest staff had shown this year did not seem as high as it had been in the past when individuals had pursued their own particular interests. That said, however, one of the tutors pointed out that teachers had pressed for a common theme 'because they felt unsure' of the precise nature of what was to be undertaken in IT-INSET.

A further three factors were found to have adversely affected the execution of some of the IT-INSET projects. One of these was lack of time. Teachers frequently commented on this. They pointed out how difficult it was to discuss the topic fully and conduct the research properly in the time allocated. The view of one teacher, that however well intentioned and potentially valuable IT-INSET might be, it was nevertheless 'an extra element in what is already a very full timetable', was widely shared. The feeling was that if the training authorities wished to presevere with this aspect of the course then 'they've got to give more time to it'. Secondly, the location of this component in the context of the training occasioned some dissatisfaction. When students were away on block teaching practice, projects had been 'left in the air' and had lost momentum. Continuity was also disrupted by the switching around of the college tutors who attended the weekly review meetings. Thirdly, the involvement of tutors was regarded as a crucial facet of the successful implementation of this component. For the student in particular it was felt that the tutors' fullest participation was 'the key element'. However, the resourcing available was insufficient to support the degree of tutor involvement which teachers regarded as necessary. It was pointed out that most of the visits made by college tutors to school 'had been primarily not about IT-INSET . . . (but) about classroom practice and organization'. The weekly review meeting was the only occasion on which participants in the IT-INSET programme could meet to discuss the future development of their projects. It was perhaps no coincidence that the most productive of the IT-INSET inquiries took place at the one school where a college tutor was able to be present for substantial periods of time.

The Course Director, while accepting that current practice with regard to IT-INSET was sometimes far from successful, nevertheless insisted, 'I would still have it'. She considered that it was valuable for the student to work in active partnership with others, and was convinced that serial school experience 'would be poorer for its removal'. She reported having been heartened by the fact that in some of the schools used the seeds of a critically questioning attitude towards practice had been sown.

The 'exchange of roles' experiment

In the final week of the course, the cohort of students under the general supervision of three tutors assumed responsibility for the complete running of a first school. The Course Director described the objectives of this innovative event as follows:

it would give students another chance to participate in school life in all its
    complexity. They would meet at the end of each day to discuss that day's
    events, and thus learn from each other what the operation of a school entailed
it would offer the students a realistic context in which they could co-operate and
    work together – as they would have to do in the future as members of the
    teaching profession
it would be 'much more of a whole situation'. It would broaden their school
    experience, filling in gaps which remained from their previous practices. They
    would, for example, be required to undertake routine administrative work
    and deal with parents.

At the same time this proposal offered a valuable opportunity for the staff of the school concerned to engage in in-service work *as a staff*. That this should be undertaken on site was a condition of the LEA's agreement. The serving staff would not, however, have anything to do with the running of the school during that week except in an emergency.

The week preceding the actual takeover was entirely devoted to final preparations. The students spent some time in the school, familiarizing themselves with its organization and ethos. Time was also set aside for developing lesson plans and preparing teaching materials.

For the exchange of roles week, students were paired and allotted to a particular class. The three tutors exercised responsibility for the three age spans into which the school was divided. The students in charge of particular classes within these age spans related directly to the designated tutor. In addition, the Course Director acted as Headteacher throughout the week. For much of their serial experience, students had had the curriculum prescribed for them. On this occasion they were given considerable freedom to develop the curriculum as they wished. A school-wide theme, 'Beginnings and Endings' was decided upon by tutors, but students were free to interpret this theme as they wished. Working co-operatively with others, an explicit aim of the training, was particularly emphasized in this experiment. Additionally, each student should not only exercise responsibility for work within the classroom – and for some this meant assuming responsibility for a classroom ancillary – but should also contribute to the running of the school as a whole.

Comments from tutors, LEA officers and the students themselves all suggested that the week ran smoothly, with only a few minor problems, and was judged a considerable success. The Course Director mentioned the following aspects with which she had been impressed:

the manner in which the students had worked together as a 'staff'. 'They were able to use their knowledge and expertise with each other, share ideas and share resources'
the imagination and originality which they had displayed in their teaching
the quality of the work which had been produced: 'As good as, or even a bit better in some cases' than many a serving teacher might produce. Practical work had been 'quite outstandingly good'
the way in which they had assumed full responsibility for nearly every aspect of the school's working life.

Coming as it did at the end of the course, the students themselves commented favourably upon having been released from the constraints which assessment imposed. 'The pressure is off', commented one. Consequently they had felt able to be more adventurous than they might otherwise have been. It meant that the course had ended on a high note. They had enjoyed the opportunity to work alongside their peers in school, and recognized that much of the success of the week was due to close teamwork. They had particularly welcomed the opportunity to gain a sense of the teacher's wider professional role, through dealing with parents on a daily basis and visitors to the school. These were aspects of the teacher's workload which had not previously featured in their training.

Some dissatisfaction was voiced, however. Some students recalled how difficult it had been to motivate themselves again at the end of a long and tightly packed course. Several were sceptical about the motives behind the venture, suggesting that it had been less a learning experience for them than 'a chance for us to demonstrate what we'd achieved' – that is, how well they had been trained and by implication how good the course had been. It was suggested that it would have been more useful to have devoted this time to filling in gaps in their training (e.g. multi-cultural education). That they had been obliged to operate within a specified theme was something which frustrated a substantial number of them. They would have preferred to have been even more independent.

Student evaluation of the school-based component

Students were unanimous in their appreciation of the varied school experience which had been incorporated into their training. They valued spending substantial amounts of time in at least three different schools and the opportunities which this brought to sample different teaching methods and approaches. They also had experience of two or more age levels. In appraising their school experience, however, they differentiated between serial experience and block practice. In the case of the former, a substantial number of students felt that their autonomy had been unduly curtailed. The block practices on the other hand were regarded as occasions when they were granted more freedom to shape their own contribution as teachers. Although they valued highly a number of aspects of their serial school experience, students did not mention that it offered opportunities for demonstrating initiative or experimentation.

Spending so much time in school was also considered to have brought sharply into focus the diverse nature of the teacher's role, and the incessant pressures under which teachers work. This was particularly valued in that it enabled students to determine whether teaching really was for them: 'It showed us really what it was going to be like.' All the students were grateful that the training had not been an easy option: 'We had to cope with so much . . . I think it prepared us for anything'. Many of them voiced a familiar complaint of so many PGCE students, namely that the time available for all the activities scheduled was inadequate. At times they had felt quite overwhelmed by requests and demands from teachers and tutors. They noted too that there was insufficient time for their own personal study. All too rarely was time set aside for them to use as they wished – going off to the library and reading around a particular topic, for example, or reflecting on something which had been introduced in a seminar. The training was perceived as a series of challenges which they had to overcome, and it was fully recognized that whether they survived was due to their own capabilities and initiatives. For those who did survive the course, this in itself was considered a noteworthy achievement.

Serial school experience

Students valued this for several reasons:

the continuity with a particular class which it offered and the long-term relationship with pupils which then became possible in these circumstances. There
was time to witness pupils' development

the rewarding relationship that many students established with their Teacher
Tutors, which led to much helpful advice and assistance being provided

the very great benefit obtained from undertaking a first block practice in the
serial experience school, and preparing for this in an environment which was
already familiar. Also, the gradual entry into teaching that a longer period of
time in a given school permitted. (We note, however, that this was not the
experience of every student.)

Students appeared to see no inconsistency between their dislike of constraint
and their approval of their predetermined phasing into the teacher's role. This
may suggest that they welcomed generalized support, but that explicit and
specific control (e.g. of lesson content) was felt to be restricting.

The major criticism made by students of the serial experience concerned their
marginal status. Some reported feeling intrusive, others that they were merely
tolerated or even made to feel redundant. Many felt constrained in both the
curriculum content that they were allowed to teach and the degree of responsibility that they might assume. A few Teacher Tutors were considered to have
been reluctant to hand over control to students. Students attributed this to the
deference which many teachers displayed towards the Course Director; also to
teachers' uncertainty about the precise nature of their responsibilities. We ourselves would suggest that it also had to do with teachers' uncertainty when faced
with a different from usual relationship with students in training. These
restrictions were regarded as particularly frustrating when students took up serial
practice again after having undertaken their first block practice. On the teaching
practice they had had some taste of professional autonomy and been granted
greater license to plan and present their own choice of curricular material. In
contrast, a small number complained at having been forced into taking on
substantial teaching responsibilities by their Teacher Tutor before they felt
ready for this. (Interestingly, where students had coped with this requirement
they tended to look back on it as a good thing!)

A second criticism students voiced of their serial experience was the exclusive
focus on classroom practice. Students' criticism here does not necessarily conflict
with their appreciation of the practical emphasis of the course, in that it is quite
compatible to value highly opportunities for actual practice in addition to
recognizing the need for a theoretical basis to that practice. Students acknowledged that the opportunities for any sustained theoretical input or for locating
their work within a broader professional context were few. They were only in

school for two days a week, during which time their priority was inevitably their teaching. In addition, the timing of Educational Theory sessions (after school) was a strong disincentive to broaden the focus of their work, for it ruled out one of the best opportunities for them to get together with teachers and engage in substantive discussion.

Block teaching practice

It will be recalled that 10 of the 12 weeks devoted to block teaching practice took place in other than the students' serial experience school. (Only the initial two-week practice was held in this school.) This arrangement had both positive and negative implications. Students recalled that the transition from serial experience to the first block practice had been relatively trouble-free since no change of school had been required. Subsequently the chance to broaden their experience by teaching in a number of schools was regarded as beneficial. However, the most welcome aspect of block practice for the student was the chances afforded them to sample 'the real world of teaching'. It was during this period that they felt themselves to be less sheltered and more able to demonstrate initiative and capabilities. Many students had not had any previous opportunity to be in charge of a whole class, and greatly welcomed the chance to assume overall responsibility for the organization and management of pupils, just as they welcomed the freedom to teach across the curriculum for a sustained period of time.

Block practice also offered the minority of students who had failed to establish a good working relationship with their Teacher Tutors a chance to make a fresh start. Nevertheless, generally speaking, students spoke less favourably of the associations which they formed with teachers in their block practice schools. Several described their supervising teachers as less sympathetic to their needs, less tolerant of their mistakes and generally less helpful than their counterparts in the serial experience school. Although Supervising Teachers were provided with a series of brief training sessions on how to approach supervision, students felt that their impact had been limited, in part because they took place during the second block practice.[5] For a small number of students at least one of the block practices proved a difficult and testing time and was perhaps of questionable value.

The second disadvantage of block practice suggested by students was organizational. Many noted that the continuity which had been built up over the Autumn term in their serial experience schools had been broken during the Spring term as a consequence of the block practice. On returning for a further 10 days of serial experience in the Spring term, considerable readjustment had been necessary. Pupils' learning had progressed in their absence, while students found it particularly trying having to come to terms with the restrictions imposed on their autonomy after the relative freedom of the teaching practice.

IT-INSET

The dual benefits claimed for undertaking an IT-INSET project in schools are, first, that investigation of some aspect of practice should have consequences for improving or developing that practice, and secondly, that the research activity itself can enhance practitioner awareness and promote the acquisition of analytic skills. Neither of these benefits was mentioned by students in their appraisal of the IT-INSET component. Instead, they valued the opportunities that IT-INSET offered to work closely with individual children in small groups and thereby get to know them more fully. There are at least two possible reasons why neither of the hoped for advantages of undertaking an IT-INSET project was volunteered by students in their assessment of this element. First, that it is more difficult to reassess practice with which one is not yet fully conversant, as would have been the case for many of the students. Secondly, that the research process itself was hampered by a number of difficulties. These included the lack of time and Teacher Tutors' lack of experience of research. From the students' point of view, therefore, motivation may have been low. It was certainly insufficient to overcome their major criticism, which was that the inclusion of the IT-INSET work detracted from the main purpose of their being in schools, which was to learn to *teach*. Thus, in this instance, the emphasis on the acquisition of classroom competence through practice, which was such a notable characteristic of the course and which the students had internalized as an important professional goal, was to the detriment of establishing the IT-INSET programme.

That the students regarded the IT-INSET inquiry as an intrusion in their acquisition of classroom skills, may suggest that they did not appreciate what it had to offer the practitioner. In part this may reflect the limited outcomes of the inquiry, generally speaking. With few exceptions students did not consider its potential had been realized. Also, it was evident that they did not fully understand what was entailed. Throughout a substantial part of the course they believed that such matters as the nature of this inquiry, the intentions and purposes behind its inclusion, its relation to other elements of the training and whether any end product would be formally assessed, had never been properly explained to them. Remarks such as the following were not unusual: 'We didn't know quite what IT-INSET was.' 'It's never been explained why we're doing it . . . it's something that's part of our ordeal if you like – that's the feeling that's prevailed.'

The students maintained that no clear explanation had been given to them; furthermore, that Teacher Tutors shared their uncertainty. In addition, very little time was available for prolonged practical inquiry. For this reason the weekly review meeting was regarded as excessive. Progress during the week was often very limited – leading to a situation in which, as one student put it, 'sometimes you feel you were thinking of things to say'.

The college-based component

It will be recalled that there were two components which made up the college-based part of the course: Curriculum Studies; and Educational Theory (including 'Method'). We examine next the teaching in these areas.

Key personnel: enactment of role

The Course Director

Given the centrality of her position, the Course Director fulfilled both professional and administrative responsibilities. It is with the former that we are concerned here.

At the centre of her professional concerns was the 'Method' session. This was timetabled twice weekly – except during block teaching practice – and was normally led by the Director herself, sometimes assisted by one or other Associate Tutor. These sessions were the principal context within which students' school experience was examined and debated. The purpose of these occasions was to generate discussion on particular aspects of educational practice. Tutors explained that their concern was not to inform students about practice, but to guide and help them to develop their own insights and conclusions, through having closely examined their own experiences in the classroom, both individually and collectively. Students were encouraged to reflect upon what they had observed or engaged in in school in order that they might develop explanations for these events. From this analysis of specific instances it was hoped that they would generate broad principles which would guide their own practices. As practitioners, they were encouraged to assume 'good' attitudes towards the teaching process. These were that teachers' educational practice was always capable of further improvement, and that they should develop the habit of constantly questioning what they had attempted in the classroom.

The teaching method employed by the Course Director and Associate Tutors was unusual. By questioning students repeatedly about their classroom practice and experience the intention was to challenge their (or those of their Teacher Tutors) taken-for-granted assumptions. At the outset of their training, students lacked the experience on which to base discussion, and consequently the Course Director had to provide some input. Time was devoted to informing students about such matters as the historical development of nursery education, classroom management, different approaches to classroom organization including vertical grouping and the integrated system – they were likely to encounter the latter in use in Northampton schools – and the importance of play in the young child's development. Once students had some firsthand experience to draw upon, however, this became the focus for analysis and discussion.

Students would be called upon to outline to the group what had taken place in their classroom during serial school experience. These accounts might address the way in which pupils had responded to a new activity, the problem of motivating pupils or the justification for having chosen certain materials for a particular learning task. The Course Director sought to challenge statements which the students made, perhaps confronting them with gaps or contradictions in their thinking. As appropriate, she would develop and extend points of particular importance. In this way students learnt to reconsider, or alternatively to reaffirm, their practical professional principles and beliefs. In repeatedly subjecting their experience to such reappraisal it was intended that students investigate the basis for the conclusions arrived at concerning good educational practice.

The role of the tutor in the 'Method' sessions was thus to 'inject statements or encourage someone to develop further something that they'd said'. A limited amount of information was communicated by tutors, but this was rarely done directly. Instead it was fed into discussion incidentally and was regarded as an adjunct to discussions rather than an essential element. The Course Director acknowledged having at the back of her mind a loose agenda of issues which she considered it was necessary that the students should address at some time during their training. These were approached by grounding the discussion in students' classroom experience. During their training, coverage of certain topics would arise quite naturally during their description of their work in schools (e.g. the organization of the classroom, the relationship between work and play, pupil groupings).

The 'Method' seminars were a major site for student learning, and a number of important points about them are recorded below:

It was the intention of the Course Director that the learning which took place in these sessions should be *active*. Students were encouraged to reflect, 'to work things out for themselves'. Passive learning, through being introduced to formal educational theory, for example, was regarded as 'not something we would like to impose on the student'. Tutors maintained that 'the best kind of theory comes largely from judicious assessment of things you have thought out for yourself'. In this part of the course the theory underlying educational practice was evolved by the students themselves, rather than being handled in the conventional way – that is, other people's ideas being passively received and accepted.

In this respect the practical professional principles that students eventually determined were 'their own'. Nevertheless, students were given a clear notion by the Course Director of what she considered to be sound primary educational practice. The way in which the sessions were conducted, the framing, structuring and sequencing of questions, suggested clearly to the students the preferred approach to education.

The emphasis throughout the sessions was characteristically on the practical activities in which students and their pupils had been engaged in the classroom. The constant reiteration of the need to reconsider their practice and strive to improve it contributed significantly to the practical competence displayed by students in the later stages of the training.

The points made by the Course Director during her interventions were discrete. In accordance with the principle of active learning it remained the students' task to systematize and make coherent the isolated principles which emerged cumulatively across a number of 'Method' sessions.

The Course Director sought to draw upon students' varied experience in their respective schools, and thus to render context-free the principles which she promoted.

The professional responsibilities of the Course Director and her Associate Tutors were also manifest in contexts other than the sessions of 'Method'. The Course Director herself taught the Curriculum Art component and there were periodic individual or small group tutorials. Such occasions offered an opportunity to examine even more closely specific students' school and classroom experiences and to discuss written assignments which the students undertook. Tutors undertook supervisory visits to schools in order to gauge students' functioning in the classroom and to assess their professional development. They also convened weekly meetings at which the progress of the IT-INSET inquiry was reviewed. Later in the training these sessions took on a broader orientation whereby students' overall school experience was monitored. Finally, we note that the Course Director exercised a general pastoral responsibility for all the students and in addition served as Personal Tutor to some of them.

The Curriculum Tutor

In the curriculum dimension of the training the Course Director chose to emphasize coverage of Arts-orientated subjects – Music, Dance/Drama, Art and Craft. (She provided the Art component herself.) This preference reflected her conviction that such subjects were crucial in the education of the young child, serving as potential entrees into the child's world, and therefore offering insights to the teacher. She would have preferred more integration of subjects under broad headings, such as 'Culture' and 'Humanities', but for the present the subjects remained distinct from each other. The greater part of the curriculum coverage was provided by tutors who were specially brought in. No fewer than seven tutors were involved, only one of whom was based at the Northampton Annexe. Under these circumstances considerable variation regarding the aims and objectives which tutors held, and how they conducted their sessions, might be anticipated. This in fact was the case, although certain generalizations can be made.

All of the tutors concerned, irrespective of their subject areas and interests, emphasized the practical rather than the theoretical aspects of teaching their subject. This is not to say that theoretical issues were neglected altogether, rather that they were secondary concerns. This practical orientation included providing students with ideas and learning resources which they could try out in school, as well as ensuring that they knew what was appropriate for children of a given primary age, and that they understood the objectives behind such work. Certain areas of the curriculum coverage were, however, approached more theoretically than others. The tutor responsible for language development described how, as part of the Language and Literacy component, he had alternated more theoretical sessions with those which focused upon practice. Thus, for example, one week he would address such topics as cognitive development and the development of language and the following week focus upon teaching techniques for promoting creative writing or stimulating language generally.

Some tutors based part of their teaching in schools. The Maths Education tutor explained how he alternated college and school-based sessions. Usually in the former he would talk about some aspect of children's mathematical development. This would be followed up the next week by the students teaching some related lesson material to small groups of children in a school. The PE tutor similarly undertook some of her teaching in school. Typically, she would talk about different aspects of Physical Education and then the students would practise appropriate exercises in the gym attached to a Teachers' Centre. The session would then be followed up in a school, the tutor working with children on a particular aspect of PE – in effect, modelling for the students – prior to students themselves working with pupils.

Secondly, tutors taking the more creative and practical subjects – Music, Dance/Drama, Art and Craft – had in common a concern to draw out and develop students' own talents in these areas. Gaining confidence, overcoming inhibitions and self-consciousness and developing personal skills, were matters which tutors recognized had to be confronted from the beginning of the course.

The Education Tutor

Three lecturers from the parent university came to the Annexe to take sessions in the disciplines of Education. Two were jointly responsible for Educational Psychology, while a third took Sociology. All three tutors had been teaching on this course for some years. (They also taught on the PGCE and other professional courses at the parent university.)

The application of psychological insights   The content of the Psychology component was determined jointly by the two tutors, although they operated independently of each other in actually teaching the material. They divided the seven sessions between them. One of them took as his theme the cognitive development of children (three sessions). The other tutor concentrated on the social and emotional aspects of child development (four sessions). After an introduction to certain cognitive processes (e.g. the relevance of short-term memory for the teacher), the first tutor reviewed various theories of cognition, particularly that of Piaget. The second tutor discussed ways of classifying observations of children's learning and behaviour. Next physical/motor development was covered and various developmental checklists and surveys examined. Finally, personality and social development were reviewed, introducing concepts such as 'identification' and 'imitation'. Also, the distinction between descriptions of behaviour and interpretations of behaviour was explored.

Both tutors recognized that this particular PGCE course differed in a number of respects from that provided at the parent university, and that this had consequences for their teaching. First, students were out in school on serial experience from the beginning of their training. From early on, students were therefore in a position to contribute from their own direct experience. Second, the sessions were open to Teacher Tutors and Heads of serial experience schools and as a consequence tutors were expected to tailor their material for a joint audience of trainees and experienced practitioners. Third, there was substantially less time at their disposal which meant that there was a need to select rigorously from the many potentially relevant topics.

Both tutors had a well-defined agenda and teaching approach. At least some part of each session consisted of their lecturing on a specific topic. Both tutors expressed concern that students should actively contribute on the basis of their experience in classrooms. Each therefore engaged students in practical tasks on which they were required to report back. For instance, one tutor asked students to undertake detailed classroom observation. The other set students the task of developing two case studies, one of an average child, the other of a child who presented difficulties.

The tutors were asked about their aims and objectives. The main concern of one was to introduce students to the basic theoretical underpinning of Educational Psychology. As for the teachers, he sought to unsettle their thinking in respect of classroom practices by, for example, questioning the assumptions which they undoubtedly held. It was also seen as important to re-acquaint them with the work of Piaget, particularly in the light of recent critical thinking and comment upon this. One of the main objectives of the other tutor was to dissuade students and teachers alike from thinking that there were ready answers and solutions to the problems of teaching and learning.

The social foundations of education   The lecturer responsible for providing the sociological input specified his main objective as being to show how Sociology, as a discipline, could contribute to the understanding of educational practice and of the school as an institution. Factors which had determined the content he covered were, as for the psychologists, the need to select rigorously because of the limited time at his disposal (four sessions) and the mixed audience. It was hoped to avoid 'the straight Sociology of Education' and to relate what was said to students' experience in schools. However, it was admitted that the content which was finally chosen reflected his own interests and expertise to a significant degree, and that in practice there was a good deal of similarity between what was covered here and on the PGCE offered at the parent university. The topics addressed were: Education and Industry; Multi-Cultural Education; Gender and Education; and Teacher Expectations.

It was the tutor's intention that the method employed would secure both student and teacher involvement. Thus, typically, after a brief lead presentation on a given topic the audience would break up into small discussion groups, amongst which the tutor would circulate. Representatives of the individual groups would then report back. Sessions would conclude with a summary by the tutor of the key points.

With regard to the students, the tutor's aim was to raise their awareness of certain issues which he regarded as critical for teachers. Race and Gender was one such issue. As for the teachers, the tutor felt it essential that schools should have some sort of policy on these matters and hoped that those present might find the sessions sufficiently stimulating and interesting to be provoked into discussing possible policy implications. He was also concerned that teachers should hear what students had to say on contentious topics such as these.

Tutors responsible for covering the disciplines of Education stressed that the time available to them was quite inadequate for what was required. There was insufficient opportunity in which to provide the necessary breadth or depth of coverage – or even to ensure that what was covered was properly learnt. All that they could hope to accomplish was to draw students' attention to some of the more salient issues. Neither these tutors nor those who taught curriculum studies had the time to devote to student or college concerns outside their timetabled commitments. They were not available for consultation nor could they provide individual tutorials. Nor did they have any real contact with the schools used for serial practice. A consequence arising from the latter was a failure on the part of some tutors to understand fully the nature of school-based training. As one admitted: 'I've got no vision of it being school-based . . . I haven't grasped what this entails . . . I'm not really sure what the implications of this are.' There was also the likelihood of commitment being less than wholehearted. Tutors from the parent university in particular acknowledged feeling somewhat peripheral to what was going on in Northampton. One spoke of the Annexe as 'a distant outpost' and described this aspect of his teaching as 'having marginality', certainly when set against his teaching overall. Although all concerned expressed a desire to make a fuller contribution, they acknowledged that given the severely restricted resources – both financial and in terms of their other commitments – this was unlikely to come about. 'It requires a bigger commitment than I feel I am able to give' was a typical comment.

Ensuring that external tutors were kept informed of developments in the core team's thinking about the training proved particularly problematic and came to be seen as a real disadvantage. Differences of opinion or perspective, minor misunderstandings and in particular a failure to understand fully what was at issue all occurred at some time or other and served to heighten tension and engender frustration. The biggest cause for concern which the Course Director and Associate Tutors experienced, however, had to do with the teaching approach employed by some external tutors. Coverage of the educational disciplines for instance was strongly didactic and thus at odds with the approach employed in other areas of the training, most notably 'Method'. It mattered not that to the tutors concerned this was the most efficient way of transmitting the maximum of information in a limited period of time. As one noted, 'The hour is too short to develop the subject – whether in group discussion or class lecture or both'. As an approach to teaching and learning it was held in low regard by the Course Director and her close colleagues, who urged a change in practice to the more discursive, seminar approach across all components of the training – to little avail, it must be said. They suggested that certain of the teaching team had seized upon the time factor as an excuse to hide behind, not relishing the element of risk and the overall challenge which the more interactive approach to teaching entailed. It also made for some difficulty, and ultimately frustration, for many of the students who, in this particular context, were essentially passive recipients of knowledge, yet elsewhere in the course were expected to be actively fashioning their own learning.

Shortage of time also prevented optimum use being made in Education Studies of the contributions of visiting teachers. The teachers were anxious to be involved and were perceived by tutors as having needs of their own which they wished to debate – most notably, concerning pupils who were presenting them with problems. In relation to such pupils they were seen to be wanting specific guidance and assistance, rather than the generalisations which comprised the substance of most of the coverage provided. Tutors also made reference to teachers' overriding concern with the practical and their tendency to dismiss theory as irrelevant. This was one reason why the Sociology tutor did not incorporate an introduction to sociological perspectives even though he considered that the students would have benefited from this. The comments of students and teachers coincided here. They were agreed that tutors had not fully met their respective needs. However, given the shortage of time, this would have been difficult to achieve.

Student evaluation of the college-based component

'Method'

Students appreciated the co-operative approach to learning which obtained throughout the course but which was particularly pronounced in the sessions of

'Method'. That a substantial portion of course time had been devoted to examining and discussing their own experiences in school as they occurred was widely regarded as a definite strength of the training. Students were, however, critical of the extent to which tutors had required them to reflect upon and analyse their own practical experience. They considered that this requirement had been excessive. Their point was that tutors had not struck the right balance between the content which they themselves provided and the substance for debate which derived from students' direct experience. The majority view was that they would have welcomed more guidance and more *direct teaching* by their tutors, particularly of classroom skills (e.g. classroom management and organization, discipline and control, organizing the timetable, motivating pupils and so on). One student commented, 'Nothing came from outside our own experience'. What students feared most about such an approach was that it could result in insufficient breadth of coverage and leave them lacking in understanding. It was a view widely shared. Although there had been ample opportunity to observe teachers teaching and to have practice at it themselves, they had not always been in a position to understand what they witnessed or did. The students wanted more by way of a theoretical basis for their everyday classroom actions and activities. They considered tutors could have been more forthcoming in this regard without having to abandon the importance which attached to having them reflect upon and analyse their experience in the classroom.

Students were in no doubt that they had been exposed to very definite notions about the nature of what constituted 'good primary practice' and had been given ideals to aim for. They had been introduced to a particular approach to teaching and learning – the integrated system, by which was meant an interdisciplinary approach to the curriculum. On the whole they welcomed the sense of direction that they had been given. They also appreciated the emphasis placed on the need to act professionally. One student spoke for many in describing as one of the main contributions of the training, 'the attitudes and expectations it gave me'.

The students were appreciative of the support which their tutors had accorded them in putting into practice the ideas and philosophies which had been acquired at college, even though in some circumstances this entailed challenging class teachers' views and practices. They did however take issue with the Course Director over her insistence that their teaching should be experimental and innovatory. It was felt that this requirement – for so it was perceived – did not take sufficient account of the circumstances which obtained in many schools. For instance, it ignored the tensions which could arise between teacher and student if the latter felt obliged to make certain changes to classroom organization and/or teaching approach yet the former would brook no substantial alterations in either area. It was also considered to take insufficient account of the lack of confidence to experiment which a good many students experienced, more especially in the first half of the training – to say nothing of the fact that they had not always known how to set about making changes. At times feelings ran high over what was perceived to be an attitude of 'change for change sake'. Possibly tutors' intentions were not always made sufficiently explicit in this regard.

There were specific areas of educational practice in which students considered they had not received sufficient instruction. These included: multi-ethnic education, dealing with parents and children with special needs. A small component covering multi-ethnic education was provided but was felt to have been limited in its scope, too general and scheduled too late in the course. Students could not recall any discussions in college on teachers' dealings with parents. They considered that the topic of meeting special educational needs had not been adequately covered either.

Curriculum Studies

The students spoke very positively about the enthusiasm which all the Curriculum Tutors had shown towards their subject. They also appreciated the specialist knowledge which these tutors had commanded and the practical nature of much of their coverage. The Language and Literacy component was particularly praised for the many practical ideas it contained, ideas which students had been able to utilize in school. The students also commended the breadth of material provided in the Curriculum Studies. 'We tended to get a little flavour of most aspects of teaching', one commented. In the limited time available most tutors were considered to have adequately conveyed to the students how to approach teaching their particular area of the curriculum within the context of primary education.

There was, however, a widespread view with respect to Curriculum Studies that 'nothing was considered in real depth' – though it was also recognized that perhaps this was unavoidable given the limitations of time. A second criticism was that many of the tutors were considered to have pitched the level of their work too frequently toward the upper primary age range and neglected the child of nursery and infant age. One student summed up the feelings of many in the following comment: 'There was very little information regarding nursery education. The lectures were aimed at the 6–8 range generally speaking.'

Students noted too that they would have preferred more timetabled sessions to have been devoted to Art and PE. With regard to Music, they considered that preparations for a musical presentation which they had put on for teachers had taken up too much time. Moreover, valuable time had been lost in developing a basic musical competence in every student, rather than focusing upon musical activities relevant to them as primary teachers. In the Maths curriculum element, they would have welcomed a review of a range of maths schemes in order to assess their respective strengths and weaknesses. They felt that too high a proportion of the time had been devoted to examining one particular scheme.

Educational Studies

It will be recalled that the majority of students attached greater importance to experience of teaching per se than to examining its theoretical foundations. It was not that they rejected educational theory per se. What they wanted was an educational theory which had immediate relevance to their work in the classroom. Students were critical of what they perceived as the over-academic nature of some of the work which they undertook in the disciplines of Education and challenged its relevance to their everyday practice.

C. The probationary year

From the course content and structure it will be recalled that the principal course aim was to train competent classroom practitioners. It was the intention of the Course Director that students completing the training should be versatile and skilled in the classroom, having proved themselves capable of executing what was deemed sound professional practice in a variety of school and classroom contexts. The wider professional concerns of the teacher such as curriculum development or school management structures did not feature explicitly in students' training. There was, however, a secondary concern which, if anything, grew in importance as the course went on. This was the evolution of a personal philosophy of education, based in part upon systematic and sustained analysis of practice. The intention here was to foster awareness, thoughtfulness and objectivity, to fashion a critical and challenging attitude in the students, both toward their own educational practices and those of others.

The extent to which each of these aims was realized will be considered by reference to the views of the probationers themselves and the senior colleagues under whom they served.

The competent classroom practitioner

The views of Headteachers and senior colleagues

There was little doubt that the course had been successful in terms of its major aim. All those students who took up teaching posts were, according to their superiors, manifestly competent classroom teachers. Quite a number were regarded as considerably above average. The benefits of the practical orientation of their training and their multiple school experience were immediately apparent. For instance:

they were able from the outset to take charge of a class and to organize and
    manage pupils on a day-to-day basis. Thus, of one it was stated by her Head:

'There are a lot of things that she knows without them having to be explained
   to her'
they demonstrated in the classroom 'a sureness and confidence', rather as if they
   had been teaching for some years
they structured the learning environment of the pupils with enthusiasm and
   initiative. Several experienced teachers spoke approvingly of the range of
   learning opportunities provided
they prepared their work thoroughly
they were conscientious and professional in their approach to their work
they had good relations with their pupils, treating them with respect. They were
   sensitive to pupils' needs and perceptive about their abilities and limitations.

Only one Headteacher voiced any substantial criticism of the training and of
the probationer in her school. In this case, although the integrated day as an
organizational approach was not completely denounced, it was felt that any
course of initial training which focused only on this approach was inadequate. 'I
think they're not aware of the diversity of primary education and that there is no
(one) right way', was how this shortcoming was referred to. More generally, it
was thought that while the training had been highly successful in terms of
transmitting the practical skills of the classroom to trainees, and that probationers displayed a degree of thoughtfulness in their everyday practice which was
impressive, nevertheless some appeared to lack understanding of the principles
underlying educational practice on occasion. Most Headteachers were, however,
extremely satisfied at the way in which probationers tackled the challenges of
their first posts. Those shortcomings which were diagnosed could justifiably be
attributed to inexperience. Foremost among these were a lack of firmness in
handling pupils and a diffidence towards parents. Probationers needed to be
'professionally competent with other adults', able to respond 'to pressures of
parents' in a way that was appropriate professionally. Also, it was noted of some
probationers that they found it hard to accept criticism.

The views of probationers

In retrospect, the probationers valued certain aspects of their training, but
voiced a number of criticisms. The school experience element of the training was
generally endorsed as having been particularly beneficial. The probationers
regarded it as valuable that they had spent time teaching in a variety of schools in
which the ethos, organization and practice did not necessarily coincide with the
ideology and viewpoints expressed in college. It was acknowledged that the
training provided 'wide experience of different schools' philosophies and how
they are reflected in practice'. As trainees, they had been able to develop their
practical skills in a range of contexts: 'I think we had a good grounding

really – actually organizing (the classroom) and teaching.' This wide-ranging practical experience was deemed not only to have fostered confidence but also to have been a sound preparation for a relatively trouble-free transition to their probationary year. 'I feel competent to do it all', was the comment of one probationer. This remark was not meant to imply that the individual concerned could successfully deal with all the exigencies of her work, but that she felt adept at handling the everyday events of classroom life. That they had been encouraged and urged to innovate was also recognized as having contributed to the confidence which they now felt within the classroom: 'We were encouraged to impress new ideas and methods of organization on the schools which were often traditional and rigid in their methods and attitudes to teaching'. The extended attachment to the continuous experience schools was mentioned specifically as having facilitated a deeper understanding of child development. It had provided 'an opportunity to work with one class over two terms, hence seeing how children progress and how the child adapts his/her work to that development'. It was also felt that spending such a high proportion of course time in school resulted in a strong awareness of the realities of teaching as a career: 'It showed us really what it was going to be like . . . and that it was not an easy option'.

It will be recalled that a related course aim was to instil in the students appropriate attitudes and values. Experienced teachers and probationers alike commended the training for ensuring that high professional standards were promoted. In addition students were presented with a clear notion of what the Course Director considered to be sound primary practice – based upon an interdisciplinary and broadly-based approach to the curriculum. Although some probationers appeared to resent the rather forceful way in which these ideals had been imparted, nevertheless, few appeared to take issue with these principles as such. Probationers affirmed that they had a vision of what they should be aiming for and were appreciative of this – even though some recognized that they might have to bide their time in their current posts before attempting to implement their ideals. Thus one probationer commented:

> Some aspects of school life are contrary to ideas I hold regarding education in young children, but at present I feel compelled to go along with these various school policies . . . However, I intend to suggest changes in these areas once I have completed my probationary year.

Most probationers made it clear that they had no intention of abandoning their educational philosophy, even though as another noted: 'The gap between the ideals we should be aiming for and what we are actually doing is enormous'. This probationer continued: 'Believing in the ideals you have been taught and striving to achieve them leaves one feeling very frustrated at how slowly they begin to be realized'.

The training was therefore seen as having given them a strong sense of direction and ideals to aim at. Such was the conviction with which the ideas and philosophical beliefs of the Course Director and Associate Tutors had been conveyed to them that they had been enabled to enter their first teaching posts with both a sense of purpose and the necessary self-confidence. None of the probationers reported having encountered serious difficulties during their first weeks as beginner teachers and only one expressed serious reservations about the methods they had been taught at college. Even here it appeared that these doubts had much to do with the particular context – and were prompted by implicit staffroom pressure rather than any fundamental reappraisal by the probationer concerned:

> I don't seem to know what I'm supposed to be achieving and if I'm going about it in the right way. I get an impression from staffroom conversation that the way I do things is not the pattern in the school.

A third aspect of their training which the probationers valued highly was the breadth of curriculum coverage. A number of curriculum areas were judged to have been thoroughly reviewed, the teaching of reading and the development of language receiving particular mention. Probationers also valued the emphasis on practical competency which was a feature of much of the curriculum work, and considered that this had enabled them to make a sound start in their first teaching posts.

As one would expect, however, there were criticisms. The superficiality of some Curriculum Studies coverage was one example cited. 'We had a smattering of most things,' was how one probationer expressed it. However, probationers recognized that in all probability this was inevitable given the limited time available and the range of content needing to be covered. There were also whole areas which, it was suggested, had been relatively neglected – although there was an indication that any deficiency here might be offset by the multiple school experience:

> At the time, we thought that there wasn't enough time spent on giving us ideas for Art and Craft, apart from what we gained in schools. Theoretically we weren't . . . given the grounding that we could have had . . . (but) we went round so many different classrooms and so many different schools, that all sorts of ideas suddenly come to you.

The major criticism of Curriculum Studies in general was that insufficient attention had been paid to the lower age range. Informative and relevant though much of this coverage had been, probationers considered that too much time had been devoted to considering the curriculum in relation to the older primary pupil. A further criticism was the failure to consider sufficiently other than the development of the normal child. As a consequence, those probationers who found themselves teaching very young children admitted to having experienced considerable uncertainty and difficulty in teaching certain areas of the curriculum. Thus, of one probationer working in nursery education the teacher responsible for that area remarked:

> – has done what she thinks is done in Reception. I don't think she has a lot of idea about why she has done it . . . She doesn't really know why she has started where she is starting and where she is going . . . She doesn't know how hard to push them . . . (or) what they should know at this stage.

More generally, several probationers reported having misjudged the level of work appropriate to the ability levels of their pupils. 'I was trained to teach competent five-year-olds to bright eight-year-olds, but I'd never had the opportunity to teach not so bright four-year-olds', was how one expressed it.

Compared with the Curriculum Studies and the Method components, the time given to Education Studies on the Northampton course was limited. This was regretted by some probationers who felt it was an important area, even though it had not been covered particularly well, being unduly academic at times and insufficiently related to their experience in school. It was not perceived by probationers as having significantly informed their professional practice.

A feature of the approach to teaching and learning which was employed in the training was the emphasis placed upon collaborative learning. The importance of this was stressed throughout the year, and was incorporated into a number of aspects of the training. Students worked in pairs on their school experience, and with the Teacher Tutor on their IT-INSET work. Although they valued this, it led to many probationers experiencing considerable difficulty in coming to terms with the isolation which characterized their first year of full-time teaching:

> I think the thing that I was least prepared for was the loneliness of being a classroom teacher – none of the school experiences prepared me for this – there has always been the opportunity to discuss what you are doing, get other people's thoughts and ideas and generally share.

As students they had not had to face the harsh fact that once their training had been completed the great majority would have to cope on their own. As one put it: 'You come out of college and there's absolutely nothing . . . Nobody cares unless you're failing.' Or as another remarked:

> There is this feeling that if anyone asks you (about your teaching) it might be misconstrued as lack of confidence in you, and conversely if I ask or talk about it it might be seen as lack of competence.

A final criticism of their training, and one which might have been anticipated, was the tightly scheduled nature of the course. Probationers complained of the lack of time for personal study, and for being able to reflect in a general way on their school experience outside sessions of 'Method'.

It will be recalled that after six weeks of teaching all probationers in the study were asked to complete a questionnaire assessing their capabilities in relation to various aspects of educational practice. Nearly all the Northampton probationers reported a growing confidence in many of the fundamental skills of the classroom. Preparing lessons and teaching materials, and disciplining and controlling pupils were examples of such skills. A considerable change in probationer self-assessment was indicated here. As students coming to the end of their course, they had recorded feeling inadequately prepared to discipline and control pupils. Now they felt much more assured of their ability in this respect. This may suggest that a relatively small period of teaching enhances confidence substantially. Similarly, experience was considered to have led to improvement in the ability to employ a range of teaching approaches. However, some limitations from their training remained in evidence. For instance, as students they had been concerned about their ability to assess pupils' progress prior to developing appropriate teaching and learning strategies. Although the proportion of probationers who admitted to weaknesses in these respects had fallen substantially, nevertheless it was still almost a third of the probationers.

At this stage in the induction year, the probationers were also asked to identify those aspects of practice which they were finding hard to master. Recognizing and catering for pupils' individual needs was one aspect cited. Probationers suggested that part of the difficulty derived from their inability to diagnose and assess pupils' strengths, limitations and achievements. They reported feeling particularly ill-equipped to determine what was a satisfactory rate of progress for individual pupils. It may be that the multiple school experience worked to their disadvantage here in that under such circumstances there was comparatively little time in which to witness pupils' development.

The teaching approach favoured by students on completion of their training was that promoted by the Course Director – the interdisciplinary, child-centred experiential approach. After six weeks in teaching a number of probationers clearly realized that this particular teaching method was not always either welcome or appreciated as *the* organizational basis of primary education. A number of probationers found themselves in situations where they were under considerable pressure to teach in a more formal manner. They were, for example, expected to engage pupils in seat work rather than in structured play. While at this stage most of them declared their intention to remain true to their ideals, nevertheless there was some evidence to suggest that they recognized the need to modify their aims and to make appropriate adjustments in the application of their ideals.

Although perceived lack of competence fell steadily in practically every area over the induction year, nevertheless by its close our questionnaire revealed that the probationers were still expressing concern in relation to assessing pupils' progress and preparing appropriate work in accordance with pupils' abilities. The proportions who considered that they lacked competence in these areas were still a quarter and a third respectively. By this stage a third related problem was reported – namely, probationers' difficulties in appraising the effectiveness of their teaching. This was somewhat surprising considering the emphasis which attached to self-appraisal of classroom practice during the training, and in spite of its having been regarded as an area of competence by a high proportion of probationers earlier in the induction year. It may be accounted for by the probationers' increased sophistication and awareness. Possibly they were more aware now of how difficult it was to isolate those factors which determine the success or failure of any teaching strategy.

The thinking aware practitioner, committed to professional development

The second major aim of the course was the development of the thinking aware practitioner, committed to professional development.

The views of Headteachers and senior colleagues

From our interview with Heads and senior colleagues it was apparent that a characteristic which many of the probationers displayed was the intention to develop and extend their educational practice, not being content simply to retain something because it seemed to work with pupils or because pupils appeared to find it enjoyable. Headteachers and senior colleagues were very impressed at this capability – 'to evaluate and assess (their) actions quite critically, and without getting depressed about it', as one practitioner described it. Thus, of another probationer it was observed: 'She looks carefully and analytically at the purpose of each activity, addressing herself to the fundamental question, ''What do I want to happen and why?'' '

The views of probationers

The need continually to reflect upon and review their practice as part of a career-long commitment to professional development was advocated by the Course Director and her two Associate Tutors in the 'Method' sessions which they conducted. The great majority of the probationers appeared to be in the habit of doing this and to value this as a basis for their practice. There was plenty of evidence to suggest that they were striving to implement this in their teaching – although it was proving much more difficult to effect because of the much greater demands on their time. An indication of this principle in action can be found in the following observation from a probationer: 'There must be other ways, other ideas . . . I've hit upon ways that seem to work but there's got to be a variety of approaches to make (learning) interesting'. It was also apparent in the increasing concern that probationers displayed over the course of the induction year toward the quality of the teaching and learning opportunities they were providing for their pupils.

However, in reviewing sessions of 'Method', probationers voiced two important criticisms:

that direct tutor input and guidance had been insufficient
that the content of the discussions had focused excessively on the classroom at
  the expense of the teacher's wider professional role.

On reflexion the unusual approach which tutors had adopted was still valued for the opportunity it afforded students to share their classroom experience. However, the emphasis on student contribution was felt to have been at the expense of direct tutorial input. Probationers commented: 'I don't think there was enough guidance in these discussions'. 'We had to come up with the ideas and end products with often very little structure.' The reluctance of the tutors to provide direction or to ensure that certain essential content areas were covered in these sessions was viewed as a definite limitation of the training. Some of the specific areas for which hard information and advice were felt to have been lacking were: classroom organization, record keeping, diagnosis and assessment. In addition the injection of educational theory was judged to have been rather thin. Although as students they had been encouraged to develop general principles through constant reflection on their practice, there had been little explicit theory provided by tutors. Probationers indicated that they would have particularly welcomed theory which could have been used as the basis for practical decision making. Pupil motivation and teacher/pupil relationships were amongst the examples cited of areas in which a more direct theoretical presentation would have been appreciated. In addition, probationers felt that reflection in the 'Method' seminars had focused too narrowly on what went on in the classroom, rather than addressing broader aspects of the teacher's role or educational issues from time to time. It should be noted however that the cohort of probationers did not hold this view unanimously. A minority considered that the emphasis of the Course Director and her close colleagues had been apt. As one noted:

> I think the course was right to concentrate on the more nebulous aspects of teaching, throwing us in at the deep end with the thematic approach, using stimulae and the environment . . . The 'basics' are really easy to pick up.

Notes

1. Hereafter referred to as the college.
2. IT-INSET: Initial Training and In-Service Education for Teachers. The principles which underpin the IT-INSET practice developed by Ashton and colleagues (Ashton

et al. 1982) formed the basis of this element of the training at Northampton, although a number of modifications were incorporated.

3. Schools in Northamptonshire LEA were used for purposes of student attachment throughout the training.

4. Six students returned to their serial experience school which was used for the 'Exchange of Roles' experiment.

5. In fact it would have been extremely difficult to have scheduled these at any other time.

3 Case Study: The University of Sussex PGCE for Secondary Specialist Teachers

A. Policy and intent

Introduction

The University of Sussex Secondary PGCE was introduced in 1964. Throughout its lifespan it has been subjected to analysis and appraisal which, in turn, has led to successive modification and refinement. Nevertheless, many of the original defining features have been retained. Two characteristics of this course stand out:

that theoretical study and practical experience should be concurrent – achieved by having students spend time in the university and out in school for much of the duration of the training
that trainee teachers should be supervised and tutored by experienced teachers in school.

In 1983/84, the year in which the course was monitored, there were places for approximately 70 students. The following subjects were offered: Biology, Chemistry, English, Geography, History, Mathematics, Physics and Social Studies.

The notion of 'school-based training' on this course was interpreted in a highly distinctive manner. During the first two terms students spent more time in selected schools – known as Tutorial schools – than in the university. Selected teachers in these schools were appointed as Tutorial fellows and worked collaboratively with university personnel, exercising a major responsibility for promoting and assisting students' professional development, including overseeing and assessing this development.

Aims of the course

The two principal aims of the Sussex PGCE were that on completion of the course all students would have:

(i) attained a reasonable level of basic competence in professional skills
(ii) developed the ability to reflect critically upon educational practice.

The first of these aims was *short term* and functional. The latter was relatively *long term* and concerned the development of a personal philosophy of education.

The aim of professional competence

By the end of their school experience it was intended that students should have demonstrated a mastery of basic classroom techniques. They were also expected to be able to operate with adequate proficiency at the level of general professional skills. That is to say, they should have become acquainted with, and gone some way towards meeting, the numerous other demands made upon teachers nowadays – the ability to fulfil pastoral duties or engage in curriculum development, for example.

The most effective means by which this aim could be attained were deemed to be:

the thorough participation by the student in all aspects of school life
the transfer of a significant part of the training process to practising teachers.

The belief that more than mere acquaintance with school personnel, procedures and structures were essential for a sound professional training lay at the heart of the Sussex course. It was the rationale for the firm preference for extended single school experience and was clearly stated in the Course Document:[1]

> Students learn the craft of teaching best by working alongside experienced colleagues and sharing the life of a school over an extended period. (The Course Document: 2)

University tutors maintained that learning the craft of teaching and what it was to function as a teacher entailed more than merely having experience of *teaching*:

> It's simply not a matter of practice – it's practice embedded in the context of school experience. (Course Director)

'School experience' was the term by which the practical component of the training was known:

> This term was chosen deliberately to distinguish it from mere teaching practice. It is understood to mean more than performance in the classroom and to embrace the whole of the student's relationships within the school community. (The Course Document: 5)

School experience was an opportunity for students to develop the skills necessary to teach their subject. However, it was also intended that students should experience at first hand other facets of the teacher's role. Prolonged immersion in a single school meant that they could accumulate a far more detailed knowledge of the many different aspects of school life than would be possible in the conventional four- or five-week block teaching practice.

The successful operationalization of the aim of both classroom and general professional competence depended in part on the quality and capabilities of teachers recruited to the scheme, and on devolving responsibility to them as joint contributors to the training. It was the teachers who could most readily transmit the craft of teaching and who could fully initiate the student into their other professional functions – liaising with parents and community-based agencies or pastoral support for example. Their fundamental contribution was formally acknowledged:

> The training is school-based: teachers in the schools are appointed as tutors by the university to take a *major responsibility* for supervising and assessing students' training experience. (The Course Document: 2, emphasis added)

The aim of critical reflection

The second major aim of the training concerned the reflective dimension of the students' development. This was defined by a faculty member as 'the ability to make informed and professional judgements about what they are doing and why'. Students, it was maintained, would necessarily 'theorize' and reflect upon their practice and in time devise their own educational philosophy. The Sussex course placed high priority on developing this reflective process. A former Course Director described this process as 'the essence of the course':

> Our ability to encourage students to adopt a critical, reflective stance towards their activities . . . to provide them with the reality of experience in the school, at the same time confronting them with ideas about the purpose of education, schooling, curriculum, etc., and demanding that they work out for themselves a supportable justification for what they are doing or intend to do.

That theory should develop out of, or 'feed off', practice was so fundamental a principal at Sussex that the theoretical component of the course was not based on any master list of topics and issues such as are usually found in courses of initial teacher training. Instead, students' 'theories' arose out of their experience in school, challenged or supported by existing beliefs, ideologies or theoretical explanations. As the Course Director explained, training as conceived at Sussex meant 'the exploration of experience rather than the transmission of a formal body of knowledge'. Its focus was 'process elements rather than (an end) product'.

The length of the school attachment was justified not only on the grounds that it allowed the student the maximum possible time in which to acquire professional skills. An extended placement also generated a substantial amount of material – that is, situations and problems which students had experienced – to be subjected to review and analysis. This material formed the basis for the development of grounded theory. Additionally it was through the concurrent alternating structure of the school attachment and time spent in the university that a creative and interactive relationship between the specifics of practice and the generalizations of theory was achieved.

> If students were to spend most of their time in the university, they might be given a vision, but one divorced from reality. If they were totally based in school . . . the realism of the experience would be incontestible but they could lose a sense of what was possible outside the walls of the Tutorial school. Our course attempts to do both simultaneously; the attempt produces its own kind of tension. (The Course Document: 11–12)

A consequence of giving precedence to a theory which was generated from practice was that students following the course might not be introduced to some of the educational theory routinely included in more conventional courses. Although it was acknowledged that 'the theory programme . . . is necessarily thin, compared with many other PGCE courses', also that 'there are important areas of educational theory which are not developed . . . or (which) are given less rigorous attention', nevertheless tutors did not appear unduly concerned at this. Developing students' own reflective abilities had to take priority. A second consequence was that it was not possible to speak of '*the* Sussex PGCE' since the development of an educational philosophy was based on personal experience. As the student was placed under the guidance of a given teacher, the Teacher Tutor, in a single school and was a member of a regularly convened seminar group, the training that any student received in terms of content could well vary. University staff and teachers enjoyed considerable autonomy regarding both the manner in which they carried out their tutoring and the content covered. As one tutor acknowledged, 'It does mean there is no common experience on the course . . . different groups have different needs, different interests and different concerns.' The only elements common to all students were that the training was school-based, that reflection on practice was strongly emphasized, and the various topics covered in plenary sessions and conferences.

Analysis and discussion in seminar and tutorial and in a Course File were the means by which this reflective process was developed. In these contexts students were required to consider their practice in depth, drawing upon theoretical perspectives derived from the educational and research literatures as appropriate.

You structure the course so that you talk about the school . . . and classroom experience. You can learn more by being in it and of it than (by) talking about it in the abstract. (Course Director)

Course structure and content

Induction

The course began with a two-week induction period, the first five days of which were spent in the university and the latter five days in the Tutorial school. Over the years a pool of 12 secondary 'Tutorial schools' had been established[2], in each of which were located groups of four to six students. During the university-based induction, students met their Personal and Curriculum Tutors and fellow members of these groups. The Personal Tutor group comprised all the students attached to a given Tutorial school. It was thus a mixed group with respect to students' main subjects. The curriculum group was subject-specific. There were meetings of both types of student group during the first week, the intention being to develop group identity and establish a teaching agenda for the term. Students also met those teachers from their tutorial schools who would be contributing most fully to their training, the Teacher Tutor and the General Tutor.

The nature of the school-based induction was left to the General Tutors in the schools to determine and was therefore likely to vary. It was regarded as a period of general familiarization, a time when students made the first contact with their subject departments and undertook some classroom observation. They should also become acquainted with the school, its practices, its pupils and the community it served.

The school-based component

For the majority of the Autumn and Spring terms, each student spent three days a week attached to his or her Tutorial school. The remaining two days each week were spent in the university. At the end of the Spring term students undertook a four-week block teaching practice in the same school. This distribution of student time reflected the high value placed on school experience by those who exercised responsibility for the training. The university also emphasized a carefully graduated entry into classroom teaching. Initially students would observe staff teaching in their own and other departments and would discuss the craft of teaching with the member of staff in their department who was formally responsible for them, their Teacher Tutor. Subsequently they would help out in the classroom in accordance with that teacher's guidance and instructions, perhaps working with individuals and small groups on materials and activities which they themselves had prepared, graduating to the point where they took their first class lesson unaided. Teacher Tutors were advised by the university that only after about four weeks should students begin to take class lessons and even then for no more than one-third of the timetable.

In addition to being eased into teaching, students should also learn about general school practices, e.g. assessment and record keeping, curriculum development, and the work of outside agencies such as the Schools Psychological Service. This work took place in seminars convened by the member of staff who exercised overall responsibility for all students attached to the particular Tutorial school, the General Tutor. Since the agenda for these seminars was to some extent negotiated between the students and the General Tutor in accordance with student interest and need, some variation in experience was likely across the overall student population.

The college-based component

As was noted above all of the students attached to a particular school were overseen by a Personal Tutor. It was the responsibility of the Personal Tutor to arrange a programme of weekly seminars which incorporated various aspects of education theory. These took place during the Autumn and Spring terms. Personal Tutors also held individual tutorials from time to time. Seminars, workshops and tutorials which focused on the pedagogy of a given subject were held by the Curriculum Tutor. Teacher Tutors were invited to attend selected seminars and to contribute on the basis of their professional experience. The student body as a whole experienced relatively few events held in common. Unlike many courses of initial training there was no common series of lectures. However, there were occasional plenary sessions and conferences throughout the course. These covered specific features of the training such as the Course File and Special Study as well as contemporary issues in education such as Education and the Inner City and Education in a Multi-ethnic Society. There was also coverage of instrumental matters such as applying for teaching posts and conditions of service.

The Summer term

At the beginning of the Summer term students who had successfully completed the practical component of the training were eligible to choose an 'Alternative Experience'. This was a three-week placement in another educational or education-related context. In 1983/84, students whose progress was followed by the team of evaluators spent time in the following settings: Colleges of Further Education; adventure playground; adult training centres; special schools; primary schools. Any student who had not satisfactorily completed his or her school experience was offered an additional teaching experience in a second school in lieu of the Alternative Experience. There followed a four-week programme of

Options for all students. Options offered included: Computer Studies; Science, Technology and Society in Education; Sexism in School and Society; Language and Literacy in School; Audio Visual Aids; Drama Workshop; and First Aid. At the same time students were expected to undertake the main body of work on their Special Study and to complete their Course File. The final week of the course was given over to assessment.

Figure 3.1 gives an outline of the programme for the year.

Figure 3.2 illustrates the nature and distribution of student activities in school and in the university.

Figure 3.3 gives the key personnel with whom the student associated.

Course personnel

Students who took the post-graduate certificate at the University of Sussex worked with four kinds of tutor. In the *school* these were the Teacher Tutor and the General Tutor; in the *university* they were the Curriculum Tutor and the Personal Tutor.

School personnel

That teachers in school had major responsibilities in preparing intending members of the profession has already been noted. That joint responsibility was formally recognized by the university in that it granted teachers considerable autonomy in this work. Broad guidelines on their tutorial responsibilities had been developed in the university and were circulated among the teachers involved. Yet they did not define or prescribe in any hard and fast way what or how the Teacher or General Tutor should contribute. A university tutor noted: 'Their (teachers') general role is well defined but the actual details are not defined.'

The Teacher Tutor

The Teacher Tutor was described in the guidelines mentioned above as the 'anchor person' in school. There was one Teacher Tutor per subject department. They were principally responsible for the classroom practice element of the student's school experience. Their role incorporated the following *professional* elements:[3]

discussing with the student their own planning and preparation and the theories and values which underpin them, prior to guiding and supervising the student's own lesson planning and preparation

supervising the student's teaching and helping the student to analyse and evaluate his or her practice

assessing the student with respect to his or her developing classroom competencies. [This was normally undertaken in conjunction with the General Tutor.]

Figure 3.1 Outline of the University of Sussex PGCE (secondary).

Term 1

Week 1	Week 2	Week 3	Week 4	Weeks 5–10
University-based Induction	School-based Induction	Tutorial school programme commenced (3 days/week)	School half term	Tutorial school programme resumed
		University programme commenced (meetings of Curriculum Group and Personal Tutor Group) (2 days/week)	University programme continued. It included a Workshop: 'Drama Across the Curriculum'	University programme included a day Conference: 'Classroom Practice and Organization' and a plenary session: 'The Course File and Special Study'

Term 2

Weeks 1–6/8–10	Week 7	Weeks 11–14
Tutorial school programme continued	School half term	Full time school experience (5 days/week)
University programme continued. It included four plenary sessions and a day Conference: 'Education and the Inner City'	University programme continued. It included a plenary session: 'Introduction to Race and Education'	

Term 3

Weeks 1–3	Weeks 4–8	Week 9
Alternative experience (5 days/week)	Individual work on Special Study and Course File. Options programme. Personal Tutor groups met. A 3-day Conference in week 8: 'Education in a Multi-Ethnic Society'	Student Assessment

Figure 3.2 Outline of main student activities in school.

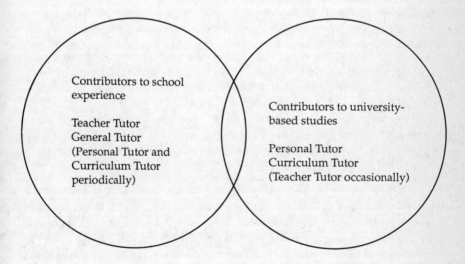

School-based activities

Observing teachers teaching
Teaching
Seminars
Tutorials
Engaging in pastoral work
Engaging in extra-curricular
activities

University-based activities

Meetings of the Personal
Tutor Group (+ individual tutorials)
Meetings of the Curriculum
Group (+ individual tutorials)
Plenary sessions
Conferences
Options

Figure 3.3 Outline of key personnel with whom students engage.

Contributors to school
experience

Teacher Tutor
General Tutor
(Personal Tutor and
Curriculum Tutor
periodically)

Contributors to university-
based studies

Personal Tutor
Curriculum Tutor
(Teacher Tutor occasionally)

The following *administrative* elements were also discharged:

initiating the student into the various aspects of departmental practice (e.g. the syllabuses used, the location of teaching resources)

arranging on the student's behalf 'access to carefully selected classes in order to give . . . a variety of experience', initially in an observational capacity but subsequently in a direct teaching role

liaising with departmental colleagues whose classes had been taken over in order to monitor the student's teaching performance and development across the age and ability range.

Implicit in much of the above was a pastoral as well as an instructional responsibility towards the student. That 'the pastoral skills of practising teachers are the missing dimension in many conventional forms of teacher training', was noted in The Course Document (p. 8). In the Sussex course the importance of this aspect of the Teacher Tutor's role was fully acknowledged.

The General Tutor

The General Tutor was responsible for the organization and management of the overall experience of the whole group of students attached to a Tutorial school. The role entailed:[4]

inducting students into the life of the school, initially within the subject department and subsequently in other areas of the school

introducing 'a general perspective on school organization' by arranging 'a sequential programme of seminar discussions' for all students attached to the school,

such as will acquaint (them) with a wider view of teaching and the process of education than can be acquired in the course of the students' teaching programme alone. The complementary role of the General Tutor requires them to introduce both a general perspective on school organization and a personal conception of the school and its community, and of the philosophical and organizational problems of making it work (extracted from Guidelines for General Tutors: 2).

By this means it was intended that practice in the classroom should be extended into school experience in structuring the students' progress and development in conjunction with the relevant Teacher Tutor, preparing an interim report on each student's classroom performance in the second term. The intention was that the report should identify any student at risk of failing to complete the school experience satisfactorily. Thereafter the General Tutor and the Teacher Tutor jointly agreed the final assessment with regard to the student's 'capacity *and potential* as a practising teacher' (The Course Document: 7, emphasis added). In addition, the General Tutor was expected to appraise the student from a wider perspective – that of a future member of the teaching profession. Hence the student's relationships with colleagues, any extra-curricular involvement with pupils and such like would also be taken into account. The General Tutor oversaw the administrative aspects of student assessment supporting and monitoring the overall practice within the school. The General Tutor was responsible for determining which colleagues became Teacher Tutors and for supporting them in this work. General Tutors had some responsibility for inducting newcomers into this role liaising with the university, mainly through the Personal Tutor. The General Tutor monitored the practice informally and discreetly, bringing to the attention of staff of the university any situation which was regarded as unsatisfactory. In addition General Tutors attended meetings held at the university to discuss the further development of the training programme.

University personnel

The Curriculum Tutor

The Curriculum Tutor, a university lecturer with a particular subject specialism, was principally concerned with 'the study of and preparation for teaching within a particular discipline or an inter-disciplinary field' (The Course Document: 9). The focus of his or her concern was subject *pedagogy*. The responsibilities of the Curriculum Tutor included:[5]

organizing weekly seminars for students. These seminars focused on questions of curriculum and method. In addition to advising and assisting students with the preparation, delivery and evaluation of lessons, Curriculum Tutors helped to expand the students' teaching skills by introducing them to the range of views which exist concerning the methodology of their subject. In so doing, they capitalized on the likely variation in departmental practices to be found in the six or seven schools in which members of the curriculum group were located

making supervisory visits to students in school – usually termly – during which they were expected to provide guidance and support for the student

liaising with the Teacher Tutor when on school visits and when the latter attended curriculum sessions at the university. In The Course Document it was explicitly stated that Curriculum Tutors should seek 'to inject from outside the school, ideas about matters of pedagogy and innovation in the teachings of the subject' (p. 10)

keeping Personal Tutors informed about the general professional development of their students. More substantial exchange of views and discussion was likely where a student encountered pronounced difficulties.

Curriculum Tutors played no formal part in the assessment of the Students' teaching, this task having been devolved to practising teachers.

The Personal Tutor

The Personal Tutor had a background in one of the education disciplines or in a subject specialism. He or she was responsible on behalf of the university for the group of students attached to a particular Tutorial school [6] and handled all university matters which concerned them. The Personal Tutor's responsibilities were:[7]

exercising pastoral responsibility for each student

liaising with the school regarding the school experience in general and the progress and assessment of each individual student in particular. For this purpose the Personal Tutor's primary contact in the school was the General Tutor

making a minimum of two supervisory visits per term to students in school

teaching the educational theory elements of the course by means of seminars and tutorials in which students' experiences in school were subjected to 'critical analysis and illuminated and extended by relevant theoretical perspectives' (The Course Document: 9). The likely differences between departments in the Tutorial school represented a particular focus of the Personal Tutor's attention in this work

providing tutorial support in the development of the Course File, ensuring that an appropriate topic was chosen as the subject of the Special Study and that a supervisor for this work was appointed

assessing the Course File. The Personal Tutor exercised sole responsibility for this.

Course assessment

That the Sussex PGCE course aimed to develop the habit of critical reflection in the student has already been discussed. Likewise that the means of training the competent practitioner was to devolve to teachers the major responsibility for the supervision and assessment of teaching competence. Both of these principles underlying the training were reflected in the assessment procedures.

Students were awarded the Certificate by the Examination Board on the basis of three pieces of evidence:

Continuous assessment of the school experience component

Written reports on school experience were received from both Teacher and General Tutors and from the student's Personal Tutor. General Tutors were required to identify in their Interim Report of the Spring term any student whom they considered to be 'at risk' of failing to complete satisfactorily their school experience. This was to allow time for remedial measures to be identified and put into operation. Where a student was formally designated 'at risk' the school experience was usually extended into the third term and in a different school. This was a real advantage which the Sussex course enjoyed over many more traditional courses wherein any extension was usually undertaken only *after* the course had formally ended.

The Course File

Students were required to maintain a Course File for the duration of the training. It was a unique feature of the Sussex course, and 'fundamental to the Sussex view of the world' (Course Director). In the Course Document it was stated of the Course File that it

> should reflect all aspects of the course, and may include papers prepared for seminars, comments on reading or lectures, group or individual research and the development of teaching sequences in school. (p. 5)

A Personal Tutor noted of its content: 'It should be more than descriptive . . . it should reflect your ability to analyse and evaluate what has happened to you'. In a guideline on the File which was circulated to students they were advised that their entries should reveal evidence of 'understanding, analytic skill, critical insight and acumen and the application of theory to the issues of practice'. C. Wright Mills' (1959) concept of 'intellectual craftsmanship' was cited: 'You must learn to use your life experience in your intellectual work – continually to examine and interpret it. In this sense, craftsmanship is the centre of yourself'. The Course File was a major means by which students could demonstrate the evolution of their ability to reflect critically upon all aspects of the training. In principle only the Personal Tutor who was assigned responsibility for assessing it, had access to the whole File. Sections of Files could be read by the Curriculum Tutor, while the Course Director and External Examiners also read the Files of a cross-section of students. The main reason for this restricted access was that it was intended to preserve the sense of personal audience which tutors maintained was paramount.

The special study

This was a substantial piece of work which commenced in the second term and which could take many forms. It entailed inquiry either specific to a subject discipline or more generally to an educational issue or issues. The intention was 'to relate practice to theory in a particular aspect of education' (The Course Document: 6).

Student support programme

Another unique aspect of the Sussex PGCE was the existence of a comprehensive and systematic network of support which could be made available should the need arise. That such a facility existed arguably was only appropriate given the early attachment to the Tutorial school for students on this course. It was, however, pointed out that the various support services were not merely remedial; they had a preventative function too. The Course Director explained that these services 'were not there necessarily for those who need a crutch. Even the best students can be made better'. Intervention to prevent minor anxieties or misunderstandings becoming major problems was seen as the key. In order for it to be successful there was a need for prompt and accurate assessment of a student's circumstances coupled with swift action.

In the normal run of events, with encouragement and assistance from their Teacher Tutor, students should gradually acquire insights into the nature of teaching and learning and develop the basic classroom competences. A small minority, however, were likely to experience difficulties in this regard. For these students forms of additional support – termed 'first response' – might be necessary.

> Such first response may vary from additional observation of the student together with tutorials, to sessions which focus on developing a particular attribute (e.g. questioning techniques, lesson planning, class control. . .).
> (From *PGCE Student Support Programme and the Student 'At Risk'*)

The range of 'first responses' was considerable. Personal and/or Curriculum Tutors were sometimes involved in their planning. Even so there might be students who, despite this additional support from school personnel, appeared to be moving toward a situation where they could be formally designated 'at risk'. For these students three broad areas of support could be drawn upon:

workshops on voice production/presentation of self: designed 'to develop aspects such as verbal and non-verbal elements of communication, interpersonal awareness and . . . "with-it-ness" in the classroom context'. These were provided in the latter part of the Autumn term and early in the Spring term

video feedback: provided for students who persistently seemed unable to benefit from analysis of their performance in the classroom by the Teacher or General Tutor

short-term support tutor: an experienced teacher trainer and teacher worked alongside the student in the school on a one-to-one basis and free of the issues of assessment.

Course administration

The PGCE was located organizationally within the Education Area of the university and its policy determined by the PGCE Programme Group which functioned as an executive committee. This Group met once a term or more frequently if necessary. Membership of the Group was open to all university-based tutors on the course. Since it was impossible for all school-based tutors to participate, six representatives of the Teacher and General Tutors were invited to serve on the Programme Group. There were also two student representatives. The PGCE Examination Board consisted of: the nominee of the Chairman of the Education Area as Chairman; two External Examiners; the Course Director; six representatives of the university-based tutors; and six representatives of the school-based tutors, nominated by the Chairman of the Education Area. (The school-based tutor representatives also served on the PGCE Programme Group.) While policy matters and planning decisions were formally ratified by the Programme Group, the strong commitment to the principle of participation which obtained within the Education Area meant that all tutors, both school and university-based, would have been actively consulted beforehand.

Day-to-day management of the PGCE rested with the Course Director. This position was held for a period of three years and was filled by a faculty member attached to the Education Area. The post was principally an administrative one and involved determining the deployment of resources allocated to the course, deciding with tutorial schools how they should be involved in the course, approaching lecturers and negotiating their contribution to the course, and so forth. While the Course Director's formal authority was relatively restricted, in practice he or she could exert influence through the distribution of the course teaching-time and finances.

Resourcing

In the schools

In 1983/84, East Sussex LEA, one of the two Authorities approached, agreed to invest additional resources in the two schools participating in the evaluation, and each was given an extra 0.3 of a teacher. The other LEA whose schools took in students from the University, West Sussex, felt unable to contribute in this way. This additional resourcing was intended to ease the problem for teachers of finding enough time for tutoring students. It was also regarded as some compensation for staff for the stress resulting from having their day-to-day activities scrutinized by the research team. The extent of the resourcing, it was emphasized, was all that the Authority could afford in the present climate and had been obtained only by 'juggling with resources'. In effect this meant that its scope for encouraging initiatives in other schools was reduced.

The two resourced schools differed in how they deployed this additional resourcing. In one school, each Teacher Tutor was given between two and three free periods a fortnight for the purpose of working with or on behalf of students. Exactly how teachers chose to use this time was a matter for each individual to decide, although the General Tutor sought to ensure that it was utilized for the benefit of the students, either directly or indirectly. The General Tutor also benefited slightly, even though responsibility for students was formally built into her job description and reflected in her timetable. In the second school, the additional resourcing went into the school's general staffing allocation. In effect it served to reduce the scale of the cutback in staffing occasioned by falling rolls.

In the university

The number of hours the Course Director had at his disposal for staffing the PGCE was based on the number of students enrolled. For 1983/84 this figure was 6.33 posts, one post being the equivalent of 280 hours of contact time. The Course Director had first to estimate the desirable contribution of each of his colleagues to the PGCE and then negotiate with each individual what he/she was able to give. Curriculum Tutors received differing teaching allowances depending on the number of students in their tutor group. The allocation for Personal Tutors was somewhat higher in recognition of their greater commitment of time – providing individual tutorials as well as convening seminars and visiting schools more frequently, for example.

The selection of schools

As will have become clear by now, the university placed great emphasis upon working in partnership with schools, turning over considerable responsibility for training student teachers to practitioners in the field. Because of the extent of this responsibility, and the complexity of the role which practising teachers were expected to discharge, the university exercised care in selecting those schools with which to link.

When considering whether a school should be admitted to the pool of tutorial schools, a series of visits and meetings involving representatives of the school and the university would occur. This procedure usually extended over several months. Members of the university maintained that it was essential that school staffs not be left in any doubt about the onerous nature of what the responsibility entailed. For their part they needed to be reassured of a genuine desire on the part of the school to be involved and a willingness to commit themselves fully. Other factors taken into account in determining whether or not to enter into partnership with a school included:

the 'climate' or ethos of the school

evidence of awareness and of a thoughtful, challenging, possibly even self-critical attitude toward the nature and purpose of education on the part of at least some staff

the shared belief that the Sussex approach to initial training was the right way to go about training intending teachers

a desire to work collaboratively with the university.

Tutors were, however, honest enough to admit that what they were looking for ideally and what it was realistic to ask for were not one and the same. They acknowledged that the perfect placement was not what they were seeking. Schools were highly complex organizations and in a state of constant flux. It was highly improbable that any school could be satisfactory in every respect. Tutors maintained that likely blemishes would be more than counteracted by the school experience being subjected to close scrutiny and analysis. They made far more of the analytical skills of the students and of their own subtle interventions in the development of these skills than of the qualities obtaining at the level of school or department. One university tutor, for example, remarked of the school which he was responsible for liaising with, 'It's an ordinary sort of school, it's got lots of problems but it's up to the student to discover these and deal with them'. He conceived of his responsibility in part as enabling students 'to understand the strengths of the situation in which they are going to work'. Except in extreme circumstances the 'goodness' or 'badness' of a school or department was not of undue concern: 'If we can't get the best teacher-tutors we're not shattered by this because the experience is critically appraised.' This was echoed by the Course Director who maintained that for learning to occur and be of value it was not necessary to have only good experiences: 'Students feel they can't have good experience unless it's all going brilliantly . . . (but) out of the biggest disasters can come the finest (learning) experiences'.

B. Implementation of the course

The school-based component

As has been noted, students undertaking their PGCE training at the University of Sussex were assigned to four kinds of tutors, each of whom had a characteristic role to play. How these tutors perceived and executed their responsibilities is considered in the following sections.

Key personnel: enactment of role

The Teacher Tutor

There were eight Teacher Tutors in the two schools monitored by the project team, three of whom were first time appointees to this position. For this reason, and in the absence of a tight role prescription by the university, differences between individuals as to how they interpreted and discharged their responsibilities might reasonably have been expected. There was in fact considerable agreement between Teacher Tutors on:

their pastoral responsibilities towards the students in their charge
the focus of their professional concerns as collaborators in teacher training.

All Teacher Tutors regarded it as an important function of their office to support and encourage students. Students needed to be cushioned but not feather-bedded. They should be helped through 'the confidence barrier' – that is the lack of confidence initially – to the point where they could survive in the classroom. Several tutors reported exercising great care in selecting classes for students, for although they subscribed to the view that students should teach across the age and ability range, they were reluctant to risk placing them with a class which was recognized as 'difficult'. They also felt that there was a balance to be kept between providing guidance and support and at the same time allowing students the freedom to demonstrate initiative and thus gain a sense of personal achievement. Most Teacher Tutors regarded it as important that students should experiment. A typical piece of advice from teacher to student was as follows: 'Be dramatic, risk your own personality . . . make yourself vulnerable. If you don't do it as a student, the chances are much more limited that you will as a teacher.' Training was seen as a time when, as another teacher put it, 'one can afford to experiment to see the effect of dynamic lessons'. Teacher Tutors stressed the value of being frank but also of framing their criticisms as constructively as possible when discussing students' teaching with them. It was also apparent that a good many Teacher Tutors did not assume that they had a monopoly of practitioner wisdom. As one senior teacher put it: 'The Sussex way encourages questions to be asked – and answered – non-defensively.'

The second area of agreement between Teacher Tutors reflected their commitment to professional practice. By common consent, competence in basic practical techniques of classroom teaching was seen as more desirable than theoretical sophistication. There was little point in debating, say, different philosophies of education if students were not capable of delivering lessons with some proficiency. Several Teacher Tutors expressly stated that they were not concerned about educational theory or the theoretical aspects of teaching. These were viewed more properly as the province of the university. There was some evidence to suggest that some of the teachers involved believed that what went on in school was the more crucial experience for the neophyte teacher. As one put it: 'The time you really learn to be a teacher is when you're in school.'

All Teacher Tutors held tutorials weekly throughout the attachment. Typically, discussion initially focused on basic classroom practicalities, e.g. drawing up lesson plans, discipline and control, preparation of worksheets, use of blackboard, presentation of self. In addition attention was paid to the unique problems of particular subject areas. Teacher Tutors in the Sciences, for example, stressed the importance of adequate safety precautions in the laboratory. At first then, the content of tutorials was specific, instrumental and of immediate relevance for the novice teacher.

The practices of Teacher Tutors differed most in the degree to which they sought to extend the students' learning and vision beyond the confines of their immediate classroom experiences. Some continued to reiterate the details of practice even when their students had acquired an adequate repertoire of basic skills and had established themselves as teachers in their own right. That discussion to some extent would become more sophisticated over time was to be expected since the students' needs and concerns evolved over the training period, and this was reflected in the issues and problems which they themselves raised with their Teacher Tutors. A minority of Teacher Tutors, however, actively sought to elevate and expand the students' interests and awareness by attempting to generalize beyond the particular. This was achieved in three main ways:

by arranging for students to observe other teachers or meet remedial specialists
by raising questions which would generate more sophisticated inquiry and
   analysis (e.g. about the principles on which a syllabus is selected, the construc-
   tion and use of diagnostic tests, the recommendations of government-
   commissioned inquiries such as Cockroft, 1982)
by challenging the received wisdom by introducing a theoretical dimension – as
   one Teacher Tutor put it, by trying to take 'some sort of midway position. In a
   sense I act as a bridge between the more academic view of things and the more
   everyday, practical sort of situation'.

The intentions behind such actions were variously described as providing students with the 'wherewithal to go on thinking throughout their career' or producing teachers 'who through their career will continue to be examining what they're doing and why they're doing it'.

In most of the tutorials throughout the two terms, however, discussion rarely strayed from concerns immediate and practical. To our knowledge there were few attempts to locate students' comments and experiences within the body of relevant educational theory. One Teacher Tutor who did attempt this justified his actions on the grounds that training based within a single school ran the risk of being unduly narrow: 'I don't think one school is a good enough reflection of all the sorts of issues that exist'. What is underlined by this finding is the critical importance of the theoretical dimension introduced in the university-based studies.

The General Tutor

The two General Tutors studied acknowledged their overall responsibility for the students placed in their schools, but they differed in the way in which they translated this responsibility into action. They were agreed that the role entailed:

ensuring that students made a sound start in their placement, which necessitated their being intensively involved during the induction period
fostering student awareness of issues beyond the classroom through seminar
   discussions and encouraging them to take on school-wide commitments
keeping informed of student progress and development during the attachment
   through regular contact with the Teacher Tutor. Assessing all students and
   supporting any who experienced particular difficulties
contributing to the success of the practice in general by maintaining communication with the university.

However, while tutors may retain a deep personal commitment to their duties, circumstances may oblige them to compromise or even to waive them. This was the case for one of the General Tutors. As a consequence, the experience of the students varied rather between the two schools. We might reasonably have anticipated even greater contrasts had our evaluation extended across all of the Tutorial schools.

Induction   The induction programmes at the two schools were generally similar. Both General Tutors placed major emphasis on the students acquiring a broad perspective. As one explained, it would be 'the easiest thing' for students 'to get stuck into the process of teaching their subject'. This tutor maintained that there would be ample time for this later in the attachment. It was considered essential that students first gain an understanding of the institution as a whole, that they acquired 'a sense of the complexity of the place'. Accordingly, they were introduced to a number of key personnel (e.g. Head Teacher, Head of Upper School, Head of Resources) and school practices (e.g. pupil assessment, the pastoral system). They attended a tutor group meeting, explored the immediate neighbourhood in order to acquire some understanding of the catchment area served by the school, and they each followed a second year pupil for a day – sitting in on lessons, and generally 'experiencing the day as the child experiences it', with the aim of 'getting back to the child's perspective'. In the second school, the students visited the three separate sites. They also visited a feeder primary school in order to obtain a sense of the continuity of the educational process. They were given a worksheet which was intended to challenge and stimulate their observations. In both schools students spent the final days of the induction period in their respective subject departments under the direction of their Teacher Tutors, observing or assisting in the classroom and discussing their future teaching and gradual involvement in departmental practices.

Developing the school experience   On completion of the induction period, the General Tutor in one of the schools continued to play a major part in determining and overseeing the nature of the school experiences: convening regular seminars, encouraging students to assume pastoral responsibilities and to engage in extra-curricular activities. This tutor monitored the handling of students by the Teacher Tutors closely, albeit discreetly and with great sensitivity. A particularly strong commitment was articulated to any student at risk of failing the practical component of the school experience. Alternative arrangements which would give them a chance to succeed and re-establish their confidence and commitment would be made. As part of this, this General Tutor made time to observe each student teaching at least once. Close contact was maintained with the university, the tutor attending all relevant meetings and keeping the Personal Tutor informed of the circumstances of each student.

The second General Tutor, having also been active in planning and organizing the initial period, thereafter participated less in the day-to-day events of the practice. Seminars were held only intermittently and few opportunities were, in the end, made available for students to engage in wider professional activities such as curriculum development or pastoral care. This tutor was not in a position to be able to monitor students' progress closely, nor to plan and execute remedial action when circumstances seemed to warrant it. In fact there was limited contact with the students – this in spite of the tutor's expressed intention of observing each student teach and of discussing them individually with their respective Teacher Tutors. Retrospectively, this tutor agreed that there had been a tendency to operate on the assumption that anything untoward would be brought to his attention, and that if this did not occur, that the practice was proceeding satisfactorily for all concerned.

There were at least two factors which clearly contributed to the disparity in how these General Tutors undertook their duties. The first concerned their respective experience. One of the tutors, whose particular responsibility was staffing, had been one of the school's three Deputy Heads for a number of years and had considerable experience in managing student programmes. The second tutor, in contrast, was new to both the position of Vice Principal and General Tutor. Such a senior position brought with it a great many pressures and demands on his time. In addition, during the course of the year he became involved in a curriculum development project and attended a 20-week course on Management. Also, time to prepare in advance of the student attachment commencing had been relatively limited since his predecessor had left late on in the previous term. Once the programme was underway this tutor experienced great difficulty in finding the time to devote to the role. Also, compared to his counterpart in the other school he was disadvantaged by not having any previous relevant experience to draw upon. In the early stages of the practice in particular he admitted to having been uncertain about the philosophy underlying the practice and about the content of seminars to be organized. He had also been unsure about the extent to which students' teaching should be monitored and the overall procedure for student assessment. Although there had been opportunities to discuss these and other matters with the Personal Tutor, and he had been given a number of documents which the university had prepared, he maintained that none of these could match having had some prior firsthand experience to draw upon.

The second factor which served to constrain enactment of the role was the context in which the General Tutors operated. The Head Teacher and senior colleagues of the first tutor were strongly committed to the principle that schools should be active partners in the training of future generations of teachers, and arranged a timetable allowance for the management of the student programme. In the case of the second tutor, initial training did not command such a priority at institutional level. The Principal stated that it was not possible to justify diverting scarce resources from other areas in order that the General Tutor's limited timetabling allowance be supplemented. Additionally, the school was on three sites, which meant that monitoring the practice as a whole was both difficult and time consuming.

In noting some of the factors which intervened between intention and actualization, the difficulty of putting into operation a school-based training programme is highlighted.

A possible lack of congruence between the ideal professional collaboration as envisaged by the training institution and the more limited contribution which may be all that school personnel can make, is the more critical under the school-based model than under the traditional approach to training, where much less of the substance of the training is devolved upon the schools. The above account clearly illustrates how demanding and unsettling it can be to undertake this responsibility for the first time. It is also apparent that the students attached to these schools will have had contrasting school experiences. In one case the training proceeded in a highly supportive environment and was rich and broadly based. In the other, as a consequence of the General Tutor being unable to arrange various activities which could have supplemented their classroom practice, students' school experience was less diverse and rewarding.

Seminars It was intended that General Tutors should convene seminars in school on a regular (fortnightly) basis for all students attached to their school. Seminars were in fact only held with any regularity in one of the schools, and even then not as frequently as this. This discrepancy between intention and realization – both tutors intended to arrange regular meetings – was attributed to the pressures which all parties were under, or to unforeseen events which necessitated cancelling meetings at the last minute. In those seminars which did take place, a variety of topics were covered. They included: systems of pastoral care, curriculum development, assessment and record keeping and language across the secondary curriculum. Later in the Spring term some time was devoted to helping students obtain teaching posts. In both schools the programme was devised initially by the General Tutor, but students were subsequently invited to propose topics for future consideration. Although the General Tutors were responsible for organizing these seminars, they were not always directly involved themselves. One tutor explained that the intention behind convening the seminars was not only to provide students with information about different aspects of school practice but also to generalize incidents and issues by locating them within wider secondary school practice, or by drawing out the principles underlying them or introducing a theoretical perspective. This tutor admitted to a lack of confidence about providing the theoretical dimension however.

Student evaluation of the school-based component

In the following section students' evaluations of the different dimensions of the school-based component are presented. Their comments derive from two main sources: questionnaires administered at the beginning and the end of the training and interviews conducted at regular intervals throughout the course. In assessing this data it is important to remember that students' views of the training which they are experiencing are inevitably partial. Moreover, as anyone who has undertaken course evaluation will know, students find it easier to express their criticism of a course than their appreciation of it. Nevertheless their views are important in that they give an alternative, though not perhaps definitive, perspective on the training process.

Teacher tutoring

In general, students attached to the two schools monitored most closely were satisfied with the quality of the tutoring that they had received. Fifteen of the 18 students completed questionaires, and the following account is based on those returned. Students were asked:

to rate teachers' ability on various dimensions of the tutorial role
to indicate their satisfaction or dissatisfaction with how their time in school was
     utilized
to state how well they felt they had been prepared on various dimensions of
     educational practice.

Regarding the tutorial competence of those teachers, principally Teacher

Tutors, with whom students had most contact, the picture that emerged was highly satisfactory to the extent that the tutorial requirements were located in the classroom. Over four-fifths of the students considered the teachers to be able or very able to comment constructively on any teaching they had observed. Almost as many regarded teachers as able or very able to help them without being unduly prescriptive. However, when asked to rate teachers' ability to relate classroom practice to wider educational principles, more than two-thirds of the students in one of the schools considered their teachers either not very able or unable to do this. It was this item which differentiated most strongly between the two schools, for in the other school staff were rated competent on this aspect of their tutorial role.

How students' time within school was deployed was largely determined by Teacher Tutors. There was some indication of incompatibility here with students' preferences. Students derived most satisfaction from class teaching, two-thirds of them indicating that the right proportion of time had been allocated for this. A substantial number, however, expressed the wish that more time had been devoted to team teaching and to teaching individual pupils.

Clearly all these commitments cannot be met simultaneously. Nevertheless the students' comments do suggest that the assumptions on which student timetables are constructed could have been reviewed and greater variation regarding size of pupil grouping introduced. Likewise their views on discussion were irreconcilable. Nearly all students regarded the proportion of time spent on discussion appropriate and approved its practical focus, yet nearly three-quarters of them felt too little time had been given over to discussion of educational theory. The majority of students were of the opinion that teachers did not regard theoretical considerations as particularly relevant, commenting for example: 'You don't get the kind of constructive criticism at a theoretical level that you need'.

Preparedness in practical skills was the third area investigated. Students were given a list of dimensions of educational practice and asked to rate how well prepared they felt themselves to have been on these. The items were of three kinds: basic teaching skills; more advanced or general competencies; and broader aspects of the teacher's role. In general, students were reasonably satisfied with their preparation in basic teaching skills. Over three-quarters now felt competent to teach their subject across the secondary age range.[8] More than two-thirds considered themselves to be well prepared in the preparation of lessons and teaching materials, in disciplining and controlling pupils and in questioning and explaining. Only in two of the basic skills – assessing pupil progress and holding effective discussions – did a majority of students admit to feeling inadequately prepared. The level of satisfaction with their training fell away, however, as the areas of competence became more complex. For instance, about two-thirds of the students felt they had been well prepared with respect to understanding the importance of language across the curriculum, employing a range of teaching approaches and teaching less able children. However, strong dissatisfaction with their preparation was expressed by nearly three-quarters of the students in relation to teaching in a programme of integrated studies, developing learning strategies appropriate to pupils' needs and individualizing their teaching, for example. With reference to the broader aspects of the teacher's role, responses were less consistent. All students felt well prepared to undertake pastoral work. They felt inadequately prepared, however, to deal with parents or support agencies. In part this may of course reflect the responsibilities which, as students, they encountered.

In addition the students were asked who had contributed significantly to the various aspects of their school experience, and the range of skills quoted illustrates the demanding nature of the Teacher Tutor's role. That the teacher's major contribution lies in transmitting the craft of teaching (e.g. organizing the classroom, marking pupils' work and assessing pupil progress) was again confirmed. The importance which teachers attached to pastoral care was also noted. Although university tutors were seen to have had some part to play in helping students to master basic classroom competencies, their true interests were perceived to be outside the classroom. Their main contribution was seen to be in promoting understanding of the principles underlying educational issues. The following were mentioned by over three-quarters of the students as areas in which staff of the university had enhanced understanding: inequality and educational achievement; the principles underlying the curriculum; and the structure and organization of the educational system. Students did not, however, consider themselves to have been well prepared in terms of understanding the principles underlying issues directly related to classroom practice such as the nature of intelligence, language development or motivation. It should, however, be emphasized that training in these theoretical domains was not a high priority in this course. The emphasis in Personal Tutor Group meetings was on the development of students' reflective abilities, not on the communication of theoretical knowledge. It is hardly surprising therefore that students should feel inadequately prepared in these areas.

More general observations

Students' comments attested to considerable variation in the way in which the school-based element of the course was put into operation and by implication in the quality of the placement. This variation was found both across schools and between departments within the same school.

Some Tutorial schools were identified as having adhered closely to university policy whereas others were perceived 'to disregard the letter of the course'. Students in both of the monitored schools considered that on the whole they had been made to feel welcome, and that staff in general – not just the Teacher and General Tutors – had been sincerely interested in them and concerned and willing to promote their professional development. They were, however, aware of some among their peer group who had been less fortunate. This was confirmed in group discussion involving other students. It was alleged that:

some Teachers Tutors had had very limited contact with their students, had rarely observed them teaching and had been unduly negative in comments they had made. One student observed: 'Some Teacher Tutors seemed to think that writing three reports was all they had to do'
some Teacher Tutors appeared to have very little understanding of their responsibilities toward students
some General Tutors had been only marginally involved
there had been limited communication between General Tutor and Teacher Tutors.

These and other perceived shortcomings were felt to have contributed to an unsatisfactory and at times fairly unpleasant school experience in the case of a small minority of students. The university was seen to bear some responsibility for this. Except in instances of near crisis, when prompt and decisive action had been taken, the students detected a reluctance to intervene. As one put it: 'I think it's only in cases of extreme difficulty that something is actually done'. Another commented: 'When the system does start to break down the university does seem to step in quickly'. The Course Director, explaining how the university approached handling potentially delicate situations and circumstances, stressed that in a partnership it was necessary for both parties to exercise responsibility. Rather than the university being expected always to resolve problematic situations there was a need to get teachers 'to accept ownership of the problem'.

While a minority of students were very satisfied with the supervision they received, a substantial number expressed dissatisfaction. This item differentiated between the two monitored schools. In one school, all students were observed teaching regularly by their Teacher Tutors throughout the placement, and from time to time by other teachers. In addition, all were seen teaching at least once by the General Tutor. In the other school there was considerable variation in the quality of supervision according to subject department. Some of the students considered that their Teacher Tutors could have been more systematic and rigorous in their supervision. Others felt that their progress was closely and fairly monitored.

Finally, the way in which the students' teaching load was handled was investigated. There were some sharp contrasts in students' experience here. Some had experienced a carefully graduated entry into teaching, each stage having been discussed or even negotiated with their Teacher Tutors. Others felt they had been 'expected to act as teachers almost from the first', that they had been pushed into class teaching prematurely, and consequently had been obliged to adopt survival strategies. As one noted: 'I think the less preparation you have, you adopt survival strategies, which become so inbuilt because it is always the first thing you do . . . It's only survival at the cost of the kids or yourself . . . they're not actually good teaching strategies'. It emerged that this student's experience was not an isolated one. Other complaints concerning their teaching allocation included: being given difficult classes while still lacking experience and confidence; having to retain difficult classes with which they had experienced problems; the – sometimes unjustified – assumption that being graduates they possessed certain subject knowledge; and being so heavily timetabled that they lacked preparation time and in particular time for reflection.

On the basis of students' comments, it is possible to develop an identikit of the 'good' Teacher Tutor – that is to say, the type of tutor who in the students' view would have contributed most fully and constructively to their professional development. A number of personal qualities were mentioned: a sound commitment to the students' cause and being sensitive and responsive to their needs, being examples. This sensitivity was clearly felt to be lacking on occasions: 'You know you made a mistake but there's no need for them to harp on it all the time', and 'It can be easily done to be over-critical', were observations made by students. Often teachers were felt to have been niggardly with their praise, even after a successful lesson. Also mentioned was the need for teachers to empathize with students, particularly early on in the training when student anxiety and naivety was at its height. Such comments as, 'They need to be aware of pressures on students from all sides' or 'They should be aware of the students' needs and the support they require', imply that students expected teachers to have considerable powers of identification. Nevertheless it would appear that some teachers did not take into account the fact that students on this course were placed in schools at the very outset of their training.

In addition to cultivating these personal qualities, the model Teacher Tutor would also be able to tutor effectively. This was felt to entail being well organized, actively advising and guiding, selecting pertinent issues to debate, and displaying skill in leading discussions. It was emphasized that a good Teacher Tutor should also be specific when commenting on students' teaching, and should show integrity in his or her assessment of it. On this course teachers had a major responsibility for assessing students and some doubts emerged regarding their impartiality and diligence in this regard. A number of students felt that personal predilections had been allowed to intervene in what should have been an objective judgement. They were particularly aggrieved at being assessed on what they considered to be inadequate evidence – teachers having appraised their performance without having witnessed a fair and representative sample of lessons. Students also felt that if their rate of progress was considered unsatisfactory they should be notified of this in good time.

In view of these comments, students from the two schools were asked whether they felt teachers needed any particular preparation prior to taking on tutoring responsibilities and, if so, in what respects. No student considered that teachers needed to be trained as such, a finding which perhaps reflected their expectations that teachers' concerns were firmly located in the classroom and that they were well able to articulate their own basic beliefs and practices. However, the students felt that there was a need for tutors to be more fully informed about the course and the nature of their role. 'They need to know what is expected of them and they should be monitored more by the university', 'Guidelines on their responsibilities need to be more detailed and clearer', 'They need to know what the university has done and what is left to the school', were typical comments. The need for greater liaison between university and school personnel – particularly between the Curriculum and Teacher Tutors – was also specifically mentioned, and was confirmed by the teachers themselves.

The college-based component

Key personnel: enactment of role

The Curriculum Tutor

The way in which Curriculum Tutors worked closely matched the specification set out in The Course Document. All eight tutors acknowledged that they had one principal function, which was to develop students' awareness of the place of their subject within the secondary curriculum and to inform the teaching of it with a body of relevant principles. To this end:

they held curriculum seminars in the university
they made termly visits to students in the Tutorial schools.

Seminars   The aims of seminar discussion were:

to provide students with the skills and knowledge relevant to the stage reached
   in their training
to 'transcend the specificity of the experience'
to challenge existing practice where appropriate.

The Curriculum Tutors recognized that the needs and concerns of students varied over the training period and that this had consequences for their curriculum work. In the first term, they perceived that students wanted only 'to talk about specifics'. Their concern was with 'the here and now', and it was seen as necessary to reflect this when devising seminar coverage. The seminar agenda of Curriculum Tutors for the first term showed themes which paralleled the current experiences of students: e.g. the aims and objectives of teaching their subject; formulating lesson plans; the different pedagogical approaches that their subject afforded; the use of resources; the purposes and nature of assessment. At this stage, the student's survival in the classroom was paramount, and initially the work of Curriculum Tutors was directed towards ensuring this. The student was seen to require 'the kind of basic apparatus which you need to go in with as a teacher', as one tutor put it. Their responsibility was 'to provide them to some extent with a survival kit', another tutor observed. Towards the end of the first term, and certainly in the second term, Curriculum Tutors began to focus more and more on the students' longer term development. Thus, they began to use the seminars as a vehicle for extending student awareness 'beyond the particular', 'to open up their horizons about what is entailed in (subject) teaching', to develop in students 'a sense of what they're doing and why'.

At this stage tutors saw themselves as responsible for extending the limited subject-based pedagogical experiences of each student beyond the specific departmental practices of the Tutorial school. This was achieved firstly by capitalizing on the variation in the experiences of the members of the curriculum group who were dispersed across several Tutorial schools. In this way different examples of teaching method in a given subject were explored, the contrasts and variations reflected upon and common themes extracted. Secondly, teachers with a particular interest or expertise were invited to attend selected seminars, not necessarily as formal presenters but rather to comment generally, drawing on their relevant experience. Thirdly, the understanding of the students could be broadened by reference to theory and research.

Some tutors used the curriculum seminars as an opportunity to expose students to ideas and opinions which would 'call into question their experience in the classroom'. This notion of discrepancy, challenging current practice, was advocated as a valuable learning device which forced students to confront issues and grapple with them. Tutors were not unduly concerned if the practices in schools did not coincide with the ideals that were promoted in the university. For example, it was recognized that students placed in a particular department in one Tutorial school had had a limited and somewhat impoverished experience, but their Curriculum Tutor accepted this as realistic:

> It would be a very unrealistic course if students were only in departments which actually consolidated the particular theories that the university might hold, or the Curriculum Tutor . . . It's a much more interesting kind of tension . . . to have many different models of (subject teaching) . . . if the students can hold it and live through it and learn from it.

Curriculum Tutors saw their task as distinct from that of Teacher Tutors. The responsibility of the latter was 'to give immediate day-to-day help with the actual teaching that the student is engaged in'. The focus of the Teacher Tutor was the particular – particular lessons or aspects of pedagogy involving particular classes in a particular school. Their own concern, in contrast, was with the more general aspects of subject teaching. Of course, the emphasis which they placed on the wider principles of subject pedagogy reflected their concern to train students to teach in the educational system in general, rather than in any given school. It also signified their awareness that the Sussex course, with its single school experience, could carry the danger of fostering parochialism.

Visits to Tutorial schools   The purpose of the Curriculum Tutors' visits to the Tutorial schools was described in The Course Document as 'to give support and guidance to the work of students and Teacher Tutors' (p. 10). They therefore had a dual function. With respect to the students, these visits could be seen as an extension of the curriculum seminar in that, where possible, tutors hoped to see the students applying in the classroom some of the ideas and practices which had been examined and debated in seminar discussions. Their observations of the students' teaching were followed up with both a verbal and written critique which could, on occasion, be very detailed. The visits also served as an opportunity to hear the views of the Teacher Tutors on students' development and progress and to discuss any tutoring problems they might be experiencing. The Course Document specified that Curriculum Tutors should attach greater importance to meeting Teacher Tutors than to seeing students when visiting schools. However, tutors did not always contact the Teacher Tutors on these visits and wherever liaison with teachers was mentioned it was invariably in the context of student learning. Discussion of the teachers' tutorial function was largely ignored. As long as there were no critical developments, Curriculum Tutors appeared to be satisfied to let well alone and not to examine circumstances in detail.

The Personal Tutor

The Personal Tutor was a central figure on the Sussex course, a 'linch-pin' for student and tutor alike and 'a godfather' to the students placed in the particular Tutorial school. In their capacity as Personal Tutor, lecturers were charged with the well-being of the group of students in the Tutorial school. They were also responsible for developing the theoretical and reflective awareness of members of their tutor group. To this end, the Personal Tutors:

held weekly seminars for the tutor group
held individual tutorials periodically
made regular visits to the Tutorial school to see both students and teachers
advised and assisted the students in the preparation of the Course File and
    monitored its development.

Meetings of the Personal Tutor Group   The most regular contact between Personal Tutor and students was the weekly meeting of the tutor group. The Course Document described the principal purpose of these meetings as to introduce elements of educational theory in order to facilitate critical analysis of students' school experience.

The precise content of the theory elements was not specified but was left to individual tutors to determine. There was deliberately no set agenda in order that issues which students raised could be incorporated into the sessions. This practice reflected the belief that 'theory only makes sense when it's related to actual experience' in that it allowed the student to voice problems or pursue points of interest arising out of school experience. Such a policy meant that there was no agreed content across the whole cohort of students. Even among the various Personal Tutors there appeared to be no agreement on whether there was a core of educational theory which contributed essential content matter for students undergoing initial training. Consequently, student experience could show considerable variation regarding the actual educational issues dealt with. Additionally, tutors were accorded considerable autonomy as to how they conducted these sessions. Thus the disparity between groups could be reinforced. This was not disputed by the Personal Tutors, although one suggested that the content covered by the different groups in fact was not as discrepant as it might appear: 'My impression is that there is a kind of common ground as far as content is concerned, but I suspect that the teaching method differs considerably across the course'. In short, tutors shared a common aim, that of creating 'some kind of dialogue between experience and theory', although how they set about this probably differed.

It will be recalled that the university placed great emphasis upon establishing a sound basis for sustained longer term professional development. The aim was to develop 'aware, self-questioning and sensitive teachers'. It was not sufficient that students simply should have experienced school life and practices, important though these were. As one Personal Tutor observed: 'There is a tendency for people to say that experience is enough . . . Experience is okay . . . but you only learn from it if you reflect upon it'. In the words of the Course Director: 'We will invest in process and exploration of experience rather than the transmission of a formal body of knowledge'. It was in these Personal Tutor Group meetings more than anywhere else in the training that this more advanced aim was pursued.

Both Personal Tutors studied were asked what they hoped to achieve in meetings of their tutor group. Three main objectives were espoused:

analysing and debating educational issues: 'To provide a kind of formal structure in which a number of issues which are important to (students) get debated'

constructing a personal 'philosophy of education', by engaging in debate and through critical analysis of and reflection upon school experience, both at first and secondhand

encouraging group members to exercise self-responsibility – 'to have responsibility for their own learning'. This was linked to fostering autonomy – 'getting people to the point where they can take decisions about things'.

Thus, the Personal Tutors saw themselves striving to enhance students' awareness of issues of professional concern and to promote their ability to develop a set of personal educational principles. The meeting of the tutor group and to a lesser extent the individual tutorial were key sites for the development of students' critical and reflective capacities. Once these skills had begun to be developed it was hoped that students would apply them to other aspects of their training, particularly in developing their Course Files.

Both tutors placed considerable emphasis upon developing a programme of topics for discussion which related to the interests and experiences of the students, and in both cases students had some influence in determining the substance of seminar coverage. The two tutors differed, however, in their views as to how much influence students should have. One tutor largely turned over the selection of topics to the students. He acknowledged having at the back of his mind 'a kind of agenda' of what he considered to be 'the essentials' and if necessary was prepared to manipulate them onto the programme of seminar coverage. He noted that the list of topics which the students had suggested, apart from one or two surprising omissions, was more or less what other groups had identified over the years. He had added to the list a number of titles. They included: What are Schools for? The Role of the Teacher; Pupil Subcultures; Comparative Education; the Curriculum of the Secondary School; Adolescence; Home-School Links; Language Across the Curriculum; Deschooling; and Recent Developments in the Secondary Curriculum. From this master list of suggestions students selected the actual topics to be addressed.

The second tutor took a more explicitly interventionist approach, although this varied in accordance with the stage reached in the course. In the Autumn term he considered that students were sufficiently preoccupied with preparing their first lessons. Rather than their having to undertake seminar presentations in addition, he took it upon himself to determine the agenda and lead discussion. If students had any time left over he preferred that they follow up some of the references which he provided. He admitted to being 'opportunist', latching on to incidents as they arose. He maintained that what mattered was not the content per se but how the discussion of the content was handled. In the Spring term he handed over more responsibility for determining the agenda and leading some of the sessions to group members.

The two tutors also differed with respect to the pattern which their respective seminars followed. The seminars run by this second tutor typically had three components. To begin with students were asked to focus upon some facet of their school experience of the preceding week, such as a problematic encounter with a pupil or an aspect of departmental practice. 'We collectivize that', the tutor stated. The tutor himself would provide the topic if necessary – 'something that's currently in the news to do with education'. They would then move on to the main business which was a presentation of and debate upon the scheduled topic of the day. Sessions would conclude with a few minutes in which anyone present could raise any matter of concern or interest to them.

For the first tutor, the main item each week was a student-led presentation on a topic chosen in advance. Initially, individual students volunteered to research an issue and speak on it. Later on, however, topics were jointly presented by up to four students. The tutor met the presenting students beforehand in order to hear their ideas and offer advice. He also provided source material and references. In addition he specified one relevant reading which group members should consult beforehand. By this means it was hoped to avoid limiting the discussion to student experience in the Tutorial school. This tutor maintained that without having recourse to the literature there was a real danger that 'all you get is an exchange of anecdotal evidence'.

The two tutors also differed with respect to the part each played in the seminar. The first tutor was deliberately restrained in his interventions during the first few meetings. He would intervene over matters of content, inaccurate statements for instance, but not over the learning process itself. This was deliberate and had the aim of deflecting attention from himself as the organizer of learning. He was keen that the students should exercise responsibility for and control over their own learning. He acknowledged that at first many of the group found his behaviour baffling, if not frustrating, and experienced difficulty in recognizing what was required of them. After several weeks they would discuss as a group how the sessions were going and agree any necessary changes. It was not uncommon for him subsequently to become more interventionist – but from the standpoint of group member rather than 'expert'. Overall, he saw his role as that of facilitating and contributing to debate by means of critical and probing questioning of the issues, set within the broader framework which the accompanying literature provided. The second tutor, besides assuming more responsibility for presentation, was more interventionist in debate, frequently over-stating his case in order to force a response from students and openly challenging their contributions.

Although both tutors regarded as important the development of the skills of analysis and reflection, they appeared to differ with respect to whether this 'consciousness raising' was sufficient in itself or whether it should be extended as far as an open challenge to the status quo. The second of the tutors believed that schools currently failed the majority of pupils and regarded it as incumbent upon him to ensure that the students were aware that they could legitimately challenge the broad consensus of values which obtained amongst the teaching profession.

Visits to Tutorial schools The second main task of the Personal Tutor was to visit the Tutorial school at least twice a term. These visits had two functions, concerning students and teacher respectively. They were an opportunity to ensure that all was well with the students, to resolve any initial anxieties or difficulties and later, to observe students in the classroom. The students' progress would be discussed with the General Tutor in the first instance and perhaps subsequently with the Teacher Tutor.

As regards the teachers, the Personal Tutors recognized that they were, in effect, ambassadors of the university and had the task of facilitating communication between the two institutions. Their more particular concerns included ensuring that teachers understood the intentions behind the long-term attachment of students to the school and the unique contribution expected of them. This could entail giving information, listening and responding to any difficulties which teachers might have experienced, offering advice and generally providing reassurance. The two tutors differed in the extent to which they regarded it as their responsibility to assist teachers – particularly newcomers – to fulfil their tutorial duties. The first tutor stated explicitly that he had an obligation to ease new tutors into their role, ensuring that they mastered what it entailed as quickly as possible. The second tutor, while acknowledging a responsibility for forwarding information to the General Tutor, maintained that it was not his brief to seek to shape teacher practice. He argued that the subject culture which Teacher Tutors and Curriculum Tutors shared was extremely potent and that his curriculum colleagues were the crucial partners for the Teacher Tutors. The Personal Tutors also had responsibility for overseeing the training in the Tutorial school in a general sense. The intention was that any unsatisfactory circumstance be brought to the attention of the General Tutor who, ideally, would take appropriate action. However, it was recognized that this could not be guaranteed, in which case the university would have no option but to intervene, albeit tactfully and with the utmost sensitivity.

Individual tutorials   These were held periodically and on an ad hoc basis, and could be convened by either a student or tutor. For instance, a student experiencing problems could request a tutorial. The tutor might arrange a tutorial as a follow up to a school visit or to investigate more fully a problem identified by a General Tutor. The pastoral responsibilities of the Personal Tutor extended to functioning as the students' advocate in instances of disagreement with the school. 'Implicit is that the Personal Tutor is the students' friend', commented one such tutor, while a second remarked more colourfully: 'It's our job to make sure that the students don't get more than the odd flesh wound'. Tutorials also could be convened in order to discuss the preparation of the Course File.

The two tutors differed as to the relative importance each attached to the educational and pastoral aspects of the role. The first tutor invested considerable time and energy in his pastoral duties, holding regular 'surgeries' which students were free to come along to if they wished. In addition, he convened several workshops designed to assist students with their Special Study and periodically scheduled tutorials at which the evolving Course File was discussed. He closely supervised the students in school, visiting frequently in the Autumn term to ensure that they had settled in. He maintained close links with the General Tutor in his Tutorial school in an attempt to remain fully informed of the developing practice. The second tutor, in contrast, gave precedence to his teaching commitments, of which the PGCE was only one strand. Within this he directed his energies into tutor group meetings, concentrating upon promoting and developing critical understanding in his students.

Student evaluation of the college-based component

Curriculum Studies

Generally speaking, the majority of students were well satisfied with the content of their Curriculum Studies. They approved the way in which their tutors had related their material to the stage reached in the training. Initially time was allowed for discussion of the basic practicalities of subject teaching. Yet the meetings were not devoted entirely to such matters, for this could have duplicated the work of the Teacher Tutor. In the second term, the topics which were covered were of a more general nature – for example, the teaching of scientific reasoning or the interrelations between different subjects.

The Curriculum Tutors differed in the extent to which they stressed the utilitarian or the theoretical aspects of teaching their subject. Some tended towards the view that the acquisition of classroom competence should take precedence in training and that there would be plenty of time subsequently to develop a philosophy of the subject. Certain others, however, maintained that it was more crucial to develop this philosophy, from which practice could be derived. They argued that if not developed during training, a philosophy was unlikely to evolve subsequently. One tutor particularly emphasized the philosophical aspects of his subject, concerning himself primarily with conveying to the students his sophisticated vision of what the teacher of his subject should be striving to achieve. Although they appreciated having had the opportunity to be party to his views and convictions, nevertheless some of his students felt that these discursive explorations of his ideals were not exactly what they most needed at the time and had led to limited development of their teaching techniques.

Some students criticized the single subject approach to teaching which predominated in the training. They contrasted this with the increasingly interdisciplinary nature of the school curriculum. In fact there were periodic joint sessions for students in the Humanities, while students pursuing Science subjects came together on a weekly basis for practical workshop sessions. A more severe criticism than the lack of integration across disciplines was that of the level of this work. Students considered that the tone of the Curriculum seminars was often too general. However, given the very limited time available to them, it is difficult to see how Curriculum Tutors could have been anything other than somewhat superficial in the treatment of their material on occasion.

The structure and conduct of Curriculum Studies seminars met with students' approval in some respects, not in others. Particularly valued was the forum that these meetings provided for students to discuss together any challenges or anxieties that arose out of their school experience. It was seen as an advantage that members of the group were placed in different Tutorial schools, and thus able to compare practice across their respective departments. Science students particularly commented favourably on the small size of their group, and suggested that this contributed to an ease in debating and to the frank exchange of views. The detrimental influence of the size of the group on members' participation in discussion was compounded on occasion by the presence of teachers, students reported. On such occasions the teachers usually contributed on the basis of their experience, though sometimes they led the sessions. Several students recalled some interesting and inspirational contributions from outside speakers, but also mentioned occasions when a small number of teachers had tended to dominate the debate.

Students were especially appreciative of well-organized Curriculum courses in which a clear agenda had been drawn up and was closely adhered to. They also approved being given tasks relating to their school experience as part of their Curriculum Studies. A small number of courses were found to be lacking in both these respects and this occasioned dissatisfaction. As a student observed: 'When you are training you want direction'.

Meetings of the Personal Tutor Group

Students spoke very positively about Personal Tutor Group meetings. For two terms members of these groups shared a school experience and it is hardly surprising perhaps that a strong group identity and a high level of mutual support should have been developed. This was particularly true of one of the groups wherein students with a mix of 'Arts' and 'Science' subject backgrounds supported each other and contributed both intellectually and socially to the development of an unusually pronounced shared identity. Several members of this group volunteered that this had been the best aspect of their training.

It will be recalled that the agenda of Personal Tutor Group sessions was deliberately kept fairly flexible in order that students might spontaneously introduce ideas of relevance and interest to them. This was highly approved of, students valuing having had their interests and needs recognized in this manner. They also approved the way in which they had been encouraged to filter their firsthand school experience through a sieve of educational theory. The content of seminars was found to be both stimulating and challenging. A typical comment was: 'It's almost always very good, very thought provoking . . . On the whole they just make you think in a very different way, or perhaps challenge common assumptions teachers have'.

However, there were criticisms. Some students felt that the theory input was too limited and that too much emphasis was placed on their school experience. Discussion could become parochial and anecdotal. Tutors had deliberately sought to counteract this by encouraging students to undertake set background reading. Given their crowded timetables, however, it proved difficult for many students to complete even a minimum of reading.

Undoubtedly the task facing the Personal Tutor was both delicate and demanding. Personal Tutors had to strive to inject a theoretical dimension into debate, at the same time referring back constantly to students' activities and experiences in school. Also, the requirement that they assume responsibility for introducing appropriate educational theory was sometimes hard to reconcile with the importance attached at Sussex to student autonomy and self-learning. In both tutor groups the initial feeling among students was that a more definite structure ought to have been imposed by the tutor. Discussion was seen 'to wander a bit' in both groups, though for different reasons. In the one case the tutor had quite deliberately pursued a policy of limited intervention in the early stages of the training. The second tutor, on occasion, was perceived to have allowed debate to become sidetracked into interesting although not always strictly relevant matters. Subsequently, however, both sets of students praised their tutors for the manner in which they had handled these sessions. A typical assessment of the style of leadership which one of the tutors employed is captured in the following student comment: 'He strikes a good balance between leading the session and being an informed presence'.

In addition to tutors' style, the lack of available time was seen as a factor which partially determined the benefit that students could derive from these sessions – and indeed from university-based studies as a whole. The problem of fitting in even a small amount of preparatory reading has already been referred to. The lack of time also prevented thorough debate. 'It's very difficult to follow anything up. Sometimes issues which are really interesting are left hanging in the air', a frustrated student observed. The principle that everyone had a right to voice his or her opinion, which was implicit in the context of seminars, was considered to compound matters so that it became 'very difficult to develop arguments fully'.

The Course File

Of the two written assignments on the course, the Special Study and the Course File, it was the latter which attracted the weight of student comment – not surprisingly perhaps given its central place in the philosophy of the course and its time-consuming nature. The majority of the students whose progress was followed in some detail encountered considerable difficulty in coming to terms with what was required of the File. As late as March there were still some who expressed confusion about this element. In spite of its having been the subject of a plenary session, being well documented, and having been discussed by Personal Tutors at various stages in the course, students still indicated that they did not fully understand what was required. They perceived this guidance as too nebulous and complained that they had needed more specific help.

Many of the students appeared to have begun by keeping a diary. Some gradually realized that this was insufficient. Others maintained that they had completed the training without ever really feeling that they had come to terms with the task. Even when students understood what was required, they still experienced difficulty in finding the time to record their reflections. Indeed, there was every indication that a great deal of thinking was going on but, as one student observed, 'It's actually getting down and writing it that's the problem'. School experience and Course Files were competing for a finite amount of time and it was widely acknowledged that the File was 'the last priority' – that 'lessons come first' and university studies and assignments were secondary. 'It's supposed to be a continuous reflection throughout the course, whereas I didn't make the time to spend an hour every evening, I was too tired', was a typical admission. In practice, weekends, half-terms and vacations were commonly the occasions when chunks of writing were undertaken in an attempt to bring the File up to date.

Personal Tutors were responsible for reviewing the Course Files at different stages during the year. In fact, the two tutors differed in the frequency with which they undertook this task. One saw the Files on a termly basis, the other reviewed them once, midway through the course. This tutor later explained that he assumed students were adult enough to approach him if they had any anxieties or uncertainties. We heard of other Personal Tutors who took the Files in each month. Irrespective of the actual practice, students considered that tutors' comments were too general in nature and that it would have been useful to have received some specific criticisms.

Maintaining the Course File was regarded by some students as a chore. The students who benefited most were those who had understood what was required, for whom it made sense to approach this task with diligence and determination. One such student commented that the exercise had been 'invaluable and absorbing'.

In discussion, Personal Tutors acknowledged that many students had experienced considerable difficulty in coming to terms with what was sought. 'Students find it very difficult to move from the descriptive into the analytic and particularly the self-evaluative', one noted. A second felt that this year his students had been 'terribly insecure' about the content of their Files. Part of the difficulty was seen to be that students clung to the notion of 'the model File' and refused to believe tutors' insistence that since it was 'a personal statement' there could be no prescribed format. 'I think you need to give students a lot of support . . . but I never want to give them the impression that there is one way of doing it', observed one Personal Tutor.

Asked what they were looking for when judging the Course File, tutors stressed three main aspects. First, evidence that the exercise had been of value and that the student had learnt from it. Secondly, it should demonstrate 'engagement in the course as a whole' – furthermore, engagement of a critical and interactive nature. The File should record 'what has happened to you and (should) communicate this to the reader . . . that development of yourself and your thinking' a tutor noted. There should be 'a pick up of themes and follow through'. Thirdly, there should be evidence of reading undertaken and of having used this to inform or review firsthand experience.

In the year of our evaluation a student from each of the tutor groups had his File rejected at the end of the course. Both Personal Tutors maintained that this was quite unusual and were clearly distressed by this. In each case the major problem was seen to have been the failure to engage critically with the material that had accumulated. One of the tutors went on to state that on the whole he had found the Files 'a bit disappointing' this year. His colleague was more satisfied with what his students had presented and maintained that it was apparent from the Course Files that students had reflected long and hard upon their lived experience and more widely upon schooling and education.

Other aspects of the university-based studies

There were three other areas of study which made up the university-based component of the training. These were Plenaries, the Alternative Experience and Options.

Plenaries   The most memorable of the plenary sessions during the course were the two conferences on Teaching in the Inner City and Education in a Multi-ethnic Society. Both were praised by students as very interesting, relevant and useful. The timing of the second of these conferences, at the very end of the course, attracted criticism however. Students read this as indicative of 'the marginalization of the issue', as one put it. 'Race has been invisible for the rest of the year' and 'It's really tokenistic having it right at the end. I don't think they (lecturers) realized just how ignorant people were (about race)', were two other forceful responses. Reacting to this criticism, tutors noted that one of the main difficulties which they had struggled to overcome was that of accommodating a three-day conference within a course which was heavily school-based. They suggested that students were unaware of the logistical problems involved.

Although these two plenary sessions were praised, students were critical of others. They challenged the inclusion of several topics and also suggested that some items could have been dealt with in a fraction of the time that was taken. The session on the Special Study was one instance cited. It was also felt that their timing could have been improved. Science students, for example, sometimes found a plenary session overlapping with Science Workshops which they were expected to attend. Such a clash of commitments could not easily be resolved.

The Alternative Experience   The aim of the Alternative Experience was to broaden students' experience of the educational process. Since the nature of the attachment was chosen by students themselves they were likely to be reasonably positive about the outcomes, and indeed practice tended to bear this out. In general students valued this aspect of the training and were highly appreciative of the opportunity to follow their own interests.

A breakdown of how this time was spent by students from the two tutor groups is given below:

5 went into colleges of further education
3 undertook placements in special schools
2 undertook a practice in sixth form colleges
2 spent time in other secondary schools
2 went into primary schools.

The remainder were attached to a variety of establishments: a training centre, an adventure playground, an adult education centre and an EFL school. No serious dissatisfactions were voiced to us. All students reported that this attachment had been productive, mainly it seemed because it constituted added experience in another – and often sharply contrasting – educational context to that of the Tutorial school.

Options   A wide range of Options were available. The most popular in terms of students enlisted was that on Science, Technology and Society in Education. Other well-subscribed Options were: Sexism in School and Society, Computer Studies, Audio Visual Aids, Drama Workshop and TEFL. Opinions as to their value differed considerably, as one might expect. Generally, students considered the Options a good idea but scheduled too late in the course and too short to allow of any substantial development. Clearly, the course organizers are faced with considerable problems in incorporating the various elements into the training, such that some items inevitably must come late in the day – a perspective which students either appeared not to possess or overlooked.

Some more general observations on the training

The demanding nature of the course   The demands that any PGCE course makes of students are heavy. The single academic year has for some time been widely regarded as an inadequate period in which to cover the practical and theoretical content usually regarded as essential for teacher training. Whether the demands of the Sussex course were greater than for any other school-based course is difficult to say. They were certainly very heavy. The continual need to adjust and readjust to being a university student and a fledgling teacher within the same week imposed particular pressures. In the words of one student: 'I found myself having to switch from being a teacher to being a student – I felt I couldn't make that transition'. That this adjustment had to be made for virtually two-thirds of the course proved extremely wearing. The need to keep up to date with teaching preparation could not be shirked. There was, however, the temptation to regard university studies as 'light relief', as one put it, and to neglect these. This attitude could be fuelled by the occasional remark from an unthinking teacher, to the effect that the university-based studies were 'a doddle'. There is a certain irony in the fact that the degree of involvement in school which many students experienced was what the university was aiming for, yet simultaneously it threatened to undermine their university-based studies. As one student observed: 'You can get so involved in the school, feel yourself part of the school, that these two days (at the university) can become an irrelevance'. Students complained strongly about the lack of time for personal study and for reading. Many pointed out that one of the fundamental aims of the course – that of critical reflection – was an activity for which time was essential. Yet, as one noted, 'The amount of time you've got to be reflective is very limited . . . you become quite manic'.

Achieving coherence in the course   As has been noted above, the students' time and attention were divided between school and university. The responsibility for training was also divided, being shared between teachers and university tutors. That this juggling of commitments could threaten the coherence of the course was recognized by the more perceptive students: 'A danger of this course is the tendency to compartmentalize – that you don't see the two (i.e. university-based studies and school experience) as fitting together in any way'. Since the demands of the school could not be ignored, there was a tendency for these to take precedence. For some students this did not matter and any disjuncture between the two parts of the course was ignored. 'I deliberately chose this course because of the emphasis placed on the practical aspect. I knew that the academic side would suffer or take second place, and I was quite happy with that because I felt that I had come here to teach', one stated. For others, however, that the training inclined to the practical and pragmatic occasioned some dissatisfaction and even difficulties. There was concern that professional development could be impeded by a lack of theoretical awareness. Some students cited the lack of psychological theory, for example. Tutors made no attempt to be comprehensive in their theoretical coverage and, in the limited time at their disposal, this would hardly have been possible. Teachers on the other hand rarely mentioned theory and their lack of concern for theory was noted and remarked upon by students.

In spite of their criticisms, students spoke very favourably of the course in general and of its school-based nature in particular. The opportunity their school experience provided to become familiar with the nature of teaching and the complexity and variability of the teacher's role was highly valued. At the end of their training very few students harboured any misconceptions about teaching or about schools as organizations, and they were in a position to know whether they wished to persevere with teaching, at least in the short term.

Major constraints upon practice

There were at least two factors which intervened between aim and implementation on the Sussex course: time and communication. These will be discussed in turn with reference to the schools and to the university.

School personnel: the constraint of time In spite of the strong commitment to the scheme by the majority of the teachers involved (whether as Teacher Tutors or as General Tutors), as a group they were unanimous that the major constraint with which they had to contend was insufficient time to do justice to the task. That the added pressures imposed on teachers who took on tutoring responsibilities were not shortlived served to compound matters further: 'It's a long-term commitment from October to Easter'. Every teacher to whom we spoke emphasized that the scheme needed to be resourced at a more realistic level.

The shortfall in time had a number of negative consequences:

teachers were under considerable stress
preparing for seminars and tutorials in advance tended to go by the board and
    consequently these became rather ad hoc
students were perceived to be disadvantaged.

Regarding the first of the above points, one participating teacher commented: 'It's fine in theory, the training on the job, but you're superimposing it on an already full workload'. Another, a newcomer to the programme, found the constant living on one's nerves difficult to come to terms with: 'You tend to work hand to mouth in the day-to-day of the school . . . it's just surviving really from day-to-day'.

As regards the second point above, the possibility of preparing for seminars and tutorials in advance was extremely limited. 'One of the weaknesses of this scheme', a teacher pointed out, was that resourcing 'only covers teachers' *contact* time with students' (emphasis added). In consequence, day-to-day practice tended to be ad hoc. 'It's done on an ad hoc basis . . . a little bit here and there and no time to do it properly.' It was felt that unless they could be given additional release time in order to read around a particular topic and prepare a thorough and balanced seminar presentation, what was actually delivered would very likely be lacking in certain important respects. Teachers similarly felt themselves forced into commenting off the cuff on students' lessons. Only a small minority were able to prepare their feedback with care.

In their meetings with students many teachers were forced to rely upon a combination of personal experience, commonsense and inspiration to see them through. Some took their lead from the students, improvising in addressing concerns and issues which the students themselves raised.

Predictably, circumstances were most problematic wherever teachers sought to introduce an element of educational theory into these discussions. The experience of one such Teacher Tutor is illustrative here. He referred to the considerable drain on both his time and energy which this entailed – such that over time his commitment fell away, in spite of his passionate belief in the scheme. In a diary which he kept an early entry read as follows:

> The existence of a tutorial heavily weighted the rest of the day. I would not be able to regularly afford this amount of time although I think it necessary to do the job properly.

Later he noted:

> I must retreat a little from student work now because it is taking up a disproportionate amount of my time.

He reported at the time having given over to the students two of his own free periods, in addition to the time formally set aside for them, and was aware of neglecting his departmental duties in consequence. He also made reference to his frustration at not being able to make a better job of the task at hand. Alluding to some materials which he had prepared on the topic of Assessment he commented: 'I had the resources to do something good on Assessment, but not the time or the energy'.

If Teacher Tutors needed time to prepare for their more formal interactions with students, this was even more true of General Tutors, whose responsibility it was to focus on issues beyond the classroom. One of the General Tutors admitted to keeping to the tried and tested seminar topics irrespective of whether they were what the students wanted or needed. This tutor pointed out that consulting the relevant literature would be necessary if the range of topics was to be broadened. Reading would also strengthen the theoretical input. In the circumstances obtaining, however, this was simply unrealistic.

Turning now to the third consequence, the student was seen to lose out as the quality of the tutoring was jeopardized. 'There is need for more time to actually sit down and give the students priority . . . and not just have them coming in as something extra to our burden', was a typical viewpoint. A number of teachers admitted to feelings of frustration that only rarely were they able to give students the sustained attention that they felt they deserved. The reality, one noted, was that 'You have to think students in short, sharp bursts'. Teachers' lack of time to give to students was felt most acutely in the early stages of the attachment when students were at their most vulnerable and very dependent on their Teacher Tutors for information and support. Teacher Tutors found that students' need of them decreased as they gained in both competence and confidence and as they formed relationships with other staff in their departments. Nevertheless, there was still insufficient time for them to undertake certain aspects of the job as they would ideally have liked. This was particularly the case with regard to providing students with feedback on their teaching. Teachers attached great importance to a swift response after having observed a student lesson: 'Possibly most valuable of all is being able to talk about your lesson when it's happened'. The importance of promptly carrying out an analysis of any problems encountered was particularly emphasized: 'Only about 10 per cent of the crises are actually resolved, because of lack of time. Usually the moment has passed'. Most students fully recognized the pressures that Teacher Tutors were under. One student spoke for many in commenting: 'I feel extremely sorry for them. I feel that they are being asked to do more than they can do'.

Furthermore, if students were to get the best out of their school experience, and to be assessed objectively, Teacher Tutors also needed time to consult colleagues about student performance. Opportunities for such discussions were few. 'You put them with other teachers and you rely on those teachers to tell you how it has gone', one observed. It was the General Tutors' responsibility to consult Teacher Tutors on student progress and also to monitor the overall success of the practice. In one of the two schools certain problems arose which only subsequently came to the General Tutor's attention. This tutor later admitted: 'I was a little unaware of some of the problems until they had become quite deep-rooted'. With hindsight, the tutor recognized that even allowing for the split-site nature of the school, which made communication difficult, monitoring practice more rigorously in future would be necessary. In addition, Teacher Tutors should be left in no doubt that it was their duty to report back at regular interviews.

School personnel: the constraint of inadequate communication   Staff involved in the scheme, both in schools and in the university, were fully aware of the crucial importance of effective communication. The infrequency of the personal contact between university tutors and school personnel was acknowledged by one member of the university as 'the great failure with the course', while a colleague noted: 'You can never get it right', for the simple reason that there was not the time to devote to it. University tutors sought to make up for the limitations in their firsthand exchanges with school personnel by developing a range of written guidelines for school staff which were widely circulated. However, the feeling remained, both in the schools and university, that in spite of the undoubted improvements in both the quality of the documentation and in its circulation, more still needed to be done.

It will be recalled that the formal links were envisaged as being between: General Tutor and Personal Tutor, Teacher Tutor and Curriculum Tutor. The two General Tutors were quite satisfied with both the nature and the level of their contact with their counterparts from the university. While in an ideal world their association might be closer and more active, a sense of realism prevailed. Both sets of tutors were busy, but found time nevertheless to meet periodically.

Teacher Tutors were markedly less satisfied however. Six out of the eight explicitly mentioned how infrequent was their contact with their subject counterparts from the university. This was in spite of the intention that visits by tutors to the two schools participating in the evaluation would be doubled during the year of the evaluation. That contact had increased was acknowledged – for example, one Teacher Tutor remarked, 'I've certainly had much more contact and there's been more interlinking of what's going on'. Nevertheless this was considered still insufficient. The prevalent feeling was one of considerable dissatisfaction. Teacher Tutors described their contacts with the relevant Curriculum Tutors thus: 'Fairly brief and vague', and 'We've only exchanged brief words . . . Through nobody's fault somehow there is a lack of contact'.

University tutors, it seems, often came and went without always meeting the Teacher Tutor. (Undoubtedly there were good reasons for this on occasion – teachers holding classes during the tutor's visit for instance, or being on a different site.) Invariably tutors were in a hurry: 'It's always a snatched 10 minutes here, 10 minutes there, and then they're rushing off somewhere else' . . . 'He was in and out before I knew it'. In the limited time available Curriculum Tutors could do no more than 'get an impression' from their brief observations of students' teaching. This being so, Teacher Tutors felt that there was every reason for their being consulted over students' progress.

Whatever pressures of time dogged the university tutors, their behaviour was seen to give the lie to the espousal that teachers had a major part to play in facilitating students' professional development. University tutors were seen by school staff to want to spend time with their students principally, rather than being concerned to deal with their needs. Yet a good many Teacher Tutors confessed to having needs which went largely unmet: e.g. how to assess student performance in the classroom in a way that was sufficiently rigorous and objective; whether the various experiences which they had arranged for students complemented those which took place in the university. Often there was only a very hazy notion of the content of the students' university-based studies. This point was frequently raised and more information from the university clearly would have been welcomed. Teachers also would have liked more guidance on the precise nature of their role. Even some of the more experienced Teacher Tutors remarked on 'a lack of clarity, a lack of liaison about what we are about'. One such teacher commented: 'I think I've devised my own role as it were, rather than being completely clear about what the university expects from me'. He would have preferred that 'what experiences students must have, whose responsibility it is to make sure what has to be done is done, and who actually does it', be specified.

Predictably, it was those with the least experience of tutoring who felt most unsettled by the limitations in communication. The main problem was diagnosed as one of over-generalization. One newcomer to the role noticed:

> . . . General discussion about the direction of the course, but it was apparent that my programme . . . would be very much up to my discretion. Responding to need is obviously important but as a starting tutor one feels a little in the air.

He pinpointed areas in which he would have welcomed more guidance: e.g. how to handle the students' introduction into departmental practice, most especially the phasing of their entry into teaching, and what to provide in tutorials. During the period of the evaluation an induction for newcomers to the scheme was provided by the university. This focused on two main topics: what to look for when observing students teaching; and assessing student performance and developing constructive but critical feedback.

That the teachers desired more explicit information may have been a reflection of lack of confidence in their ability to assume a tutoring role. The perceived paucity of their knowledge caused anxiety. For instance, some teachers, while accepting a degree of responsibility for facilitating students' basic teaching competence, were of the opinion that the university also had responsibilities in this regard. Yet, as university tutors pointed out, a feature of the training was that this was substantially delegated to schools. Tutors further maintained that attempting to prescribe what teachers should do would have contravened the philosophy underpinning the course. In addition, they noted that there were alternative channels by which information was communicated, e.g. the twice yearly meetings of General and Personal Tutors, annual meetings of Teacher Tutors and Curriculum Tutors. In addition, Teacher Tutors were invited to selected curriculum seminars. There were also the various Guidelines which the university issued.

Regarding the latter, although teachers appreciated that the university meant well and was attempting by this means to promote knowledge and under-standing, their criticisms of this documentation nevertheless were very forceful. 'Verbose and not very helpful', 'Very turgid and long-winded', 'If you give anyone more than one side of A4 nobody will read it anyway', were a selection of comments. One of the most experienced of Teacher Tutors observed that all too often what was down in print was 'too vague, and unrelated to the reality of what one actually does'. He added: 'In spite of what is said on paper, there are still key issues which are not very clear.' Whatever the assets and short-comings of the available literature it was not, of itself, acclaimed as the complete answer by the university. The Course Director spoke of the documentation as part of the process of 'familiarization', insisting that a fuller understanding of the philo-sophy of the course could only be 'forged through dialogue'. This would only come about over time and as good relationships between both parties were developed further.

University personnel: the constraint of time   Members of the university had only limited time available for their PGCE work. For the majority the PGCE was only one of several teaching commitments and it was acknowledged by the Course Director that the demands of PGCE tutoring far exceeded the time set aside for it: 'There is no relationship between the logistic that's given and the time that's needed to do the job'. For instance, no time was allowed for travelling to and from schools. Nor was an allowance made for seeing students who got into difficulty in school and who needed additional guidance and support and possibly counselling. Curriculum Tutors were faced with a particular problem in that there was a prescribed curriculum content which they had to cover with students in a limited period of time. It was, however, pointed out that the major expenditure of time was on preparation and not the actual contact time with students. As one tutor observed: 'The PGCE runs away with our time in a way that other courses never do'.

The limited time available had direct consequences for the operating of the scheme. Curriculum Tutors, for instance, had no choice but to rely heavily on Teacher Tutors for information as to how students were progressing. They were simply unable to make regular school visits. However, as their visits were relatively infrequent and brief, opportunities for detailed discussion with teachers were substantially reduced. In turn this carried the danger of a lessened response from teachers. As one member of faculty noted regretfully: 'I have seen an increasing trend of even the most committed Teacher Tutors not seeking our help because they know we can't give it'.

It had long been recognized that the extent to which university faculty were able to maintain close contact with teachers in school was critical for the success of the scheme. The level of supervision which current resourcing permitted was widely regarded as inadequate by both university faculty and teachers and was acknowledged as a potential weakness of the practice.

University tutors: the constraint of communication   In the past, communication between Teacher Tutors and Curriculum Tutors had been to some extent facilitated through their meeting at selected curriculum seminars. These seminars were still open to teachers, and teachers continued to attend, but attendance had fallen away of late. This was widely regretted. One Curriculum Tutor for example commented: 'The whole course depends upon this exchange – me going out to school and the Teacher Tutor coming into the university'. One reason for this fall off in attendance was thought to be the abolition in 1983 of the practice of paying teachers a fee (£125.00 per annum) for undertaking tutorial responsibilities. The discontinuation of this fee was a consequence of financial restrictions imposed by the University Grants Committee. The sum of £25.00 was now paid to each Teacher Tutor's department – a token recognition of the fact that taking on a tutoring role required time and energy.[9] As an embarrassed university spokesman acknowledged: 'We are aware of the enormous demands it requires . . . (such as to warrant) real resources rather than token ones'.

C: The probationary year

From the course content and structure were derived two principal aims for the Sussex course:

that the student would attain a reasonable level of basic competence in professional skills

that the student would develop the ability to reflect critically upon educational
practice.

The extent to which each of these aims was realized will now be considered, by
referring first to the opinions of teachers under whom they served and then to
the views of the probationers themselves.

Basic competence in professional skills

The views of Headteachers and senior colleagues

For four of the five students whose progress during the induction year was closely
charted there was indirect evidence to suggest that their training had had a
considerable influence on their professional attitudes and practices. Headteachers and senior teachers with responsibility for overseeing their progress
throughout the probationary period commented positively on the qualities they
perceived in them. They noted of these probationers that:

they were immediately at home in the school
they had been well schooled in practical skills
their educational interests extended beyond the classroom.

That they appeared to be quite at home in their respective schools perhaps
reflects their long hours of familiarization during school experience. These
former students quickly settled into departmental and school practices and were
able to fit in at both these levels. Thus, of one it was stated: 'He doesn't need to
be told to do things. He sees they need to be done and he does them'. Of
another it was noted that he seemed able 'to anticipate what he needs to know'.
It would appear too that the probationers' extended experience in school also led
to their being relaxed in the classroom and to their having become relatively
skilled in handling a class. The observations of senior teachers suggested that
they had acquired a repertoire of practical techniques. The following were
typical assessments: 'The traditional problems of probation . . . lesson preparation, discipline . . . he's not had'; 'She hasn't got any of those probationers'
problems such as collecting materials or what she's going to do in a lesson'.

Their close involvement with Teacher Tutors during training was seen to have
led probationers to have a realistic attitude towards teaching and learning. They
had acquired the terminology of the seasoned professional and used it appropriately. They were perceived as having been schooled in professional rather
than academic knowledge. Thus one Headteacher noted of a probationer, 'He
seemed to have his feet solidly on the ground'; while the Head of Department,
having first alluded to the 'woolly headed ideas' about subject teaching which

probationers frequently displayed commented: 'He gets down to the nitty gritty of what he's supposed to be doing.'

The views of probationers

Having put some distance between themselves and their training, and having acquired considerably more experience of schools and teaching, probationers were in a much stronger position than as students to review what their training had achieved. This they did at some length.

School experience   Probationers were extremely approving of their long training in basic classroom skills and the close contact with practising teachers. The prolonged and continuous placement in the Tutorial school was viewed as invaluable. Sustained immersion in the daily life of a school was seen as sound preparation in that the knowledge and understanding it brought had enabled them to commence their teaching careers with a degree of confidence. The breadth of the school experience had led to their 'being part of a school and a department, actually being part of a system' – they knew what the process of schooling entailed. 'I had more than just a classroom knowledge of how a school works and knew what I would be expected to do outside of my normal lessons', was a typical observation. For most of them, having observed and in some instances participated in such activities as staff meetings, tutor group periods, and parents evenings, there was little in day-to-day school life with which they were totally unfamiliar. 'School was not so much of an unknown to me', as one probationer put it.

During their training they had, of course, acquired much more than this general familiarity with the working of the school as an organization. Their close association with teachers was valued for its practical utility. The teachers worked on the job and knew both the problems of the classroom and many of the solutions to them. Working at length and in close conjunction with teachers, and learning the craft of the classroom from them, was regarded as highly beneficial. Teachers were perceived as 'very down to earth' and were accorded greater credibility than were university tutors who were seen to have a 'very academic emphasis'. There were numerous comments indicating the extent to which, as students, they had relied on teachers. 'I put a lot of faith in what they told me', 'The best advice was what I was told in school' and 'Teachers can give the most appropriate form of advice . . . they know the class, the children and the situation you're in . . . (Their advice was) fresh and apt and immediate', were typical comments. Since the initial anxieties of students on school experience are likely to focus on class control and management, the practicality of teachers' advice was particularly appreciated. Examples cited included: 'Be organized. Know what course of action you're going to take for any event', and 'Deal thoroughly with the small organizational matters first'.

Four of the five Sussex probationers followed in depth, recalled how, in their training, they had acquired the confidence to discuss their fears and failings honestly and openly. This had been a valuable means of learning, since it elicited support and guidance from experienced colleagues. A number of the probationers continued to employ this strategy, although it was not always as successful. Nor were they all sure that it was a sensible thing to do. Two probationers who encountered more severe difficulties were more reticent, preferring not to advertise their predicaments too publicly. One stated: 'At the university we were encouraged to bare our souls. While I feel reasonably comfortable within the Department, I wouldn't dream of doing so outside the Department.'

University-based studies　The probationers' training had clearly stood them in good stead in many respects. They were, however, critical of certain weaknesses in their training of which they were now more aware. They considered that there had been a number of omissions and inadequacies. There were, for example, complaints that certain fundamental areas of the curriculum had been neglected. For instance, integrated approaches to the teaching of science had received scant coverage at the university. This omission had caused one probationer who was required to teach it to public examination level severe anxiety and not a little difficulty. The light weighting given to the principles of teaching method was another example quoted. A third concerned the teaching and assessment of CSE Mode 3 work.

Although probationers had spent a high proportion of their training in school, they felt ill-prepared in certain non-teaching tasks. Writing reports, pastoral and tutorial work and general administration were mentioned in this respect. This is not exactly surprising. The tasks mentioned above – taking examination classes and meeting parents were also cited – are those which, as students, they were unlikely to have undertaken independently to any great extent, and in which they therefore might be expected to feel relatively unprepared. Take pastoral care for example. That students should engage in this during school experience had been the intention of the university, but it was at the discretion of school personnel and Tutorial schools varied in this respect. In one of the two monitored schools there was very little by way of practical involvement in this. In the other, every student was attached to a tutor group for approximately a term. Some recalled that this had been a useful experience. Others disagreed. One commented: 'I'm at a loss as to what I should be doing in tutor periods'. He, like some of the others, found himself expected to hold active tutorials and felt uneasy and ignorant about how to tackle this. The point is that schools differ considerably in respect of pastoral systems and practices. Also, pastoral care is an altogether more delicate area for the novitiate to be introduced into.

Students were also critical of Curriculum Tutors' preoccupation with content at the expense of method. Tutors who 'were concerned about how you should present things' were compared unfavourably to teachers whose 'main concern was that you survived'. One probationer felt that the omission from their university studies of what was termed 'sound teaching advice' was a serious limitation: 'Classroom management is vital to success in lessons. Routine is important and need not necessarily be boring. There was not sufficient emphasis placed on these aspects of the job'. It was also felt that curriculum seminars 'should have been on the nuts and bolts of presenting materials in the classroom . . . It was asking too much to expect school to cover all the practical side'.

A further related criticism was that some university tutors were out of touch with the realities of the classroom. The underlying philosophy of the training to a degree implies a division of responsibility between tutors and teachers, the former being more concerned with the theoretical and philosophical aspects of training and the latter with the day-to-day practicalities of the classroom. Probationers were divided on the wisdom of this arrangement. One probationer noted of tutors: 'We all felt that a lot of them didn't have much experience in the classroom . . . There is this growing feeling at the back of your mind that the people who are telling you to try something haven't really done it themselves'. On occasion tutors' advice was thought to have been unrealistic – for instance, being encouraged to experiment and innovate 'before we had established ourselves in the classroom', as one expressed it. Another probationer recalled having had doubts about the advice given by a tutor in relation to programming less able pupils. 'My ideas about the practicability of his ideas have been confirmed subsequently by my experience in school.' A third probationer referred to assessment and marking having been considered in their Curriculum Studies but from the standpoint of 'whether it is possible to achieve consensus on what we mean by "literary quality" '. This had been of limited value in the development of practical principles.

However, at least one probationer, with the benefit of hindsight, appreciated the merit of her Curriculum Tutor's approach in particular, and that of the course in general. She now recognized the value of the tutor's attempt to inspire students and to give them a vision to which subject teaching might aspire.

> Where it succeeded was that it gave us a coherent, very acceptable philosophy of . . . teaching, so that you have a focal point that your attention can always go back to when you're considering what your objectives are and how you're trying to achieve them.

Although the intellectual and philosophical orientation of much of their Curriculum Studies

> seemed irrelevant to some extent at the time – I was desperate for practical advice – in retrospect they have given me a solid foundation and a continuing questioning and a wish for more knowledge about education.

Nevertheless, this probationer still maintained, 'It was not enough that it was inspirational . . . We needed more of the nitty gritty'. Both university-based studies and their school experience had been deficient in this regard.

Finally, experience of but a single school and of only a single block teaching practice also attracted some criticism. For some, their teaching experience had been relatively narrow. One probationer recalled how, due to difficulties over timetabling, he had never experienced anything approaching having to teach a full timetable or the full range of pupil abilities. This had left him seriously unprepared for the pressures of teaching a full timetable and across the ability range for a sustained period. Some probationers made reference to the fact that only having had experience in one school, they were not very capable of developing general principles about teaching and learning. They had only learnt of the similarities and differences to be found in schools and classrooms by vicarious means, through having listened to the accounts of their tutors and their peers' experience.

Probationers' assessment of their basic competence in professional skills   On two occasions during their induction year – after six weeks and at the end of the year – probationers were given a checklist of items covering both specific classroom skills and broader issues of professional practice and were asked to rate their capabilities. As is noted in the Appendix this was the same checklist which was completed at the end of the training year. As might have been expected, seven of the eight areas in which they felt most competent some six weeks into teaching were among the areas of practice in which they had considered themselves to be well prepared at the end of their training. In most cases they reported that their skills in these areas had substantially increased. In only one respect did their two self-assessments differ – namely, the ability to appraise the effectiveness of their teaching. As students they had not rated their training highly on this dimension despite the importance which tutors attached to it. However, after only six weeks teaching they felt much more confident in this regard.

There was no similar degree of coincidence between preparation and performance in those areas in which, as beginning teachers, they now felt themselves to be less competent. For example, at the end of their training, these probationers – then students – had considered themselves well prepared to teach mixed ability groups, to question pupils effectively, and to engage in pastoral work. That these were areas in which, after a few weeks teaching, they felt less skilled is difficult to explain. It has already been suggested that they may not have undertaken much pastoral work during their training. Equally, the realities of trying to motivate and teach a mixed ability class may have been a novel experience. Perceived difficulties in questioning pupils effectively could be attributed to their gaining in perception as teachers. Perhaps only when they began regularly to do this did they come to realize what *effective* questioning meant. It may be surmised that as students they would have asked questions without being aware of the ways in which those questions could be used to structure response or to control deviant behaviour. Other areas in which the probationers still felt inadequate after six weeks' teaching included: preparing schemes for an extended period of time; individualizing teaching and learning strategies according to pupil attainment and need; and employing a range of teaching approaches. The first two of these they had earlier regarded as weaknesses of their training.

By the close of the induction year, sheer experience had brought about some improvement in all of these dimensions of teaching. This was especially so in the case of pastoral work and preparing schemes of work for an extended period. However, at the end of their probationary period, teaching mixed ability groups was still a matter of concern for over half the respondents. By this time, a new problem had also emerged – that of motivating pupils. Although this was an area in which, as novices, they had considered themselves to be reasonably well prepared it would appear that the reality of having to deal with disaffected pupils had induced a more realistic assessment. It cannot be known whether or not the probationers felt this to be a temporary inadequacy on their part, a shortlived lack of skill which in time they might hope to remedy.

The Reflective Practitioner

The second aim of the course was the development of the 'Reflective Practitioner'.

The views of Headteachers and senior colleagues

Several of the Headteachers interviewed recalled having been impressed by the level and breadth of awareness of educational matters which candidates from Sussex had displayed. In particular:

they had exhibited a personal philosophy of education
it was apparent that they had subjected their teaching and school experience to
   close and continuous analysis
they placed a premium upon professional development.

The Heads and their colleagues noted that these probationers held coherent educational objectives which they were able to articulate and defend in discussion. Their contributions indicated that they understood what they were seeking to achieve. One Head of Department commented of a probationer:

Often when someone comes in as a probationer . . . they're full of good intentions (but) they haven't actually thought through any kind of aesthetic, any kind of philosophy behind what they're doing . . . What —— is able to do . . . is to do something and then reflect on it constructively . . . Basically what she's got is educational principles.

Another Headteacher, recalling the interview noted: '(He) was able to speak from understanding rather than from regurgitated knowledge.' This probationer had 'come over as a guy who knew what he was talking about, who did know what his teaching was about'. These probationers were seen as having acquired the habit and skill of reflection, which was such a central principle of the Sussex course. Headteachers and Heads of Department also noted that the probationers displayed personal qualities which together contributed to a strong commitment to professional development – qualities which, in all likelihood, had been generated, or at least husbanded, by the Sussex course. It will be recalled that students were encouraged to be frank and open in discussing their school experience. The honesty which the probationers displayed in discussing their capabilities and shortcomings was commented upon several times. For instance, one Head of Department referred to the 'intellectual honesty' which her probationer displayed. Of another it was observed early in the induction year: 'He's not happy to get by. He's trying to push a bit further toward this super teacher'. These probationers were also seen to be resilient when lessons went badly and well able to contend with pressure. A typical comment was: 'He shows no sign of being intimidated by the job'. They were adjudged for the most part to have very accurate views of their strengths and weaknesses and to have capitalized upon their strengths.

The views of probationers

From our interviews with probationers it was apparent that the habit of reflective awareness clearly had become ingrained and had influenced their practices. Three of the five studied in depth had come to recognize that (as one of them put it) 'the teacher's relationship with the pupils is at the heart of effective teaching'. One spoke at length of how teaching was an act, a performance – and in doing so illustrated very clearly the outcome of reflection on practice.

> You learn to conduct yourself in a particular way . . . Now I'm aware of how you need to be to make a lesson work.

It entailed, 'huge amounts of energy' and

> giving it out in a certain way . . . Being energetic, enthusiastic about what you're talking about, being slightly hard and bright . . . encouraging and not irritable, prickly, tense . . . It's some kind of happiness that you need to show whether or not you feel it really.

Others spoke about their ideals – of how they had come under siege and had had to be tempered by a new realism. 'I think my ideals are becoming a bit more realistic . . . I'm changing them, but I'm not losing sight of them', stated one, while a second commented: 'I'm now aware that to realize those ideals it's going to take a lot more time and effort than I expected'. Initial problems had been experienced by one, as a consequence of 'having set my sights a little too high', as he put it. A vision of what to aim for had been retained, but this was now modified by a more realistic assessment of what was attainable: 'My ideas about what education *should* be about haven't changed. My ideas about what education *is* about maybe have' (emphasis added).

Notes

1. The Course Document was a basic guide to the structure, organization and philosophy of the course. It was drawn up in 1982 in order to provide information for all those involved in the Sussex course.
2. Normally, not every Tutorial school would be used by the university in any given year.
3. The dimensions of the Teacher Tutor's role listed in this section were derived from interviews with Teacher Tutors, Curriculum Tutors and with the Course Director, as well as from observation and course documentation.
4. The dimensions of the General Tutor's role were derived from interviews with General Tutors, Personal Tutors and the Course Director, as well as from observation and course documentation.
5. The dimensions of the Curriculum Tutor's role were derived from interviews with Curriculum Tutors and with the Course Director, and from observation and course documentation.
6. A viable size for the Personal Tutor Group was considered to be about eight students. When fewer than six students were placed in a Tutorial school the Personal Tutor was likely to assume responsibility for two schools.
7. The dimensions of the Personal Tutor's role were derived from interviews with Personal Tutors and with the Course Director, and from observation and course documentation.
8. In this and subsequent observations, it is recognized that *perceived* preparedness is not necessarily *actual* preparedness.
9. In addition Teacher and General Tutors were designated as 'Tutorial Fellows' of the University.

4 An Analytical Framework

Introduction

At the simplest level, PGCE courses can be understood as consisting of three major elements:

(a) Curriculum Studies Methods work, focusing on the pedagogy of particular school subjects or curriculum areas
(b) Education Studies, derived from the 'foundation disciplines' of sociology of education, psychology of education, philosophy of education and history of education
(c) School practice

In the most traditional of courses these three elements have been seen as largely distinct, representing discrete elements of professional preparation. As was noted in Chapter 1, however, in recent years more complex courses, stressing the inter-relations of the various elements, have been developed as the case studies in the previous two chapters have clearly shown. Yet it is interesting to note that despite considerable changes in the structure and organization of the innovative school-based courses we studied, the distinctive contributions of the three original major elements still remained. In all four of the courses it was possible to discern areas of work that could be characterized as predominantly curriculum studies, education studies or school practice.

In trying to understand the way in which these innovative courses differed from each other and from more traditional forms of training, and the significance of school-based work within them, it therefore became apparent that we needed to develop a much more sophisticated framework for analysis. The primary purpose of this chapter is to set out a framework or model that we developed through our research. In the next chapter we attempt to demonstrate the value of this model by using it to assess and make evaluative judgments about the two courses not yet considered.

We begin, however, by outlining a number of concepts derived from two authors who have been influential on our thinking. These are, first, the work analysis of the nature of professional practice by Schön (1983), and secondly, Bernstein's (1971) concepts of classification and framing. Both of these authors' writings are particularly significant as a background to our analysis.

The nature of professional practice

In his book *The Reflective Practitioner* Schön (1983) sets out to analyse in some detail the nature of professional practice. His purpose is to establish what he calls a new 'epistemology of practice'. Traditionally, he argues, the relationship between professional knowledge and action has been understood in terms of technical rationality; professional activity has been seen as a process of instrumental problem solving 'made rigorous by the application of scientific theory and technique' (p. 21). Professionals have been seen as 'experts' in that they possess a body of abstract knowledge which they 'apply', in a rule-governed way, to the real world.

Schön argues that there is a current crisis of confidence amongst contemporary professionals which can be attributed to the fact that this is an entirely inadequate understanding of the way professionals actually work. They may have a body of specialized knowledge, but they do not simply 'apply' it in a rule-governed way, nor is it appropriate to draw an analogy with scientific technologies. Professional activity has a rationality of its own; it is more akin to an artistic performance than a direct following of rules. The practitioner

> responds to the complexity . . . in what seems like a simple spontaneous way. His artistry is evident in his selective management of large amounts of information, his ability to spin out long lines of invention and inference and his capacity to hold several ways of looking at things at once without disrupting the flow of inquiry. (p. 130)

This 'artistry' has an epistemology of its own which Schön characterizes as 'reflection-in-action'.

In understanding the 'artistry' of professional practice Schön begins by emphasizing that professionals constantly find themselves facing situations which are unique. For example, teachers have to cope with the fact that no two groups of pupils they may have to teach are the same; even with pupils with whom they are familiar, the teacher is constantly having to present new material which raises its own unique problems of explanation and understanding. What the professional brings to these unique situations is a stock of experiences at many different levels of practical and theoretical sophistication.

> The practitioner has built up a repertoire of examples, images, understandings and actions . . . (which) includes the whole of his experience in so far as it is accessible to him for understanding and action. (p. 138)

Yet Schön argues that it is not a process of 'applying' this knowledge to the new situation. The teacher does not try to fit *this* group of pupils rigidly into some kind of pre-existing pattern of understanding that will simply tell him or her what to do. Rather, past experiences are used as a metaphor or exemplar.

> When a practitioner makes sense of a situation he perceives to be unique he sees it as something actually present in his repertoire. To see *this* site as *that* one is not to subsume the first under a familiar category or rule. It is rather to see the unfamiliar, unique situation as both similar to and different from the familiar one, without at first being able to say similar or different with respect to what. The familiar situation functions as a precedent, or a metaphor or . . . an exemplar for the unfamiliar one. (p. 138)

In drawing on his or her past experience the professional imposes a structure or 'definition'[1] on the problem at hand. 'Defining' a problem is an active process. It involves interpreting the situation in *this* way as opposed to countless *other* possible ways, shaping it to the definition. For example, a teacher may define a standard situation by interpreting a child's difficult behaviour as the result of a combination of the distinct factors seen to be operating in previous cases. To draw on one's understanding and experience is to begin with an interpretation which to some degree shapes the situation one faces. But this defining process, Schön argues, has to be seen as experimental; one imposes meaning by actually taking action and then evaluating the consequences. The teacher interprets the child's behaviour and responds in a way which leads to many consequences and that may result in the changing of the definition. Imposing a definition therefore leads to a

> web of moves, discovered consequences, implications, appreciations and further moves. Within the larger web, individual moves yield phenomena to be understood, problems to be solved or opportunities to be exploited. (p. 131)

There will also be unintended consequences; to 'excuse' the behaviour of one child may affect the behaviour of the whole class. The situation 'speaks back' to the practitioner, demanding more reflection and further action.

Engaging in professional activity is therefore a 'transactional' process. The professional

> shapes the situation, but in conversation with it, so that his own models and appreciations are also shaped by the situation. The phenomena that he seeks to understand are partly of his own making; he is *in* the situation that he seeks to understand. (p. 151)

In short, 'the unique and uncertain situation comes to be understood through the attempt to change it and is changed through the attempt to understand it' (p. 132).

Schön argues that using professional knowledge is always therefore a reflective process even if that reflection is not raised to the level of consciousness. The definition is constantly monitored for its 'fit' with the situation at hand; if it does not work an alternative or supplementary definition has to be employed. The professional also has to evaluate the consequences, both intended and unintended, of his or her actions. For example, professionals must decide

> whether they can solve the problem they have set, whether they value what they get when they solve it (or what they can make of what they get); whether they achieve in the situation a coherence of artifact and idea, a congruence with their fundamental theories and values; whether they can keep enquiry moving. (p. 141)

Professional activity is therefore a constant process of interpretation, action, reflection and adjustment. As such it is very different from the rule-governed application of scientific knowledge to produce predictable results.

Classification and framing in the PGCE

If Schön's characterization of professional activity as reflection-in-action is accepted, it has important implications for our understanding of the nature of professional training. As has already been mentioned, traditional PGCE courses would seem to reflect a rationalist rule-governed model of professional activity. In the college or university there is an emphasis on 'preparation' in curriculum and education studies which one learns to apply on teaching practice. It is our contention that the move to school-based training, at least potentially, implies a rather different epistemology, one that may more closely resemble Schön's notion of reflection-in-action.

In order to understand the changes involved in school-based training more clearly we found it helpful to begin by drawing on Bernstein's (1971) concepts of classification and framing of educational knowledge. For Bernstein there are three fundamental topics for inquiry in relation to any educational course – the *curriculum*, which defines what counts as valid knowledge; *pedagogy*, which defines what counts as the valid transmission of knowledge; and *evaluation*, which defines what counts as a valid realization of this knowledge on the part of the taught. In understanding the changes implicit within the move to school-based training, the first two of these – the curriculum and pedagogy – are of particular importance.

In relation to the curriculum, Bernstein suggests that a critical question to be asked of any course is not only what appears on the curriculum, and by implication what is left out, but also how different elements of that content stand in relation to one another; whether the boundary between different contents is clear cut or blurred. The degree of boundary maintenance between different contents is known as the *classification* of educational knowledge. If the contents of a course are well insulated from each other, i.e. when the course is characterized by *strong* classification, Bernstein describes the curriculum as a 'collection code'; it is made up of the discrete study of segregated elements. On the other hand if the boundaries between different contents are less clear cut, i.e. if there is *weak* classification, then Bernstein characterizes this as an 'integrated code'.

A curriculum may therefore exhibit either strong or weak classification in relation to its constituent parts. But the degree of insulation or integration between contents is not the only factor of significance in analysing the curriculum of particular educational courses. Equally important, Bernstein argues, is the *'framing'* of this knowledge. By framing, he refers to the degree of control teachers and pupils possess over the selection, organization and pacing of knowledge transmitted and received in the pedagogical relationship. Once again, framing may be *strong* or *weak*. When it is strong, the teacher or lecturer maintains tight control over the knowledge that is transmitted; the pedagogy is traditionally didactic. Where the framing is weaker, the students have more power. In such cases the pedagogy is more frequently individual or group based.

Thus in ideal terms, a curriculum may be characterized as being one of four different types, depending on whether it exhibits strong or weak classification and strong or weak framing. With *strong classification* and *strong framing* there is a strict demarcation between the boundaries of different contents and a clear control by the teacher or lecturer over the selection, pacing and organization of knowledge. Alternatively with *strong classification* and *weak framing* students are given some control over the selection, pacing and organization of knowledge within traditionally defined and separated subject areas. *Weak classification* with *strong framing* leads to the boundaries between contents being blurred, but with a didactic relationship between the teachers and taught. Finally, with *weak classification* and *weak framing* traditional boundaries as well as control over knowledge are challenged.

If one applies the concepts of classification and framing to traditional PGCE courses one can see that in ideal typical terms they constituted a strong form of collection code with strong classification and strong framing. We would suggest that it was precisely because it was a collection code that its implicit epistemology was one of technical rationality where students were inducted into existing knowledge and then expected to 'apply' that knowledge during their practical work in school.

Because in the traditional course the classification of different elements of the curriculum was strong, education studies (sociology, psychology, philosophy and history) were clearly demarcated from each other as well as from curriculum or methods work. Perhaps most crucial of all, they were clearly insulated from work undertaken in school; students were initially 'prepared' in the training institution and only at a later date did they enter the classroom for teaching practice. Framing in the traditional course was equally strong; the pedagogy was typically didactic (despite the frequent use of discussion-based work in curriculum or methods work) in that lecturers retained tight control over the selection, pacing and organization of knowledge. This strong framing also contributed to the dissociation between 'theory' and 'practice' because of what Bernstein describes as the 'deep structure' of educational codes. He argues that the deep structure of a collection code means that students are inducted into existing hierarchies of knowledge. As learners, they are relatively powerless; they do not have the opportunity to learn how the knowledge they are required to master is produced. The emphasis in such a curriculum is on 'states of knowledge' rather than on 'ways of knowing'. As Bernstein notes, within the collection code it is only the most advanced learners who have the opportunity to engage in knowledge production themselves. Within the traditional PGCE this was seldom possible. Students simply had to learn what they were taught within their training institution and *apply* it as best they could during teaching practice.

By contrast it would seem to us that a curriculum appropriate to the epistemology of professional practice put forward by Schön would be more likely to approximate to an integrated code. As Bernstein notes

> The underlying theory of learning of collection is likely to be didactic, whilst the underlying theory of learning in integrated codes may well be more group or self regulated. *This arises out of a different concept of what counts as having knowledge which in turn leads to a different concept of how knowledge is to be acquired.* (p. 61, emphasis added)

If professional activity is not about the technical following of rules but is more akin to an artistic performance, then this indeed demands a change in the sort of knowledge that is valued. This in turn must lead to a change in how that knowledge is acquired.

The recognition that teaching is an interactive process whereby one draws on one's past experiences and understandings to experimentally impose meaning on a situation applies equally to the novice as to the experienced practitioner. Even the most naive student therefore comes to the PGCE with a stock of knowledge with which to 'define' classroom situations, as well as certain practical skills with which to deal with children. However inadequately, most students can 'survive' in the classroom even from the earliest days of training. Professional training may therefore be seen as process of sophisticating students' pre-existing skills and understandings. From this point of view students are not being asked to 'apply' the rules they have learned in a different context. Rather the primary purpose of training is to help them bring the 'constant process of interpretation, action, reflection and adjustment' that is necessarily involved in professional activity increasingly under their own control and understanding.

Such an approach would seem to necessitate, first, that practical activity is placed at the very heart of training. Moreover, if the main purpose of other elements of the PGCE is indeed to help students sophisticate their skills, knowledge and understandings in relation to such practical work, then this will also demand weaker forms of classification and framing. Weaker classification would mean that education studies and curriculum studies could be more closely related to each other and most particularly to work undertaken in school. A pedagogy derived from weaker framing in which students have greater control over the selection, pacing and organization of knowledge would also seem more appropriate. As Bernstein suggests, within an integrated code, lecturers 'will be less concerned to emphasize *states* of knowledge but will be more concerned to emphasize *how* knowledge is created' (p. 60). If professional activity is an interactive process then students actually need training in the 'creation' rather than the application of knowledge. This is only likely to be achieved by moving away from didactic pedagogies.

The need for an analytical framework

A move towards an integrated code within the PGCE would therefore seem to us to be a logical consequence of following Schön's characterization of professional practice as 'reflection-in-action'. In trying to understand the changes in the school-based courses we examined we must therefore ask whether they did indeed move in this direction and how was this achieved. To what extent did they adopt an integrated code where different contents (theoretical, professional and practical) were brought into closer relation with each other; to what extent was there a changed, more active pedagogy? Given the complexity of professional training courses, if these questions were to be answered in a meaningful way we needed some kind of analytical framework with which to analyse our data.

Though superficially the four courses under study still retained many traditional features (course elements with familiar labels such as curriculum studies or education studies), they did indeed involve contents that were new and there were sustained attempts to bring these contents into new relationships with one another; in many cases there was also a deliberate move away from didactic pedagogies. Therefore to have analysed them merely in terms of the titles of specific course elements would have been to overlook much that was innovative about them. We also found that Bernstein's notions of classification and framing, although useful at a general level did not capture all the changes that we saw. Questions about moves towards integration were central, but in themselves such questions cannot reveal, at the level of detail, how those moves are actually achieved, nor all of their consequences. In order to understand the distinctive way in which each of these courses developed students' professional expertise we have therefore found it necessary to develop our own framework for analysing them. The remainder of this chapter is devoted to outlining the key concepts that we developed.

Our framework for comparing the four courses has been developed both inductively and deductively. Throughout the project the team was involved in a process of 'constant comparison' (Glaser and Strauss, 1967) of the data. The four courses were continually discussed and compared, both with each other and with other training courses with which team members were familiar. During the analysis stage of the project this process was undertaken more systematically and the constituent elements of each course rigorously compared. In this sense the framework outlined below may be seen as a form of 'grounded theory' – it was in part developed inductively from the fieldwork data. However, grounded theory never emerges within a vacuum; questions posed of the data must be derived from somewhere. In developing the framework, three theoretical influences were significant. The work of Bernstein (1971) and Schön (1983) has already been mentioned. Also significant was the work of Hirst (1983) in his analysis of the nature of educational theory and its relationship to practice. In particular his attempt to elucidate the character of practical principles, their significance for practice and their relationship with the fundamental disciplines of educational theory, led to a number of important distinctions we came to make. As has been commented in Chapter 1, Hirst's analysis stresses the centrality for professional practice of theory developed in direct critical reflection on practice itself. But he insists too that fundamental critical examination of such theory and practice must be carried out, examining its location in wider beliefs and practices, its presuppositions and thence its more adequate rational defence. This examination he sees as demanding the use of the methods of those academic disciplines, such as philosophy, psychology and sociology, which progressively undertake and develop fundamental enquiry. It demands too the incorporation into the framework in which professional theory and practice are developed of the achievements of those disciplines.[2] These theoretical writings provided a series of questions with which the fieldwork data was addressed. The result, however, should not be seen as the mere *application* of these theories; what is presented below is derived from the inter-relationship between such theoretical questions and the fieldwork data itself. As a result, our analysis is significantly different in a number of key respects from any of these authors' works.

PGCE courses: a framework for analysis

In the previous section we suggested that our central question in relation to the four school-based courses could be expressed as a concern with the degree to which they were moving towards an integrated code. Specifically, this meant finding some way of assessing the nature of the classification and framing that each of them exhibited. As has been noted above, questions of classification deal with curriculum contents and their relationships while framing focuses on issues of pedagogy.

The content of PGCE courses

From our research it is apparent that the content of initial training courses may be seen as concerned with two distinct but interconnected areas of professional competence associated with different aspects of the teacher's role. These are:

1 The development of *classroom* competence – covering the understanding, judgements, skills and principles relating to the day to day practice of classroom teaching.
2 The development of *wider professional* competence – covering the understanding, judgements, skills and principles relating to the teacher's wider professional role within the school, the community and society at large.

Training in each of these spheres of professional competence involves students undertaking work on a variety of different topics. In relation to classroom competence, students concentrate on such topics as lesson planning or the teaching of reading. 'Curriculum studies' or 'methods work' and 'education studies' have traditionally both made a contribution here. While the teaching of a specific area of the school curriculum is almost exclusively the province of curriculum studies or methods work, there are many aspects of classroom management and pedagogy that may be considered either common to all areas of the curriculum or concerned with integrated activities in the school. It is these common aspects of teaching (such as discipline, motivation, language) that in some institutions are addressed together within general 'education' courses; in other institutions they may be considered separately in relation to particular subject areas.

Topics covered in relation to developing students' wider professional competence may be more diverse. For example, students may spend time developing an institutional perspective on schools (examining pastoral care or curriculum policies); they may cover the relationship between schools and their community (considering parent/teacher relationships, the social class intake of schools). Wider professional training may also involve a consideration of the school in society at large (learning about the structure and organization of the educational system as a whole, examining the relationship between schooling and the economic basis of society).

Many different topics could potentially be covered within these two general areas and a particular course will have to make a selection from all of those that are possible. One key question in examining any particular course, therefore, concerns the *selection* of topics covered within these areas as well as the relative *weighting* given to these different dimensions of professional competence. For example, until recently, many courses, both primary and secondary, focused almost exclusively on the development of classroom competence, comparatively little attention being paid to the teacher's broader professional role. More recently, because of the changing role of specialist graduate teachers, training in this second area has become an increasingly important focus of attention (a factor reflected in three of our four courses). The *selection* and *weighting* of topics to be covered is, therefore, a key factor to consider when making comparative judgements about PGCE courses.

But the *content* of a course cannot only be understood in terms of the topics addressed for as our courses revealed any one topic may be covered in a variety of different ways. Learning may take place experientially within school or be part of the taught course. Within the taught course there can also be important differences in how a topic is considered. On any topic, for example, lesson planning or the teaching of number or pastoral care, different kinds of knowledge and skills can be the object of training, ranging from the very practical to the highly theoretical. More formally, this can be expressed as training at different 'levels'.

In analysing the curriculum of any particular course our research would suggest that it is necessary to assess the character of the training provided, not merely in terms of topics that are covered, but also in terms of the levels across which it ranges. We have, therefore, used our research in order to refine our understanding of what these different levels of training actually are. In presenting the results of our analysis we have sought too, not to refine the categories in any way beyond what seemed to us strictly necessary to bring out these general issues, fearing that over-elaboration of detail might obscure the enterprise.

'Levels of training'

One of the weaknesses of Schön's model of professional practice as a basis for considering professional training is that he is very unclear about the nature of the stock of knowledge and skills professionals use to 'define' teaching situations. From our research, it is apparent that it may be of many different kinds. For example, it may include direct experiential understanding of particular classes, knowledge of other professionals' work (e.g. about schemes of work, or disciplinary techniques and their consequences) as well as professional knowledge of a more abstract, principled kind (e.g. ideas about what ought to be done in 'this type of situation' with 'these sorts of pupils', or ideas about what sorts of activities, in general, motivate children). Professional knowledge, practical skills and principles are of course themselves based on fundamental values and educational theories and these too may form part of the teacher's explicit stock of knowledge; alternatively, such assumptions may be merely implicit. Professional expertise can therefore be developed at a variety of different levels from the most concrete and practical to the most fundamental and theoretical, each of which may be a focus in specific forms of training. For the purpose of comparing these four courses we found it necessary to distinguish four different levels of training.

Level (a) Direct practice

At this level, training involves the development of understanding, judgement and skills through direct practical experience in the classroom, school or community context. Understanding, judgement and skills are here essentially acquired by students in immediate first-hand experience; issues of professional principle and theory are entirely implicit. Students may be helped in developing their practical understanding, judgement and skills through forms of systematic or informal supervision either by teachers or lecturers. Through such supervision students may become more detailed in their understanding, more sensitive in their judgements and able to exercise more complex skills. However, at this level their training remains rooted in the specifics of particular concrete situations.

Level (b) Indirect practice

Training at this level also concerns the acquisition of practical understanding, judgement and skills but in detached contexts rather than through direct practical experience. In these contexts, students are not involved in professional practice itself. At this level of training, the knowledge and understanding of concrete practice that students develop is essentially 'second-hand'; it is derived from talks, books, videos, discussions etc. The training in skills they receive is essentially detached or simulated, taking place in workshops or micro-teaching situations. Although concerned with practice, work at this level is therefore divorced from at least some of the complexities of application in a particular context. Once again, issues of theory and principle are implicit. Through training of this sort, students are intended to develop a repertoire of specific skills and ideas which they can utilize in their own teaching. Taken together, Levels (a) and (b) may also be used as a basis for more principled and theoretical forms of training addressed at Levels (c) and (d).

Level (c) Practical principles

Training at this level involves the acquisition of knowledge of the principles behind different professional practices and reflection on their use and justification. Through reflection or direct teaching, students become explicitly aware of the general principles which underlie differing practices encountered at Levels (a) and (b). They thus come to understand, not only the overt details of these practices, but the general principles that are governing what is done in particular circumstances. Such principles, which suggest, say, how best to teach fractions or handle children who interrupt the work of others, may of course not be agreed by all teachers. Some are well founded, others are not. At this level, therefore, students begin to understand that, of their nature, principles require justification. They begin to understand also that practical principles are inevitably general, suggesting what ought to be done in certain kinds of circumstances, not prescribing because any given situation may be unique in crucial respects. Work at this level develops students' overt critical reflection on practice, their own and others. It is here that the principles implicit in training at Levels (a) and (b) are made explicit. It is at this level that Schön's 'reflective practitioner' sees the practical implications of the principles in different ways of 'defining' problems, becomes consciously aware of how definitions open up reflective practice and sees the need for the justification of the principles that responsible professionalism requires.

Level (d) Disciplinary theory

Levels (a), (b) and (c) are all concerned with professional understanding, judgements, skills and principles. As such, they are themselves based on many implicit value judgements and theoretical assumptions. Work at Level (d) is of a different order in that its purpose is to make explicit and critically examine such value judgements and theoretical assumptions by reference to the foundation disciplines (philosophy of education, psychology of education, sociology of education and history of education). Training at this level may have a number of objectives. Its purpose may be didactic, introducing students to an essential content of theoretical knowledge. Psychologists, for example, continue to argue that students must have at least a passing acquaintance with the work of Piaget; sociologists are equally insistent on the importance of students knowing of the relationship between social class and educational achievement. Such courses may be seen as contributing to a minimum package of 'academic cultural capital' that all teachers need.

But learning of a content is not the only objective of training at this level. When related to work at the other levels, theoretical work may also be used in developing students' own skills of reflection and analysis. Helping students critically to appreciate the value judgements and theoretical assumptions implicit in 'defining' practical problems is, in some courses, seen as a key to advanced professional development. In Schön's terms, such analysis will raise students' consciousness of the character and significance of reflection-in-action, their own and others, at the most fundamental level and thereby bring their own professional activity more directly under their control.

Clearly, from what has been said to characterize these levels, each, but particularly (c) and (d), could readily be divided to produce a more detailed analysis of training. However, for the present purposes of considering the significance of school-based work in training we decided not to pursue that detail further for fear of overburdening the study with distinctions not central to our purpose.

Each of the above levels of work may be developed in relation to both classroom competence and wider professional competence. These different levels and areas of work may be briefly summarized as in Figure 4.1.

Students may therefore be offered training on any one topic within their course at a variety of different levels; curriculum studies, education studies and school

Figure 4.1 Levels of professional training.

Level (a) Direct Practice
Practical training through direct experience in schools and classrooms.

Level (b) Indirect Practice
'Detached' training in practical matters usually conducted in classes or workshops within training institutions.

Level (c) Practical Principles
Critical study of the principles of practice and their use.

Level (d) Disciplinary Theory
Critical study of practice and its principles in the light of fundamental theory and research.

---

experience may all make a contribution in their different ways. However, given the limited time available within the PGCE, not every topic can be approached at all four levels, neither can different levels of work all be given the same emphasis. Once again, selections have to be made. The growing importance of training in relation to the teachers' wider professional role has already been noted. However, this is not necessarily attributable to the development of school-based training. One general feature of school-based, as opposed to traditional courses, however, is that they are likely to involve a greater proportion of work at Level (a) with proportionately less emphasis on other levels of training. Precisely what has been sacrificed from the traditional course to provide this additional time for practical work varies from course to course.

The integration of Levels

Although our research shows that it is possible to analyse the training of students at a variety of different levels it must of course be remembered that these divisions are artificial. The expertise on which teachers draw in the process of 'defining' the practical situations they face will always include elements of concrete and detached understanding, judgement and skill and these are themselves based on certain principles. They also involve fundamental social, psychological and philosophical assumptions which can themselves be called into question. If students are to bring the process of reflection-in-action more explicitly under their own control then it is apparent that they will need training at all of these different levels. However, if for the purpose of training, different levels are separated out then we must ask how linkage or integration between these elements is also achieved for their appropriate and effective operation in professional practice. It will be recalled that central to Schön's analysis of professional activity is the idea that detached or abstract knowledge cannot properly be simply applied to concrete situations in a rule-governed way. Using what training can provide at the different levels in professional activity is a complex process of trans-action and students will, therefore, need the course to integrate work at the different levels so as to result in practice responsibly and critically undertaken.

In evaluating professional courses such as the PGCE, Bernstein's questions about the classification of educational knowledge do not, therefore, simply direct us to ask how far different *topics* within a particular course are integrated with or separated from each other. It is also essential to ask how far different levels of training *within the same topic* are integrated with each other and how this is achieved. On any one topic one must ask, for example, how a student's concrete classroom experience is related to some understanding of professional principles; what precisely is the role of educational theory and research and how are they related to educational practice? If one is to understand the nature of the training made available in our four courses it is necessary to disentangle for the chosen topics of content the different levels of training provided and their integration. Being concerned in particular with the school-based elements of the training it is necessary to disentangle the training given at the most concrete level in school experience and how work at other levels relates to this throughout the programme.

In the most traditional form of PGCE course, the different areas and levels of training outlined above were carried out in three course elements. Direct practi-cal training at Level (a) took place entirely in block teaching practice. Curricu-lum studies or methods work, concerned with certain areas of classroom practice, ranged across Levels (b) and (c) with perhaps some attention to Level (d). Education studies was concerned with certain other, more general classroom topics and wider professional issues at Levels (c) and (d); above all education studies stressed Level (d) work from the foundation disciplines.

Though there was some linkage of levels and areas of work, as has already been noted, the structure of the course firmly institutionalized particular separations of major significance. Curriculum studies or 'methods' work and education studies were taught within the training institution and were sharply divorced from each other, being taught by distinct groups of lecturers with different forms of expertise. What is more, both elements were strongly separated from the practical training being given in schools. Thus, although all these elements clearly had a common aim (the development of competent and knowledgeable practitioners) the *structure* of the course and the expertise of the different *personnel* responsible for different dimensions of training inhibited any systematic integration of the different levels. It is, therefore, not surprising that a repeated criticism of this model was that there was an unbridgeable gap between 'theory' and 'practice'. Integration was something that was in many respects left to the students themselves to achieve rather than a principle that informed course planning. The implicit assumption behind the course model was that knowledge derived from college and university-based studies could simply be 'applied' by students themselves in school practice. The reality was that once students started teaching practice they 'forgot' all that they had learned in their training institution and simply got on with the business of teaching as best they could.

In recent years, as was noted in Chapter 1, the strict separation of these particular course elements has been challenged in many PGCE courses. For example, practising classroom teachers now often contribute to curriculum studies courses. Lecturers may undertake frequent supervision of students on school experience. In the area of education studies the traditional model has also been challenged with the development of new courses which aim to link educational theory with the close study of school and classroom practice. School-based courses potentially offer the opportunity to integrate levels of work much further. However, before we could make evaluative judgements about these four courses it first became necessary to develop a clearer understanding of the means by which such integration can be established. From our analysis of the four courses, it became apparent that two factors were of particular significance in moves towards integration. These were firstly the *personnel* responsible for different aspects of training and secondly the *structure* of the course itself.

Personnel

From an analysis of our four courses it is apparent that an examination of the personnel assigned responsibility for different aspects of training within a PGCE is significant in that different sorts of professional are typically in a position to contribute only certain levels of expertise. For example, by virtue of their own training and experience, most of the teachers we observed had different forms of expertise from lecturers; the training that these two groups of professionals were able to offer on the 'same' topic was therefore frequently of a very different character. Given that teachers are involved, day in day out, in the minutiae of work with particular children in a particular school with a particular syllabus then the nature of the expertise they have to offer students is most likely to be rooted in those specific contexts; it is likely to be a form of training at Level (a). This is not to deny that for idiosyncratic reasons some teachers do have access to other levels of expertise. It is, however, to recognize that such teachers are always likely to be in a minority.

By contrast, method or curriculum lecturers do have the opportunity to witness a wide range of different forms of practice; they also have the opportunity to explore the principles upon which practice might be based. They are, therefore, more frequently in a position to offer training at Levels (b) and (c). However, their opportunity to develop a detailed understanding of the specific contexts in which their students are placed for school experience is extremely limited. Lecturers usually visit their students during teaching practice once a week at most – in many cases it is far less frequent. There is therefore little possibility that they can develop the detailed, context specific knowledge necessary for effective training at Level (a). *Almost by definition this is a task that only teachers regularly working within a specific school can undertake.* When curriculum or methods lecturers do visit students during their work in school, then the nature of their supervision is likely to be of a different character; it is more likely to be concerned with relating what they have seen to other forms of practice (Level (b)) or the principles of practice (Level (c)).

In trying to understand the levels of training that students are offered it is, therefore, necessary to look carefully at the expertise particular professionals have at their disposal. Different sorts of teacher (classroom teachers, heads of departments, senior staff) are likely to have access to different contents; they each have access to a different perspective on school life. Different categories of lecturer (curriculum or methods lecturers, and education lecturers) are also likely to differ in their possible contributions.

Structure

In assessing the character of the training made available within a particular course our research has indicated that it is necessary to begin by examining the personnel involved in each aspect of the programme for they will in large part set the limits to the levels of training made available to students on particular topics. However, these four courses also demonstrated that the *structure* of a particular course is equally important in determining the character of the training. By structure we refer to such factors as the way in which the major elements, or 'sites' of training, (curriculum studies, serial practice, block practice etc.) are weighted and organized in relation to each other as well as their physical location. Structures are significant because amongst other things they help determine the possibilities for integration of different levels of training.

Our analysis revealed that the *relative weighting* given to different parts of a course was clearly significant in determining the character of training. Given the very limited time available within a one-year programme, a course which places great emphasis on direct practical experience must either neglect some aspects of traditional content or try to approach them through direct experience itself. The courses we observed varied significantly in the weighting they gave to different aspects of training and in the changes they had made to achieve greater time in school.

The way in which course elements are organized, i.e. the *pattern of the course*, is also important. For example we have already noted that the most traditional form of PGCE pattern, with one term wholly in college, one term in school and then one term back in college, almost by definition prohibited any significant integration of Levels (b), (c) and (d) with the students' direct practical experience at Level (a). By contrast, the progressive movement towards concurrent patterns of training which these courses revealed, with students spending two or three days a week of 'serial practice' in school and then two or three days a week in the training institution, at least established the possibility of some forms of integration. Equally important in the pattern of the course is the sequencing, length and number of block practices.

We also found that the *range* of schools students teach in on serial and block practice is significant. If students experience several schools at first hand then they are likely to develop a wider repertoire of direct practical skills and knowledge at Level (a). If the schools are carefully chosen to provide them with significantly contrasting experiences this may also help them to recognize important differences of principle (at Level (c)) implicit within practice. Alternatively a sustained experience in a single school can establish the possibility for a more in depth understanding of teaching, allowing the student to watch pupils develop over a period of time, giving the student time to establish an understanding of the school in its full complexity as an institution.

Finally, the *physical location* of various training activities was also found to be significant. Running a seminar in a school may not *in itself* mean that the content is necessarily any more integrated with students' own direct experience, nevertheless it does set up the possibility in a way that is much more difficult to achieve within the training institution.

Pedagogy

In what has been said so far we have been concerned to draw out the significance of the *content* of training courses and the way in which different dimensions of that content were linked or integrated with each other. In Bernstein's terms this can be expressed as a concern with the *classification* of educational knowledge. However, as was argued at the beginning of this chapter, equally important in determining the character of training in any course is the *framing* of educational knowledge. That leads us to a consideration of pedagogy.

According to Bernstein, 'framing' concerns the selection, pacing and organization of educational knowledge. In traditional courses very different pedagogies were adopted within the training institution as opposed to the school. Within the training institution decisions about what counted as valid knowledge and what was to be learned were almost entirely within the hands of lecturers. Even in discussion based workshop sessions it was typically the lecturers who decided the agenda of topics to be covered; it was they who established, albeit often indirectly, what students should learn. Despite the fact that the surface form of the teaching style was discursive and students were active, the underlying pedagogy of the taught course was in almost all cases entirely didactic. When it came to work in school, however, a very different pedagogic style was adopted in that students were frequently left to themselves to apply what they had learned. They were expected to observe other teachers and use them as role models but for the most part they were expected to apply what they had learned in the training institution through trial and error with only occasional supervisory visits from their lecturers. As was suggested above, the pedagogy employed in both dimensions of the traditional course (college based and teaching practice) was derived from an understanding of professional activity as a technical following of rules; in Schön's terms it implied a rationalist epistemology.

As has already been argued, the recognition that teaching is not a technical activity but an interactive process, where one draws on one's past experiences and understandings *experimentally* to impose meaning on a situation, would appear to demand a different pedagogy. If professional activity is not the *application* of knowledge, didactic training is not enough. It may be the case that at certain points of their training students do indeed need didactic teaching; most teacher educators remain convinced that there are things students must be taught. During their time in school, learning by trial and error and by modelling themselves on others will also remain important. But if professional activity is an interactive process in the way Schön suggests then students need training in the 'creation' rather than the mere application of knowledge. They must be reflective and analytical in relation to their own teaching. In the training institution this may demand some movement away from didactic pedagogies with students at times being given greater control over the selection, pacing and organization of what they learn. Only in this way can they develop the *skills* necessary to bring their teaching increasingly under their own control. Within the school it may mean establishing a less laissez faire pedagogy where students are encouraged to reflect systematically on and analyse the teaching in which they are engaged.

From trying to disentangle the different pedagogic styles employed within the four school-based courses we studied, we came to recognize the importance of a number of different dimensions of teaching and learning style. Within formally taught sessions, whether held in the training institution or the school, we found three questions to be important. The first concerns whether students are expected to be *active* or *passive*. As has already been noted, much teaching, even in traditional courses, has actively involved students by means of discussions, workshop activities etc.; this alone is therefore not enough. An equally important question concerns the choice of *agenda*. In some parts of our courses we saw examples of the selection of the agenda of topics to be covered being turned over substantially to the students. In other cases the agenda was open to negotiation between the lecturers and students while in yet other cases the choice of topics remained with the lecturers. The final and most significant question concerns who determines *what is appropriate knowledge* within any training session. Even where the selection of topics is assigned to students it is still possible for lecturers to control *what* students should learn on any one topic. The answers to each of these questions significantly affects the degree to which the pedagogic style moves away from the traditionally didactic to a more analytical, reflective approach. Such changes, we would suggest, have a profound effect on *what* students actually learn.

As we have already noted, there is also a pedagogic style implicit in students' direct practical experience in school. Critical questions here concern the degree to which students are expected to *model* themselves on the teachers with whom they work; the extent to which they are expected to learn for themselves, by means of *trial and error* and the extent to which there is *active tutoring* in relation to their teaching. Where there is active tutoring then once again it becomes important to ask whether it is didactic or analytical.

Summary and conclusions

In trying to analyse the nature of training made available in any PGCE course we therefore suggest that it is necessary to consider the following three factors.

1 The *personnel* responsible for different dimensions of training. Because different personnel typically are able to contribute only specific forms of expertise, the *levels* of training involved in any particular session will, at least in part, be determined by the personnel responsible.
2 The *structure* of the course (pattern, weighting, physical location etc.). This is significant because it helps establish the possibilities for integration between different contents and *levels* of training.
3 The *pedagogy* employed in different course elements. This is important in that it will determine the degree to which course content remains an externalized body of knowledge to be applied or whether the course provides the opportunity for students to develop the skills of reflection and analysis in relation to their own developing practice.

Using this framework it is now possible to summarize two ideal typical models of training, one based on a traditional, rationalist epistemology and the other based on Schön's notions of reflection-in-action. In the traditional model we would expect different *contents* within the course and different *levels* of training within each content to be well insulated from each other. The responsibilities of the *personnel* involved would be clearly demarcated and the *structure* of the course would inhibit any moves towards integration. Such a course is also likely to be characterized in its taught elements by a *didactic* pedagogy. On the other hand, during teaching practice there is likely to be little emphasis on *active tutoring* with students largely being left to themselves to apply what they have learned in the training institution.

At the other end of the continuum we might expect a course which based itself on Schön's notions to place explicitly students' direct practical experience (Level (a)) at the centre of training. Such a course would then try to establish a *structure* and *pedagogy* so that the different levels of training provided by different *personnel* could be integrated with students' own practical work in schools.

As has already been noted, many courses in recent years have moved increasingly towards the latter model. In this sense school-based courses are nothing new, they merely offer the opportunity to take that movement even further than before. However, having established a clear basis for understanding the changes implicit in this type of training we were then in a position to analyse the courses in these terms and to make evaluative judgements about them. The purpose of the next chapter is to illustrate that process by presenting 'analytical and evaluative' case studies of the two remaining courses.

Notes

1. Schön's actual term for this process is 'framing' and in many ways this is more appropriate. However, in order to avoid confusion with Bernstein's (1971) quite different concept of 'framing' discussed below we have adopted the term 'defining'.
2. Hirst's attempt to make explicit the role of the academic disciplines of educational theory in the development of professional theory and practice is, of course, controversial; a rather different position is often taken by those working in different strands of the 'action research' tradition (see for example Elliott (1985), Carr and Kemmis (1983)). Hirst's particular approach has recently been discussed in the context of the Gadamer–Habermas debate about the nature of Critical Theory (see Elliott (1987)). What is not at all clear however, is whether there is any substantive dispute about the procedure and content of this fundamental examination rather than how best to describe that exercise. In following Hirst's analysis we have primarily wished to emphasize the crucial importance within any adequate exercise of critical reflection of work at this fundamental level rather than any particular account of its nature.

5 Evaluating School-based Training

In the last chapter we set out an analytical framework which we developed during our research in order to clarify the nature of school-based training and establish a clear basis for making evaluative judgements about particular courses. We began by suggesting that the courses we studied implicitly challenged the 'rationalist' model of professional activity at the centre of traditional courses. We argued that in the past, teaching has been seen as a rule-governed activity for which students could be 'prepared' in advance; training courses based on such a model would seem to have as their objective the preparation of the competent technician. By contrast school-based courses seemed to us to imply a different view of the relationship between professional knowledge and action; one that can be characterized by Schön's (1983) phrase – 'reflection-in-action'.

We suggested that a training course based on this alternative 'epistemology of practice' would, in ideal terms, approximate to Bernstein's 'integrated code'; it would embody a weak 'classification' and weak 'framing' of educational knowledge. Students' direct practical experience (what we have termed Level (a)) would be placed at the heart of the training programme. Such a course would then try to establish a *structure* and *pedagogy* so that other 'levels' of training, made available by different *personnel*, could be integrated with students' own practical work in schools.

The outcome of this form of training would not then be the production of the competent follower of rules; rather it would be what Schön calls the 'reflective practitioner'. The notion of the reflective practitioner is one that is currently widely canvassed;[1] not surprisingly each advocate has their own particular characterization of what such a teacher is. From our own model of training set out in Chapter 4 we would suggest that a 'reflective practitioner' is a teacher who has developed a wide repertoire of practical skills appropriate to many different situations, is able to bring his or her professional activity under self-conscious control and is able to understand and justify that activity at progressively more fundamental levels.

Having used our research to develop a model of what school-based training ideally is we must now turn to the question of how far the courses we studied actually achieved this ideal. To what extent did these courses adopt an integrated code? Were different contents brought into closer relationship with each other? Was there an opportunity for students to develop the skills necessary to integrate these different levels of training with their *own* work in schools?

In order to answer these questions the next step in our research procedure was to construct a series of 'analytical case studies'. This involved taking the major dimensions of each course (serial and block practice, curriculum studies, education studies etc.) and analysing them by using our framework. For each of these major dimensions of training (or training 'sites' as we called them) we attempted to disentangle the way in which the course structure, personnel and pedagogy were used to establish different contents and levels of training and the forms of integration that were achieved. We were particularly interested in the way in which other levels of training were integrated with students' own direct practical experience at Level (a). Once each training 'site' had been analysed in this way it was then possible to go on to make some evaluative judgements about it in relation to our ideal model.

Given the complexity of the four courses we have studied it is not possible to present all four of our analytical case studies in this volume. We have therefore chosen to present those relating to the remaining two courses not considered earlier, i.e. Leeds Polytechnic and Roehampton Institute of Higher Education. At a general level they reveal that moves towards developing an 'integrated code' were only partially achieved. This, however, is hardly surprising since the model of school-based training we have constructed is by definition an ideal one; it represents one end of a continuum toward which these and many other courses in recent years have been moving. Establishing a course which claims to be school based may potentially offer the *opportunity* for a closer integration of 'theory' and 'practice' but institutional change is a complex and often slow process. While some aspects of the courses we studied had indeed established very close forms of integration, other dimensions of the same courses remained very traditional in philosophy and practice.[2] This 'mix' of approaches is particularly apparent in the two courses presented below.

Analytical case study – Leeds Polytechnic PGCE (upper primary)

In 1982 the School of Education at Leeds Polytechnic submitted proposals for a revised, school-based upper primary PGCE course to the Council for National Academic Awards. Although the term school based was used, the Course Leader made it clear that the new course was only intended to make limited moves in this direction. The most significant change in the structure of the course was the introduction of a regular component in school one day a week in addition to the traditional block teaching practice. Hitherto in this PGCE course, priority had been given by the course team to curriculum coverage and indeed some lecturers still regarded the introduction of additional school experience as 'essentially an interruption to the taught course' (Course Leader).

The new course was seen by the Course Leader as a tentative attempt to introduce a more school-orientated training in which practising teachers were to assume greater responsibility for the development of students' practical skills. However, as we will describe below, the curriculum dimension of students' training remained firmly in the hands of Polytechnic staff.

Twenty students accepted places on the Leeds Polytechnic upper primary course in 1984/85. This was the year in which the new course came into operation and which was monitored by the research team.

The course structure at Leeds was a traditional one in that it consisted of three main elements. These were

Practical school experience
Curriculum Studies
Education Studies.

In the past each had been primarily associated with one particular level of training with comparatively little integration between the different contents. However, the move to a school-based course had stimulated the development of new forms of integration within and between these different strands and each now included work at a variety of different levels. The pattern of the course is summarized in Figure 5.1

We now consider each of the major training 'sites' of this course under the headings of structure, personnel and pedagogy. (In some instances, where they are inseparable, two of these dimensions are considered together.)

Practical school experience

Structure

As is shown in Figure 5.1, practical school experience within the Leeds course was structured in terms of an inter-related programme of serial and block practice. After an initial period of preliminary observation, work in school was divided into two distinct phases. In Phase 1 students were attached to their main first school (school 1) visiting it one day a week for 10 weeks; this was then followed by 3 weeks' block practice in that school at the beginning of the Spring term. In Phase 2 the pattern was repeated in a second school (school 2). Students visited the school for one day a week for 8 weeks then undertook 7 weeks block practice in that school in the Summer term. Six schools were used in the consortium of co-operating schools, students being assigned to them in twos and threes. As the schools varied considerably in terms of their organization, philosophy and intake it was possible to give students direct practical experience in two contrasting educational contexts during the year.

Figure 5.1 The pattern of the Leeds Polytechnic PGCE (upper primary).

Weeks	Term 1
1 – 2	**INDUCTION**

PHASE 1

3 – 12	**CONCURRENT PROGRAMME** 4 days per week in college 1 day per week in school Curriculum studies (16 hr p/w) (school 1) Education studies (2 hr p/w)
	Term 2
13 – 16	**BLOCK PRACTICE** School 1

PHASE 2

17 – 24	**CONCURRENT PROGRAMME** 4 days per week in college 1 day per week in school Curriculum studies (16 hr p/w) (school 2) Education studies (2 hr p/w)
	Term 3
25 – 30	**BLOCK PRACTICE** School 2
31 – 33	**COLLEGE-BASED** (completion of assignments)

Block practices were organized in a more traditional way with the students progressing towards taking full responsibility for a particular class towards the end of the first block. The course leader envisaged different emphases in the two block practices. In the first one, it was intended that students would develop basic classroom competence while the second practice was to be devoted to achieving more advanced classroom skills. The weekly serial visits, on the other hand, involved two distinct activities. For half of their time students worked with the teacher whose class they were to take over during block practice: observing, teaching, assisting with group work, devising schemes of work. The remainder of their day in school was devoted to completing exercises specified in a series of 'activity booklets' designed by the course leader in consultation with teachers. These activity booklets required the students to carry out observations, investigations and discussions in relation to a range of topics. In Phase 1, the booklets focused students' attention on general aspects of classroom practice (e.g. lesson planning, classroom language). In Phase 2, broader issues were addressed (e.g. school-wide problems of assessment, the school and its community). By following the activities prescribed it was intended that students would develop a detailed insight into the practicalities of teaching and working in the schools to which they were attached. The understanding they derived was then used as the basis for follow-up work in the weekly Education seminars run within the college. As will be described below the objective was to use the booklets to establish some integration between students' direct practical experience in school (Level (a)) with other forms of analysis, at the level of principle (Level (c)) and theory (Level (d)).

It will, therefore, be apparent that the Leeds Polytechnic course was structured in such a way as to give students two different forms of direct practical training. Block practice and at least half of the time during serial practice was devoted almost entirely to the development of practical classroom skills, judgements and understandings at Level (a), only limited attention being given to wider professional issues. In addition, however, by undertaking the investigations specified within the activity booklets it was intended that students would lay the foundation for a deeper analysis of the teaching processes in which *they were engaged*, as well as develop some practical understanding in relation to their broader professional responsibilities. By being involved in both practical training and investigation in two contrasting schools, it was hoped that students would achieve both breadth and depth in both forms of experience.

Personnel and pedagogy

As has already been implied teachers themselves were extremely important in this aspect of students' training. There were however, important differences in their role and methods of teaching between serial and block practices. During serial practice students worked closely with teachers on the activity booklets, the teachers first acting as 'expert witnesses' and then discussing the students' findings with them. Teachers were also responsible for planning and supervising students' classroom work, easing them into teaching, overseeing their lesson plans etc. During serial practice, there was, therefore, an explicit emphasis on *training* in understandings, judgements and skills at Level (a) by the teachers themselves. However, when students moved into block practice, teachers were less actively involved – something which many of them regretted. During block practice the approach to students' learning may be more appropriately characterized as 'experiential'. They were expected to learn by directly engaging in the activities of teaching. In comparison with, say, the Sussex course, teachers were not expected to take a particularly active role in supervision. What students had was the benefit of previous experience and the help of teachers in serial practice, plus work at other levels in Curriculum and Education Studies that they could seek to 'apply'.

This 'experiential' approach to training within block practice arose for two principal reasons. First, in comparison with other courses evaluated, supervision was not a highly developed feature of the course structure. As has already been noted, teachers were not expected to undertake systematic supervision of their students; instead one lecturer (known as the Professional Tutor) was assigned to each school which he or she visited weekly. However, these lecturers were only granted limited time to undertake this role and they were seldom able to remain in their schools for sustained periods. As a consequence, they were precluded from adopting a strongly interventionist approach to supervision. Rather than trying to 'train' students in the practicalities of teaching at Level (a), supervisors tended to pursue the more traditional objective of supporting them so that they could learn for themselves through practical experience.

A second reason for the experiential approach was that the Course Leader did not wish to promote a particular philosophy of primary education. There was a genuine belief that there are many different approaches to professional excellence which students would benefit from by experiencing them for themselves. Schools were, therefore, chosen because they were examples of good professional practices of whatever kind, rather than because they conformed to one particular view of good practice. By carefully selecting placements, the polytechnic tried to ensure that students had experience in schools that pursued different educational philosophies. Whatever their own philosophy, students were, in the first instance, encouraged to fit in with the school. Only as their confidence grew, typically in Phase 2, were they encouraged to question what they witnessed. By immersing themselves in two schools that could differ in a variety of ways (age, structure, intake as well as philosophy) it was hoped that they would be better prepared to decide for *themselves* an approach to teaching that suited their capabilities as well as their ideals. On this issue interesting contrasts can be drawn with the Northampton course where the very active tutoring by lecturers of students' direct practical experience at Level (a) was associated with a very clear philosophy of teaching.

Commentary

From the perspective we have developed, the Leeds course seemed to have a number of advantages in terms of the practical training it offered students. By attaching students to two main schools the scheme may be seen as an attempt to forge a compromise between the multiple and the single school approaches adopted by the other courses evaluated. The objective at Leeds was to give students both breadth and depth in their practical work in schools. Breadth of experience would seem to be particularly important in primary training. Primary schools vary substantially in their structure and organization; moreover, given their size, they tend to be more homogeneous in their intake and philosophy than most secondary schools. A single school experience for primary students could, therefore, be seen as excessively narrow in terms of the training opportunities it could offer. However, if students move schools too many times there is a danger that their work will become superficial; they could be forced to spend their time 'coping' with new situations, new pupils etc., rather than developing more complex skills, more detailed understandings and more sensitive judgements. By opting for two schools with serial and block practices related to each other, the Leeds scheme involved a deliberate attempt to give depth as well as sufficient breadth in practical training at Level (a).

There were also significant advantages deriving from the use of activity booklets in relation to school experience. Because of the constraints of timetabling, lecturers were unable to spend much time in school with students during serial practice; if school-based *training* was to take place then teachers had to be drawn into the process. But there are more principled reasons for involving teachers in training students. As we suggested in Chapter 4, it is they alone who have access to the context-specific knowledge, much of it implicit, that students need to acquire in learning to teach effectively in any particular school. But what is more, they alone are in a position to train students in the art of being sensitive to many of the context-specific factors that are so critical in teaching. Training of this particular character is an essential part of professional development. However, one of the potential difficulties of involving teachers is that without very careful preparation and control, significant variations can emerge in the training received by different students; differences in terms of time spent, the areas of practice covered and the quality of analysis offered. A key advantage of the activity booklets was that they helped to establish a common and carefully considered framework of activities for students in whatever school they were working. Quite incidentally they also acted as a form of 'in-service training' for the teachers themselves, encouraging them to re-examine their own work perhaps from a slightly different perspective.

Despite these advantages there were three significant drawbacks to the scheme. First, there was the very limited time assigned to serial practice in schools. One day per week was simply not sufficient to undertake the activity booklet exercises and also prepare for teaching. Moreover, as students always visited the school on the same day each week it meant that they were restricted in the work of schools they could become engaged in. As will be noted below, the main reason for this limited time in school was the heavy demand made on students' time by the curriculum courses. Primary courses face a constant dilemma between time devoted to school activities and work on curriculum preparation; at Leeds the emphasis was very much on the latter.

A second weakness was the relatively light emphasis on supervision during block practice. The Leeds students did not receive any greater degree of systematic training at Level (a) than in traditional courses. In contrast, all three of the other courses we studied had, either by delegating responsibility to teachers or by basing lecturers more frequently in school, significantly increased the degree of direct supervision at this level. Thirdly, while the idea that students should, to a significant degree, learn by experience and come to their own conclusions as to what constitutes good practice has much to commend it, there are dangers unless systematic training at other levels directly engages with their practical classroom work. In particular, adequate judgements of good practice involve consideration of matters of principle at Level (c). In work at Level (a) alone, these principles are implicit and if not explicitly examined may result in undesirable forms of practice. Overcoming this difficulty involves somehow overcoming the gap that opens up if training in school takes place only at Level (a) and training elsewhere only at other levels. As will be noted below, the comparatively lighter emphasis on supervision was particularly significant given the relative lack of integration between Curriculum Studies and school experience.

Curriculum Studies

As was suggested above, despite the move to a more school-based form of training, the Leeds course structure remained a traditional one. This was particularly apparent in relation to Curriculum Studies work which was seen as primarily a 'preparation' for practical classroom experience; as such, it was in the majority of cases divorced from students' own practice in school.

Structure and personnel

Curriculum Studies was strongly emphasized at Leeds, taking up by far the majority of course time outside block practice. Students were offered a series of courses on different aspects of the primary school curriculum by specialist polytechnic staff. In Phase 1 all subjects covered were taught separately while in Phase 2 there was some limited integration of subjects in Humanities and Creative Arts.[3] In spite of the opportunities for concurrent training which the development of serial practice offered, Curriculum Studies remained largely divorced from students' direct practical experience in school. They were seen as a form of 'preparation' of necessity abstracted from the realities of school experience itself. Students were expected to develop the skills of how to 'apply' what they had learned in their college-based curriculum work during block teaching practice.

The main reason for these courses being divorced from the students' own work in school, on either serial or block practice, would appear to be the staffing structure of the polytechnic. In many ways the Course Leader at Leeds was in a similar position to the Course Leader at Northampton in that he had to 'buy in' staff on an hourly basis for these courses (the only difference was that he had to buy them in from other Polytechnic departments rather than from outside). No specialist Curriculum lecturers were specifically assigned to the PGCE as their major responsibility. As a consequence it was extremely difficult to devise courses that were closely integrated with students' own work in schools; the lecturers concerned had commitments elsewhere when they were not actually teaching the students.

Pedagogy

Perhaps not surprisingly, given the separation of these courses from students' own classroom practice and the expertise of the lecturers responsible for the teaching, the main emphasis in curriculum studies was on indirect practical training (Level (b)) and the study of the principles of curriculum work (Level (c)). As is traditional in such courses the pedagogy was frequently didactic in the sense that the lecturers controlled the agenda of topics to be covered and defined what was appropriate knowledge; at the same time, however, students were required to be 'active' in their learning by participating in workshops, discussions etc. It was through these active forms of learning that students acquired 'indirect' practical training in judgements and skills. At Level (c), however, though principles were made explicit and their practical significance explored, there was only limited concern with any critical assessment of them and only occasional reference to fundamental theoretical issues (Level (d)).

However, the fact that Curriculum Studies courses were divorced from serial and block practice did not mean that they had to be divorced from schooling *per se*. During the year of our evaluation some Curriculum Studies lecturers had begun to experiment with their own school-based forms of teaching by, for example, running some of their sessions within a school rather than within the polytechnic. This gave lecturers the opportunity of drawing both teachers and pupils into their training work and laid the foundation for a much closer integration between professional knowledge at Levels (b) and (c) and students' direct practical experience at Level (a). Although these experiments were very limited during the year of our evaluation, we understand that they were developed considerably in the following year.

Commentary

Curriculum courses which are detached from the complexities of integrating their training with students' own classroom teaching have the opportunity to develop a thorough and systematic approach to preparation. The very substantial amount of time devoted to Curriculum Studies at Leeds meant that students were in many ways well 'prepared' at Levels (b) and (c) in discrete areas of the curriculum. A major issue for debate, however, concerns the extent to which these forms of preparation were integrated with each other and with students' own classroom teaching. The course structure would appear to have two weaknesses here. First, given the relatively low emphasis on supervision during block practice, there was the possibility that in some curriculum areas (those taught exclusively within the polytechnic) students might receive little or no systematic support in relating curriculum preparation to practice. In a course that elects to devote so much time to curriculum preparation rather than supervised serial practice, some alternative means of integrating the different levels of professional preparation needs to be established. Only by these means can students be trained to be critically reflective about their own developing practices at Level (a). The experiments within some Curriculum Studies areas to forge closer links with schools are, therefore, to be welcomed.

A second, and related weakness, derives from the strongly segmented approach to curriculum preparation. While students were obviously well prepared in different subject areas, they received little *training* in how to integrate work in these areas within their teaching (the only exceptions were the Creative Arts and Humanities courses taught in Phase 2). For the most part, the integration of different elements in the curriculum was something that students were expected to achieve for themselves during their work in schools; it was not a specific focus of their preparation in college. In this aspect of training, interesting comparisons may be made with Northampton. Here there was relatively less emphasis on specific curriculum inputs. However, the integration of these into a coherent programme of teaching was seen as a separate and important area of preparation. The Course Director's 'Method' sessions were specifically designed to range across all aspects of teaching. As a consequence, they helped students to integrate the different curriculum elements that had been introduced in their specialist courses. Moreover, the way these sessions were organized was intended to facilitate integration with students' practical work as well. It could be argued that a slightly more segregated approach to curriculum preparation was legitimate at Leeds because it was concerned with upper primary age children. However, it is apparent that all primary students, even when teaching older children, do need some training in how to integrate the different elements of their preparation into a coherent whole. Such issues can either be addressed within the College or through school experience which is systematically supervised by lecturers or teachers; presumably a well designed course would include both. The failure of the Leeds course to provide anything more than practical experience on this aspect of training would seem to be a significant oversight.

Education Studies

In line with the traditional structure of the Leeds Polytechnic course, theoretical issues at Level (d) relating to general teaching practices and wider professional issues were mainly addressed within Education Studies. However, despite this

familiar pattern the work undertaken within these sessions was far from traditional; indeed, Education Studies seminars represented one of the most
innovative parts of the course. They were also extremely important within the
course despite the fact that only a small amount of time was devoted to them.
Their significance, as well as their innovative nature, was in part attributable to
the fact that they were taught by the Course Leader who used them as a forum to
integrate many different 'levels' of training undertaken elsewhere.

Structure

Education Studies seminars took place in the polytechnic for two hours a week
during the concurrent programme, the main focus for the discussion being the
activity booklets completed by students during their visits to schools. By following the activities prescribed in the booklets (observations, investigations and
discussions) it was intended that students develop a detailed insight into the
practicalities of teaching as well as wider professional concerns in the schools to
which they were attached. Because of the concurrent structure of the course and
the use of the activity booklets, students were able to come to the seminars with a
fund of knowledge about practice in their own schools in relation to specific
topics; this was knowledge at Level (a).

Personnel and pedagogy

The objective of the Education Studies seminars was to follow up the investigations undertaken with the activity booklets in two different ways. In the first
place, the Course Leader, who was an ex-primary school Head of very considerable experience, utilized the information students had researched in order to
broaden the groups' knowledge of practice; the process of sharing experiences
became a form of indirect practical training at Level (b). In addition, senior
teachers from the six partnership schools were also occasional visitors to these
seminars; they too contributed to the group's knowledge by describing and
debating their own practice.

   However, broadening students' knowledge base about classroom and school
practice was only a subsidiary aim. A far more important objective, as far as the
Course Leader was concerned, was to utilize these examples of practice as a
vehicle for raising issues of principle (Level (c)), and theory (Level (d)). In this
process the Course Leader was relatively didactic. He believed that there was a
body of knowledge to be 'quarried' from the foundation disciplines relating to
each topic under study which it was important that students be introduced to.
For example, in examining classroom interaction 'affective' and 'cognitive'
aspects were discussed; in considering the school and its community, notions of
social class and family background were introduced. The Course Leader used the

students' contributions of their own analysis of each topic at the level of practice to introduce a more theoretically informed agenda; pedagogically the movement was *from* considerations of practice *to* considerations of theory. Yet the Course Leader not only wanted students to learn some of the major findings derived from the foundation disciplines, he also wanted to encourage them to raise theoretical questions for themselves in reflection at the most fundamental level. By tying theoretical work to the students' *own* practical investigations and experience it was hoped that they would come to appreciate the value of such forms of questioning and even begin to engage in such questioning themselves. Students' training in this regard was taken one stage further in the assessed work associated with this aspect of the course. A 3500 word essay had to demonstrate both theoretical understanding and reflection on practical school experience.

Commentary

Our research in other courses demonstrates that students may be introduced to issues arising from the educational disciplines (what we have termed Level (d)) in a variety of contrasting ways. In the Education Studies component at Northampton the emphasis was on 'content'; students were expected to learn a particular body of knowledge derived from the educational disciplines and their contribution to the analysis of certain areas of practice. Despite the protestations of the Course Director, moving to a school-based course had not changed the fact that the teaching in this aspect of the course remained an externalized body of knowledge largely unrelated to other aspects of students' training. An alternative approach was adopted at Sussex. Here the primary objective was to use theory and research and their significance for practice in developing students' *own* skills of critical reflection and analysis. In the words of the Course Leader they emphasized 'process' rather than 'content'.

Education Studies at Leeds was interesting in that it may be seen as representing a limited but successful attempt to address both of these objectives at the same time. The activity booklets were particularly significant here for they helped to tie theoretical analysis to the students' own investigations of practice. In his presentation of theoretical ideas and their significance, the lecturer still retained a degree of didacticism. He believed there was a minimum content of educational theory that students *ought* to know, and the development of the activity booklets was, in part, an attempt to find a more effective way of *teaching* that content. However, the activity booklets also meant that students became actively involved in the learning process itself. What was being 'theoretically interrogated', was their own schools' practice which they had investigated. Participation in the seminars did not simply require a passive receiving of knowledge; students were asked to re-examine their existing knowledge at the level of concrete practice (Level (a)) in the light of experience of others, but especially from a more theoretically informed point of view. In other words, the seminars gave them some training in the processes of analysis and critical reflection themselves and linked that with their own experiences. In this way the Education component at Leeds became a key 'site' for achieving integration in the students' training.

Analytical case study: Roehampton Institute of Higher Education PGCE (secondary)

The Roehampton Institute of Higher Education (RIHE) is a federation of four colleges which dates from 1976. Up until then, each college – Digby Stuart, Froebel Institute, Southlands and Whitelands – functioned as an independent entity. With the merger of the colleges, the need to rationalize policy and practice was self-evident although it was recognized that rationalization could not come about overnight; the first common PGCE was run in 1982/83. This new course coincided with a change of validating body for the PGCE from the University of London to the University of Surrey and this opportunity was seized upon to establish an experimental school-based course to run alongside the main programme. It was hoped by the lecturers involved in the experimental programme that it would eventually become the common pattern for all secondary PGCE students at the Institute. It was the first year of this experimental programme that was monitored by the research team.

In its first year, the experimental course offered 21 places in the following subjects: Business Studies, English, Maths, Music, Religious Studies and Science (Biology and Chemistry). This experimental course catered for approximately one fifth of those taking the secondary PGCE. The major differences between the two courses were that on the experimental course:

students spent three as opposed to two days a week in school during their serial experience in the first two terms of the course
all of the students were placed in one of three co-operating schools for both serial and block practice. In each of the three schools there were therefore six to eight students (in the main programme students were more widely distributed)
students spent all of their school experience (serial and both blocks) in the same school (in the main programme students spent their second block practice in a different school)

The Education Studies programme was taught primarily in school during serial practice. To this end Education Studies lecturers were based in each of the three co-operating schools. These lecturers were also timetabled to remain in the school for up to one day each week during block practices.

As is shown in Figure 5.2, the Autumn term began with a five-week concurrent programme (three days a week in school and two days a week in college) followed by a five-week block practice. In the Spring term this pattern was repeated with a five-week concurrent programme followed by a five-week block practice. Students remained attached to the same school throughout the whole of these first two terms. The Summer term was devoted to special projects in the college and in other educational settings.

Despite the innovations outlined in Figure 5.2, the underlying structure of the RIHE course remained a traditional one. It consisted of three major elements which will be used as the framework for our analytical study. They were:

Education Studies (primarily based in school during serial practice)
Curriculum Studies (including some school-based elements during serial practice)
Block practice

Education Studies

Structure

During the year of our evaluation, Education Studies was the area of most significant innovation in the RIHE course in that much of it was taught in school. The main vehicle for this aspect of training was a programme of Education Studies seminars which took place in students' schools for 1½ days a week during serial practice and on a more occasional basis during block practice. The focus of these seminars in the Autumn term was on general issues of classroom practice, while in the Spring term wider professional issues were considered. Finally, in the Summer term, students' experience was 'rounded out' by undertaking a research project in a different educational setting. Within this single unit of the course training was provided at all four different Levels – (a), (b), (c) and (d). Education Studies was therefore intended to act as a major 'site' for integrating students' levels of training.

In order to establish the school-based Education Studies programme one Education lecturer was attached to each of the three participating schools for the first two terms of the course. These lecturers were responsible for the staffing and organization of the school-based seminar for the students working within that school. In the majority of cases the seminars took place in the students' own school, though on a number of occasions the seminar groups in all three schools combined for a joint session in one or other of the three schools. The aim of these joint sessions was to provide students some insight into practice in other schools and thereby compensate them for their single school experience.

Personnel and pedagogy

The convening of a seminar group in each school was the prime concern of one of the three Education lecturers responsible for this aspect of the course. However,

Figure 5.2 The pattern of the Roehampton Institute of Higher Education PGCE (secondary).

Weeks   Term 1

1	INDUCTION
2 – 6	CONCURRENT PROGRAMME School 1 3 days per week in school 2 days per week in college (curriculum studies)
7 – 11	BLOCK PRACTICE School 1

Term 2

| 12 – 17 | CONCURRENT PROGRAMME
School 1
3 days per week in school   2 days per week in college
(curriculum studies) |
| 18 – 22 | BLOCK PRACTICE
School 1 |

Term 3

23 – 32 The final term programme was complex. In addition to 2 days per week
         curriculum studies throughout the term, it included a range of college-
         based short courses and a 7 – 9-day research project placement either in
         the students' original school or in some 'education related setting' (primary
         school, youth centre etc.)

where this meant drawing on the schools' staff and resources, the lecturers worked in collaboration with a senior teacher, known as a General Tutor, who was designated by the school to oversee the students. Individually, Education lecturers had training in one of the educational disciplines – sociology, psychology, philosophy. The team as a whole, therefore, had access to considerable expertise at the theoretical level. However, for the purposes of actually teaching, all three lecturers took an interdisciplinary approach, drawing as necessary on their knowledge in any one of the foundation disciplines.

These school-based seminars constituted a major part of the taught course and involved a variety of different activities including videos, talks from teachers, visits to other schools as well as input from the lecturers themselves. The work undertaken was therefore complex and can be seen as covering a variety of different 'levels' of analysis. After an introduction by lecturers, each seminar typically included substantial discussion of the topic under consideration at the level of concrete practice within the students' own school. The main contributors here were teachers (the General Tutor and others) who were invited to join the seminars for short periods in order to articulate their own classroom practice or some aspect of institutional practice. Given that the students were familiar with their own particular school this constituted a form of training at Level (a). In some of the seminars there was also a deliberate attempt to broaden students' knowledge base concerning other forms of professional practice by, for example, showing videos and arranging visits to one or more of the other schools participating in the training scheme; this constituted a form of indirect practical training at Level (b). The objective in both of these forms of work was to establish a common knowledge base for the whole student group. This common first- and second-hand knowledge of professional practice was considered important in itself, but it also constituted the main 'resource' for the more theoretical analyses which followed.

As far as the Education lecturers were concerned one very important objective of their sessions was to *introduce* certain elements of educational theory that related to specific issues of professional concern (language in the classroom, the curriculum, pastoral care). In the past many of these topics had been covered in college-based courses. The change in structure to school-based work therefore gave lecturers the opportunity of developing new and more effective means of introducing students to this agenda by linking the theoretical teaching with students' own practical experience. But the aim was not simply to develop a more effective pedagogy for teaching theory. School-based Education Studies seminars established for students new forms of integration between different levels of training.

In many ways the Education lecturers were at heart didactic in their approach; they believed that there was a group of essential classroom and wider professional topics that students ought to address from a theoretical point of view. Moreover, on any one of these topics certain key theoretical issues needed to be taught. They therefore carefully controlled the agenda of topics to be covered (even the General Tutors were rarely involved in drawing up this agenda). They were also the arbiters of what students were intended to learn, their own theoretical interpretations of practice often taking precedence over those offered by teachers or students. Students themselves were perhaps unintentionally assigned a somewhat passive role in this process, in that there was so much content to be got through. Through a tightly controlled pedagogy, lecturers moved the discussion of any one topic across all four levels of analysis. After a general theoretical overview, discussion would move on to a consideration of practice in the students' own and other schools (Levels (a) and (b)), then move to the principles underlying such practice (Level (c)) and finally on to a more detailed consideration of the theoretically informed debates commonly associated with these topics (Level (d)). By this process students still learned much of the traditional Education Studies agenda; they learned of Hirst's forms of knowledge and of Barnes's work on classroom language, but the discussion of these works was directly related to an analysis of the curriculum or language policies of which they had experience in their own particular schools.

Students' familiarity with theoretical ideas was taken considerably further in the Summer term by attending a series of college-based seminars and short courses on issues of current professional interest (the 11-16 curriculum, multi-cultural and anti-racist education). In these sessions, primarily organized by the Education staff, theoretical knowledge at Level (d) was again to the fore. However, students were also given some practical experience of relating such theoretical ideas to practice in a final 'Interdisciplinary Study'. In order to carry out this study students returned to their school or were attached to another educational establishment (youth club, educational welfare office) for a period of seven to nine days. Their task in conducting their study was to examine empirically one aspect of practice and in their writing relate this to relevant theoretical and professional literature.

Commentary

The Education Studies course in the first two terms of RIHE provides an extremely interesting example of how school-based structures can be exploited to develop new forms of teaching and training. In terms of the topics covered in these seminars much of what took place would be common to many college-based courses; in terms of what students actually *learned*, the course was far from traditional. The lecturers' familiarity with their particular schools together with their wide knowledge of educational theory meant that they were able to be extremely effective in their teaching at a theoretical level. Not only was the coverage of theoretical issues both thorough and systematic, the students had the advantage of seeing the relevance of theoretical work demonstrated in an analysis of their own school context across the levels. If what is needed within a professional course is the *teaching* of educational theory and its contribution to the analysis of certain areas of practice, then the RIHE approach had much to commend it.

Yet one must ask if the 'teaching' of this content is a sufficient objective in relation to educational theory. In this regard the RIHE approach can be seen as the opposite of the Sussex course. In Sussex the objective was not to *teach* theory and its significance but to develop students' abilities to use theory in reflecting on their own practice. However, developing students' skills in this way is a time-consuming activity. As a consequence some parts of what is conventionlly taught in Education Studies courses did not get covered. Sussex lecturers recognized this potential weakness but maintained that it was more important to develop students' own skills than didactically to insist on coverage. By contrast, at RIHE, apart from their final 'Interdisciplinary Study', students had very little training in reflective analysis or opportunity to utilize what they learned of theory and theorizing in relation to their own experience. The *teaching* was certainly extremely effective, but the students were not expected to utilize what they learned in relation to an analysis of their own practice. Moreover, what they learned in their school-based seminars was still in significant measure abstracted from the 'real' world of teaching. Even though it was based in school, and dealt with educational practice, its main purpose was not the promotion of a more adequate understanding of that practice at Level (a). Concrete practice was carefully selected and 'tidied up' or interpreted for a particular theoretical purpose; in this sense it was primarily being used for understanding at Level (d).

The limitation of the RIHE approach was particularly significant in training for the wider professional role. At least in the area of classroom training, students had plenty of opportunity during teaching practice to develop practical classroom skills. However, there was no such practical training in relation to wider professional issues. Students certainly *learned about* practice in their own school on matters such as pastoral care and curriculum development. They also had some insight into practice in the other two schools. But unlike the Sussex students, they received little systematic practical training in these activities. Virtually all of their training in this area took place within the confines of the Education seminars; despite the discussion of practice it therefore remained very much an 'academic' exercise.

Therefore, while we might criticize the Sussex course for not taking the teaching of educational theory seriously enough, at RIHE it may be that 'learning' was assigned too high a priority. However, in a crowded course establishing the right balance between 'process' and 'content' is a difficult judgement. Even in a well-established course such as Sussex, the balance was constantly under scrutiny.

Curriculum Studies

Structure

Of the three days a week that students spent in school during serial practice, one was formally designated a Curriculum Studies day. However, because this was the first year of the experimental school-based course, during the year of the evaluation the opportunities for developing school-based Curriculum Studies activities on this day were not exploited. (In the year following our evaluation more use was made of this day.) In consequence, Curriculum Studies courses at RIHE remained largely divorced from any direct involvement with students' school-based work. Developing the skills, judgements and understandings of classroom teaching in a specific school context was to be achieved during block teaching practice; Curriculum Studies courses themselves were primarily concerned with *preparation* for teaching practice. In the first phase of the course, prior to the first teaching practice, preparation was for basic classroom competence, while in the second phase the emphasis was on preparation for more advanced classroom competence.

Personnel and pedagogy

As in many college-based courses, Curriculum Studies at RIHE were the sole responsibility of a group of highly experienced college lecturers; in almost all cases the PGCE constituted one of their main teaching responsibilities. They were in effect therefore primarily lecturers in pedagogy in their chosen field and brought with them a broad knowledge and experience of the teaching of their particular subject as well as an understanding of the principles on which that teaching was based. Within Curriculum Studies sessions the main focus was on preparation for classroom teaching. This involved work at two different levels – that of indirect practice (Level (b)) and that of principle (Level (c)). Even though Curriculum Studies courses were not closely related to students' *own* practical experience at Level (a), there was plenty of evidence of attempts to provide them with a preliminary base of practical skills, judgements and understandings. This was primarily achieved indirectly through input from the lecturer, visits to other schools, workshops and simulations etc.

Developing this preliminary but 'indirect' practical competence was one of the major objectives of this part of the training. Not only did such experience give students specific ideas that could be utilized during teaching practice, it also laid the basis for reflective work at the level of principle. Typically, lecturers moved back and forwards between these two levels of analysis at times drawing the principles of classroom teaching out of the examples of practice under discussion and at other times beginning with principles and giving practical illustrations of them. Students took an active role in this process as many of the teaching sessions involved discussions or workshop activities. However, the pedagogy may still be defined as primarily didactic in that it was the lecturers who controlled the agenda of topics to be considered and defined the appropriate knowledge, judgements and skills for students to learn. In so far as it was teaching in reflection itself, it was of its nature grounded in a base of Level (b) understanding.

Commentary

One of the major strengths of traditional Curriculum Studies courses of the type run at RIHE is the thoroughness and breadth of preparation that can be achieved. Students spent 1½ or even 2 days a week studying the teaching of their own particular subject; by the end of their course they had had every opportunity to develop a broad base of preliminary classroom competences (skills, understandings and judgements at Level (b)) as well as some real understanding of the principles on which such practice is based (knowledge at Level (c)). It offered them, in 'detached' form, the basis for framing situations they would face in practice. Although it was not a major feature of the RIHE scheme, there is also the possibility in such a course of systematically examining classroom principles from the perspective of educational theory at Level (d). A college-based course which is detached from the complexities of specific school contexts can be both broad ranging and systematic in its professional preparation. In this sense the RIHE students were very thoroughly 'prepared' in their Curriculum Studies work. What such courses cannot do is teach students how to *apply* that knowledge to their own classroom practice, particularly in a sensitive, reflective way. This was something that students had to achieve for themselves during block practice. As we will see below, there were only relatively limited opportunities for Curriculum Studies lecturers to take an active role in tutoring students during their block practice and the two dimensions of the course therefore remained somewhat detached.

One consequence of this relative detachment from practice was that in comparison with Sussex and Northampton, Curriculum Studies lecturers seemed less influential on students in terms of developing a particular philosophy of classroom teaching. A curriculum course which finds a mechanism of carrying its training through to the level of classroom practice can potentially be far more influential on the approach to teaching adopted by students. Given the relative detachment from schools of the RIHE curriculum courses, students had little choice but to fit in with the models of practice they met in their block teaching practice schools. The potentiality for experimenting with teaching approaches was thereby reduced and, in contrast to Sussex and Northampton, students received little practical training in how to introduce innovation and change into established classrooms.

Block practice

Structure

As has already been noted, the purpose of block practice was to give students the opportunity for developing their practical skills, judgements and understandings in relation to classroom teaching (Level (a)). In their first teaching practice students were expected to apply what they had learned in their early Curriculum Studies sessions in order to develop basic classroom competences. In their second teaching practice, which followed a further period of Curriculum Studies, students returned to the same school. In this second phase of direct classroom experience they were intended to develop more advanced classroom competences.

Pedagogy and personnel

In the development of these practical competences two distinct 'pedagogies' may be discerned. In the first place, there was a strong emphasis on experiential learning of a particular kind. Students were *prepared* for classroom teaching within Curriculum Studies courses in the college which were wide-ranging in their coverage of teaching methods, materials etc. They were then expected to *apply* this indirect practical training (Level (b)) in school. In so doing students were expected to fit in with the practice they saw around them using the teachers they worked with, as far as possible, as models. In contrast to, say, the Sussex course, teachers themselves were not specifically asked to take an active role in training;[4] students were to learn much of what was necessary by actually doing the job of teaching. The immediate responsibility of teachers was to make their classes available for student practice. Experiential learning was seen as a major component of the training; this was the rationale for a single school experience and the retention of the substantial block practices. Students, it was argued, needed to teach in one school over a sustained period if they were to develop the full range of professional competencies they would need.

During block practice, however, there was also comparatively strong emphasis on another form of training pedagogy provided in school by college lecturers. Curriculum Studies lecturers were expected to visit students on a weekly basis (in practice their visits were less frequent), while Education Studies lecturers were even more frequently available. We have already noted that during serial school experience an Education lecturer was attached to each of the three participating schools. During block practices these lecturers were also timetabled to spend up to a day a week supervising in 'their' school. The role of these lecturers was particularly interesting in this regard. Although they were not subject specialists and the nature of their supervision had to be confined to generalized issues of classroom practice, they had the specific advantage of being extremely familiar with the working practice within their particular school. They were therefore well equipped to offer non-subject-specific advice and training at the level of concrete practice (Level (a)) as well as at the more abstract level of principle (Level (c)) and theory (Level (d)). In a limited way, therefore, their work helped students integrate some other aspects of their training.

It was apparent that there was a 'tension' in the different approaches to pedagogy pursued by the Education and Curriculum strands of the course.

Ideally at least, Curriculum Studies lecturers wanted students to work alongside excellent teachers so that they could learn how to 'apply' what they had learnt in college by 'modelling' themselves on their teacher tutors. However, the participating schools were not chosen by Curriculum Studies lecturers but by Education lecturers; their criteria of choice were somewhat different. First and foremost they wanted to select *schools* that were willing to co-operate and make available the training opportunities necessary for mounting the course as a whole; the choice of teacher tutors had to take second place. As far as the Education tutors were concerned teachers were not seen as role models; as a consequence they took it upon themselves to provide a systematic training for students in their classroom work. School experience was therefore seen in two quite different ways by the two groups of lecturers, such tensions reflecting the fact that the course itself was in a stage of transition.

Commentary

In the training of students, experiential learning is an essential element and the RIHE course, which placed such strong emphasis on this approach, clearly had important strengths. The move to school basing had in no way been allowed to reduce the amount of time students spent on block practice; serial experience had been introduced *in addition* to conventional block practice. In comparison with Sussex, where block practice was more limited, it could be argued that RIHE students had a more sustained and therefore more realistic opportunity to experience the work of the teacher. However, it must be pointed out that although students spent a great deal of *time* in school they were only actually teaching during their two five-week block practice. They certainly had plenty of opportunity to learn about practice in their particular schools, but their opportunities to develop direct practical skills through teaching in the school were not significantly greater than in a traditional course.

A further benefit of the RIHE scheme was that as a result of the move to school-based work Education lecturers were available within the school during teaching practice to supervise students. Their contribution to students' training was particularly strong in that they had access to knowledge at a wide variety of different levels. Their familiarity with their particular school meant that they were able to offer students concrete advice at Level (a) while their broad knowledge of classroom practice meant that they could refer students to practice within other educational contexts (Level (b)) as well as raise issues of principle (Level (c)) and of theory (Level (d)). Education lecturers were, therefore, well placed to support students' learning at all levels of training and to provide a means of integrating many other aspects of the course with students' practical classroom experience. Although extremely demanding in terms of staff resourcing, assigning an Education lecturer to a particular school during teaching practice had very considerable advantages.

A major advantage too was the notion of development that was structured into the pattern of block practices. Because students returned to the same school, and possibly even to teaching the same classes, in their second block practice, there was a possibility of them capitalizing on their further curriculum preparation to develop more advanced teaching competencies. However, this advantage must be balanced against the fact that all of the students' direct practical experience was confined to a single educational context.

A number of other important weaknesses to this course's approach to practical classroom training must be noted. For example, the very limited involvement of teachers in all but the most minimal forms of supervision was a significant omission. However beneficial the use of Education lecturers, their contributions were limited both by their lack of time and their limited knowledge of the practicalities of actually teaching within the school. Systematic training at the direct practical level (Level (a)) must surely be in the hands of teachers and thus will require more of them than simply making over their classes to students. 'Outside' supervision cannot replace their detailed knowledge of their own particular context nor can students really 'pick up' all that they need to know simply by experience alone. Teachers clearly have a crucial contribution to make to training students in any scheme; it was therefore not surprising to us that a number of teachers within the RIHE scheme expressed dissatisfaction that they had not been granted more responsibility.

A further difficulty was that students received little systematic training in the subject-specific dimensions of practical classroom work; experiential learning was all that was really available. As in traditional courses, Curriculum Studies lecturers were only able to visit students for an hour or so each week and therefore had neither the time nor the context-specific knowledge to offer anything but the most generalized advice at Level (a). As was noted above, Education lecturers were available but could only cover general issues of a non-subject-specific nature; teachers, as has also been noted, did not have a highly developed training role. As a consequence, students had little choice but to learn through their own experience – trying to 'apply' what they had learned in their earlier Curriculum Studies courses and using the teachers they worked with as role models. As was suggested above, experiential learning is clearly a necessary element in any training but cannot be regarded as sufficient in itself. The RIHE course structure did not capitalize on the opportunity of school-based work to provide a systematic training in this aspect of practical school experience. The structure of school experience in the course would have made it possible for part of the first serial experience to be formally used as an introduction to the first block practice. Some students did follow suggestions in the Course Handbook and, with the help of teachers, established some form of induction for themselves, but a more systematic approach would have helped structure students' practical training developmentally.

Conclusion

As we noted at the beginning of this chapter, the courses we evaluated had moved towards our ideal model of school-based training in part only. In both of those outlined above it was in the Education Studies components that the most significant moves towards establishing integration had been achieved. However, the way they had utilized course structures, personnel and pedagogy to achieve that end was in each case quite different and these different approaches had a significant effect on the character of the training offered to students. The other two courses, University of Leicester (Northampton Annexe) and the University of Sussex, had achieved forms of integration over a wider number of training 'sites' illustrating other ways of developing the 'reflective practitoner'. In the next two chapters we turn our attention to exploring the implications of our model of training for course development generally and for schools and training institutions.

Notes

1. See for example, Zeichner (1981/82); Handal and Lauvas, (1987); Whitty, Barton, and Pollard (1987); Pollard and Tann (1987).
2. The reasons for these differential degrees of change are complex and were not in themselves the main focus of our research. In some cases limitations on the movement towards the 'reflective model' appeared to be for reasons of deeply held principle; course leaders or particular groups of lecturers were not convinced of the validity of the approach. In other cases the issue was not one of principle but pragmatics – resourcing, staffing and timetabling were all felt to impose their constraints on innovations that in other circumstances might be advocated.
3. Time was distributed between the various subject areas in the following way:

Maths Education	2 hr x 20 weeks
Language and Literature	2 hr x 23 weeks
Science Education	2 hr x 12 weeks
Physical Education	1 hr x 23 weeks

In addition, during Phase 1 students took

Art, Music, Drama, History, Religious Education, Geography	} 1½ hrs x 12 weeks each

During Phase 2 Art, Music and Drama were combined as Creative Arts while History, Geography and Religious Education were combined as Humanities in order to help the students 'explore the practical problems and possibilities afforded by integrated approaches to teaching and learning'. In addition French was offered to those students wishing to teach this to the upper age range in primary schools or in middle schools.

The time assigned to these additional subjects in Phase 2 was

Creative Arts	2 hr x 11 weeks
Humanities	2 hr x 11 weeks
French or Humanities	2 hr x 11 weeks

4. Some teachers, however, of their own volition, did take this role on themselves.

6 Implications for Course Development

In Chapter 4 we suggested that professional training within the PGCE may be understood as being undertaken at four different 'levels'. Level (a) is concerned with practical training through direct experience in schools and classrooms, Level (b) with 'indirect' practical training in classes and workshops usually within the training institution, Level (c) with knowledge and critical use of the principles of practice and Level (d) with the critical review of practice in the light of the foundation disciplines of Education. In the analytical studies presented in Chapter 5, we have sought to show how the character of the professional training provided in two of the courses we studied varied in relation to the opportunities made available for students to develop expertise in these four inter-related levels of skill, judgement and understanding. All of the courses we studied put major emphasis on direct practical training at Level (a) but they differed considerably in the emphasis they put on training at the other levels. Even more importantly, they differed in the inter-relationships they tried to build between these different levels. At one extreme we noted some course elements (for example, block practice elements or Education courses) that were relatively well segregated from other levels of training – they exhibited strong 'framing'. At the other extreme were course elements where there was a deliberate attempt to integrate work across all four levels combining critical reflection with direct practical training. In between there were many attempts to forge a wide variety of different links, especially between direct practical experience (Level (a)) and one or more of the other levels.

As was highlighted within the case studies, the four courses differed considerably in that they pursued different aims, established different priorities and worked within different constraints. Not surprisingly the levels of training and the relationships between them were embedded in the courses in a variety of different ways. What students learned was significantly influenced by the *structure* of the course, the *personnel* responsible for different aspects of training and the *pedagogy* adopted in any one training situation.

Throughout the analytical studies in the previous chapter we have explored the influence of these three factors – course structure, personnel and pedagogy – on the training experiences students actually received in these courses. In this chapter we seek to draw out the consequences of planning decisions about these three factors more explicitly. In doing this we hope to set out the issues which have emerged as central to all PGCE course planning and implementation. In so doing we recognize that we are making value judgements both in terms of what the key issues are and our comments on them. These professional judgements are made on the basis of the work we have undertaken during the project. They are based on the evidence collected and the continuous attempt to subject that evidence to analytical and critical review in the ways set out in the previous chapters. In keeping with the nature and constraints of the enquiry we were invited to undertake, we have endeavoured to present these implications at a level helpful to course developers and others concerned to review the degree and general character of school-based work in the PGCE.

Structure of this review

In all the four courses studied, a variety of school-based elements, usually referred to as serial and block practices, focused primarily, if not exclusively, on direct practical training at Level (a). All of the courses also had substantial elements concerned with training at other levels which were *integrated* in various ways with this practical training. These elements, usually labelled 'Curriculum Studies' or 'Methods work' and 'Education Studies', were almost all located, for the majority of their work, in the training institution. All four courses thus basically retained the traditional division between, on the one hand, school-based practical training and, on the other, institution-based work in 'Curriculum Studies', 'Methods work' and 'Education Studies'. This organization was significantly modified in only two ways where there were deliberate attempts to establish *integration* through the structure of the course. At RIHE, Education Studies were located in school and at Northampton, IT-INSET work was based in school, though it was not directly concerned with practical training. Purely for the purpose of organizing the discussion in this chapter, and without prejudice to other and perhaps more appropriate course divisions, we will therefore follow the traditional division of courses into three basic elements: School-based Practical Training, Curriculum Studies or Methods work and Education Studies. What each term covers will be qualified where necessary in relation to the different courses, and the crucial links between these elements will be considered as we proceed. In the case of each element we will be concerned with the significance of the course structure, the personnel responsible for training and the forms of pedagogy employed.

School-based Practical Training

Course structure

Weighting and diversity of Practical Training

All courses, by their structures, determine students' direct practical training in a number of major respects. First, by the weighting they give to the time spent in experience of immediate classroom and school activities at Level (a), courses provide different opportunities for direct understanding of the complexities of practical situations. Much of this understanding is a matter of tacit appreciation of situations as well as explicit attention to what is occurring. Opportunities to understand both the uniqueness of concrete teaching situations and their common features is central to developing teachers' sensitivity in practical judgement. Without extensive direct experience and the understanding which it alone can provide, professional judgement is inevitably limited. In the same way, it is only in direct experience of carrying out professional activities in the classroom that the skills and competences required can be mastered. These skills and competences take time to develop and the amount of time allowed sets a limit to the sophistication that is possible. Substantial direct practical experience is therefore highly desirable and students at Sussex and Northampton, who had more 'hands on' experience than their counterparts at RIHE and Leeds, clearly had some advantages. However, in a relatively short course, direct practical experience at Level (a) is in competition with work at all other levels. The precise amount of time devoted to such experience needs to be considered in relation to other priorities including the variety and diversity of teaching contexts students experience.

The range of situations and of activities which students can come to understand at the concrete level, and the range of practical skills and competences they can acquire, are significantly limited by the range of classes with which they have experience within any one school and the number and diversity of the schools used for classroom experience. Only by experience in a number of schools would it seem possible for students to develop practical competences that range across the demands of teaching in very different social or cultural contexts. Different schools may be necessary for working with different age or even ability ranges. In the primary phase, a particular school often has a distinctive philosophy and uses a restricted range of teaching methods.

Clearly, however, the number of schools experienced has a bearing on the quality of the practical training achieved. Too many schools can lead to superficiality, with students going back to the basic, elementary competences for merely coping, unless the similarities and differences between the schools are carefully considered. Sustained work in a stable context is necessary for developing students' sensitivity to what is happening around them and the complex skills of really good teaching.

All of these factors would suggest that some form of direct practical experience in more than one school is essential in primary courses and desirable in secondary courses. Whether it is actually essential in secondary courses depends on the weighting given to other 'indirect' forms of practical training at Level (b). Because direct practical experience in school is, by definition, specific and because it necessarily reduces the time available for other activities, courses which elect to provide only a single school experience must address the issue of how students' skills, judgements and understandings can be broadened. At RIHE, the single school experience was complemented by substantial input in terms of college-based Curriculum Studies preparation. However, at Sussex, students had a single school experience as well as very limited Curriculum Studies time. There was therefore a serious possibility that students' practical expertise was too narrowly based. The final term's 'alternative educational experience', although valuable for broadening students' perspective on the education system as a whole, did not compensate for the narrow range of practical classroom and school contexts to which they had been exposed.

Multiple school experience of some kind would seem to be most important in courses where substantial amounts of time are devoted to school experience. The Northampton course, by its major weighting of time spent in a minimum of three and often four different schools, provided the contexts for students to acquire a breadth of understanding and skills. The fact that these experiences were carefully co-ordinated and closely supervised meant that there was a real possibility for development throughout the year.

The character of serial and block experience

Course structure, in terms of the weighting and diversity of direct practical experience, therefore, has an important impact on the character of training students receive. Equally important is the pattern of serial and block practices that is established. Of its nature, serial experience is intermittent and in providing direct practical experience, the possibility for sustained work with pupils is limited. Block practice alone offers the opportunity for regular, sustained and systematic practical training for which there is no alternative. It is not surprising that in all four courses, block practices remained a significant feature of course structure, though at Sussex the time devoted to block practice was reduced to an absolute minimum.

Serial practices of one day a week, as adopted in Leeds, are very limited indeed in what they can provide by way of sustained involvement in the work of any given class. They give students little opportunity to develop the kind of tacit understanding professionals require, the appreciation of seeing the consequences of activities engaged in, and the skills that can only come from sustained practice in the same context. Evidence from the courses showed clearly that spells of serial experience that were devoted to direct practical training for one or two days a week were valuable only when they were well structured to achieve quite clear and relatively limited self-contained ends.

This is not to say that such experience does not have a very important part to play at this level, it is only to say that its use needs very careful consideration. Indeed, when appropriately structured by those supervising the work, it can clearly be used very effectively early in a course for introducing students progressively and cumulatively to particular elements of practical training (e.g. observing, with developing precision, what is happening in a given classroom; acquiring some experience of explaining a topic to one particular pupil). In both the Leeds and the Northampton courses such activities were carefully programmed and were of considerable benefit in the early stages of student training.

What particularly distinguishes serial experience from block experience, however, is that the former alone makes possible the 'concurrent' harnessing of students' work in analysis and reflection at Levels (b), (c) and (d) with the development of their own practical competence at Level (a). The sequential relationship imposed by block practice, though providing more time for preparation and sustained review, inevitably makes the integration of 'theory' and 'practice' more difficult. It is important, therefore, that periods of serial and block experience be carefully planned with their distinctive characteristics and precise purposes in mind. The developmental sequence of direct practical experiences also needs careful planning. In Northampton, returning to the same school for a second serial practice after both serial and block periods, left students unclear of the precise point of school-based work at that stage. In contrast, at RIHE there was a conscious developmental shift in the character of work in the same school during the two serial experiences, from a focus on classroom practice to a focus on wider professional matters. When used later in the course classroom-based serial practice can seem limited and contrived when compared with the full opportunities for teaching provided in block practice. In all of the courses where students were based in classrooms for a second period of serial work after a block practice, they complained about the narrowness of the experience. Classroom-based serial practice may therefore be most appropriate in the earlier phase of a course. Care also needs to be taken in planning the development of block practices. At Leeds and RIHE there was a deliberate shift of focus in the two block practices, from attention first to basic competences and then to more complex competences. In both cases this was well appreciated by students.

Personnel

The contribution of teachers

In all the courses investigated there was repeated evidence that teachers working with students were, in general, able to help them to understand in detail and with sensitivity what was happening in immediate classroom situations.

Moreover, they did this in ways that were impossible for lecturers to match, even when they visited schools regularly. The teachers were equally able to give students specific advice and help on judging what to do in particular circumstances. Yet such understanding and help demands of teachers skills of explicitly indicating to students matters which many teachers only implicitly sense and which they rarely formulate consciously. What is more, such help in understanding and practice hardly ever went beyond the immediate context to any wider consideration of other forms of professional practice (Level (b)) or to any explicit consideration of the practical principles behind their suggestions as to what ought to be done in the particular circumstances in this class or school (Level (c)). Students, therefore, were trained by teachers almost entirely by being made to attend explicitly to understanding classroom activities in immediately practical terms, and by being implicitly trained to judge and act according to the teachers' *own* practical principles.

Many, though not all, teachers were thus training students very effectively at Level (a), but hardly at all at other levels. Critical assessment of particular situations and incidents was by reference to *implicitly* accepted principles. There was little or no critical reflection that made the principles of practice *explicit* nor were those principles critically examined or looked at in terms of their more fundamental assumptions (Level (d)). Though Sussex gave very considerable responsibility for students' school-based training to teachers, thus reducing the time spent on work in the training institution, there was no evidence that in general, the work undertaken by these teachers differed in character from that undertaken by teachers elsewhere. By and large it remained rooted at Level (a). What that responsibility did do, however, was to 'legitimate' forcefully, in the eyes of the students, teachers' contribution to training, giving it at least equal standing with the contribution from lecturers. As a consequence, the importance students attached to the practical professional knowledge of teachers and of training at the level of direct practice was marked.

The contribution of lecturers

Practical training at Level (a)   Lecturers are clearly limited in what they can contribute to the development of students' competences at Level (a) because they lack the detailed and tacit knowledge necessary for effective teaching in the many classes that their students will experience. This lack of knowledge (which, by definition, is available to the regular teacher of a class), and the fact that lecturers simply are not present to be able to help students in the many situations they face, means that their help must, of its nature, be more general. Individual lecturers, particularly Curriculum or Methods lecturers, may develop such close contacts with schools that they can, to some extent, provide the same kind of detailed support as teachers. It will be recalled that this was the case at RIHE, where one Education lecturer was attached to each of the three schools participating in the scheme. However, the numbers of schools, classes and students that any one lecturer has to work with, and the time he or she has to perform these duties, usually make such training impossible. If it is to be attempted, the number of schools a course uses must be severely restricted with consequences that have already been commented on.

Yet, to suggest that lecturers cannot realistically substitute for the work undertaken by teachers is not to say that lecturers do not have a distinctive contribution to make to work at this immediate practical level. Many lecturers, particularly in Curriculum and Methods areas, are widely experienced in observing teaching in very varied circumstances. They are also experienced in doing this with conscious awareness of the practical principles on which a given teacher or student may, perhaps unconsciously, be operating. As was suggested above, this is a skill that most teachers do not at present usually possess. Perhaps in the future they may develop such skills, though the training implications are considerable. At present, some form of direct involvement of lecturers in students' direct practical training would seem to us to be advantageous. In the limited time they usually have for supervision, they may be seen as complementing the very highly specific and detailed work that teachers alone can undertake. As will be noted below, it is also in present circumstances lecturers alone who can link or integrate students' direct practical experience with other levels of training.

Relating school experience and other training   Lecturers may therefore make an important, if limited, contribution to students' school-based training at the most basic and practical level. But the most important and distinctive training contribution of lecturers at Level (a) is to integrate or link this work to other levels of training. In this work it is usually lecturers alone who have expertise. In so far as lecturers have detailed and practical knowledge of a school and of the work of a student in it, there is the possibility that they can integrate supervision at this level with other levels of training. In supervising students, they may, for example, inform them about other forms of practice engaged in elsewhere (Level (b)); it is, after all, part of their job to have an extensive knowledge of practice that no individual teacher can hope to possess. In addition, a lecturer may also explicitly draw out the principles underlying specific examples of concrete practice and discuss their appropriateness in that given context (Level (c)). At its most sophisticated, such training can include questions about the fundamental pre-suppositions that are influencing the concrete practices in the school (Level (d)).

But such 'supervision', that integrates critical reflection by the student into an analysis of his or her own practice, is a rare phenomenon in most courses. We saw only occasional examples if only because the conditions for it existed so rarely. At RIHE the presence of an Education Lecturer attached to a school during practice made such work a serious possibility. At Northampton, Sussex and Leeds, the knowledge of particular schools by certain lecturers provided some opportunities for more occasional and limited work of this kind. In general, however, the choice of schools used and the practicalities arising from shortage of time available to lecturers made such supervision impossible.

But if integrated 'on the spot' supervision of this sort is difficult to achieve, it is still important for lecturers to be as familiar as possible with students' school-based practical work so that they may establish some links with other levels of training. Serial practice is an important addition to practical training in this respect because it allows the possibility of critical reflection and analysis in the training institution to be developed in relation to the student's *own* practical experience. Block experience cannot be anything like so readily linked to work in the training institution. Indeed, without serial practice, if opportunities for integrated supervision in school are not possible, it is hard to see how the gap between practical training at Level (a) and training at other levels can be bridged. If reflection and analysis only takes place on other people's or simulated experience, we believe that there will be a serious weakness in students' professional preparation. As will be considered later, all four courses in our study sought to exploit the possibilities of serial practice for developing links across the levels. In so doing it became clear that if lecturers are involved in school supervision such links can have a vitality and value that reliance on students' own reporting of practice can not provide.

Pedagogy

At the level of direct practical experience pedagogy is primarily a question of the form of supervision of classroom and school experience. It concerns the *way* in which students are expected to learn which necessarily in turn influences *what* they learn. The pedagogic styles of teachers and lecturers therefore have considerable significance for the training students receive.

The contribution of teachers

As already indicated, the pedagogy of teachers in relation to students' direct practical experience varies widely in the degree to which explicit attention is given to increasing students' direct knowledge and understanding of practical situations. If students receive little explicit help and comment, all they can do is learn by trial and error. In these circumstances, they may be reduced to simply using teachers as 'models', following them or ignoring them as they see fit. Alternatively, they may try to 'apply' abstract skills, judgements and understandings they have developed elsewhere in their course. Traditionally much teacher training has sought the application in school of work prepared elsewhere, teachers being required either simply to give up their classes for practice or to see that students have done as instructed. These approaches to students' learning would seem, in themselves, inadequate. As has been implied above, some more active form of training by teachers in relation to students' direct practical experience is essential.

Teachers must attempt explicitly to 'train' students at this practical level. Yet, if this is done in a strongly didactic fashion, it can take on the character of apprenticeship. Fortunately most teachers experienced in work with students take on a more detached position while recognizing that their own practices must, at least to some extent, serve as models. They seek to analyse a student's own practice in terms of the particular causes of difficulties encountered and offer suggestions without seeking to restrict the initiative and judgement of the students as to what exactly they should do. By controlling, with care, the character and range of situations students face in observation and practice and by attending to the issues raised selectively and developmentally, the student's own capacities are formed in a more reflective and responsive way. In order to carry out such training teachers need a framework of implicit basic principles of what constitutes good practice, but they must accept that the expression of these is a complex matter, dependent in part on the student's own unique personal qualities.

In the four courses studied, the significance of modelling in Level (a) training varied. At Northampton, the teachers who worked most closely with students during serial practice were very carefully chosen in order to provide basic training at Level (a) of a specific form approved by the Course Director. That they could act as good role models was seen as extremely important. They were chosen in close consultation with the Course Director for their high standards of professionalism and for their broad sympathy with the child-centred approach to teaching. A similar approach was adopted at Leeds, though here the definition of what constituted good primary school teaching was more broadly conceived. In contrast, in the two secondary courses teachers were not selected on this basis as modelling was assigned a lower priority in the pedagogy of school experience. Although many teachers were indeed excellent, the basis of their selection was left to the school. What course leaders looked for was a *school* that was sympathetic and willing to participate in training. The selection of teachers was a more random affair. Bearing in mind what has been said of the practical difficulties that usually make it impossible for lecturers to contribute to students' development at this practical level in any detailed way, the importance of the choice of teachers for work with students in schools can hardly be over-estimated. Nothing in the four case studies runs counter to this conclusion. There would thus seem to be much to be said for recognizing the inevitable place of some modelling in students' early practical experience and choosing schools and teachers partly on this basis. But if training is to produce a reflective practitioner, teachers must also be able to work with students in a more open, analytical way than modelling or apprenticeship implies.

The contribution of lecturers

We have stressed that supervision by lecturers of students' school experience must, in general, serve quite a different purpose from that of teachers. The help they can offer students is necessarily an interpretation of what is occurring in classroom activities in more generalized terms than those which teachers can provide and is made from within a wider and more detached framework. Potentially they can highlight features of students' practice that are less discernible by teachers who are constantly immersed in the complexities of work with their classes. What is more, the aspects of practice they attend to are likely to be cast in a form that dissociates them from their detailed context and thus links them to explicitly formulated principles of practice.

In relating students' own practice to other forms of practice and to general principles, the pedagogy of lecturers during school experience can be either dogmatic in seeking the application of 'external' ideas or analytical and reflective in seeking to develop students' existing insights and skills. Only in this latter case does it seem that a divorce can be prevented between students' own developing practical achievements and their more theoretical work with lecturers. If analytical 'supervision' is to be asked of teachers, it is at least as important that it be asked of lecturers. What is more, it is only if teachers and lecturers can share with students a common basic conceptual framework for the analysis of practice that the training of students given by teachers at Level (a) can be adequately related to the training at all levels provided by lecturers. However, such a common framework can surely be established and applied coherently only if teachers and lecturers work in the closest collaboration with students discussing school experience. It is important therefore that ways be found in which teachers and lecturers work together in the analysis of students' practice. By these means there can be real hope that the traditional gaps between theory and practice and between training institution work and school experience can be bridged.

In the courses studied, this kind of work occurred only very infrequently. Even where teachers and lecturers regularly undertook supervision of the same students, the limited time available for lecturers to visit schools and the difficulty of arranging simultaneous observation by lecturers and teachers, meant that opportunities for integrating different levels of training in this way were seldom realized. It is perhaps because of the difficulties of establishing a framework and training style for linking practical training with other levels of training that two of the courses evaluated had begun to experiment with training materials.

The use of training materials

Increasingly significant at Level (a) is what may be called the pedagogy of training materials. Lecturers can influence their students' practical development much more systematically if they provide them with specific activities to engage in in schools and by structuring these developmentally both in observation and in teaching exercises. When lecturers devise such work, it has the limitations of externally determined practices mentioned earlier and needs to be sensitively adapted to individual practical contexts by teachers working in those contexts and to individual students by those supervising their development. As was demonstrated at RIHE, where students were left to themselves to utilize such materials as they saw fit, such careful considerations will be beyond the ability of untrained students. As the students themselves realized, the very real potential of the material available in the 'Course File' at RIHE was therefore never exploited. However, when jointly contructed by teachers and lecturers working together in the course, and used under adequate guidance of teachers who appreciate its analytical rather than didactic purpose in professional training as a whole, such structured work can become a powerful training vehicle. As was demonstrated in the case of the Leeds 'Activity Booklets', such materials can help build together what both groups of supervisors can bring to practical training in itself, and help establish the necessary practical base and common framework for other levels of professional development.

Training in Curriculum Studies and Methods work

As has been seen, although practical training is central to the professional development of students, what can be accomplished is often restricted by many purely pragmatic considerations that govern the running of courses. As a consequence, not everything that students need to learn can be realistically accomplished through direct practical experience. Practical experience is a time-consuming way of learning much that can be learnt by other means. Moreover, certain activities of professional practice and reflection (e.g. lesson preparation and marking), do not, in any case, necessarily take place in classrooms. All courses therefore devote a significant amount of time to other forms of training, ranging across what we have referred to as Levels (b), (c) and (d). As has been outlined earlier, in most courses this work is split into two major elements, Curriculum Studies or Methods work and Education Studies. As the names imply, Curriculum Studies or Methods work has traditionally been concerned with teaching methods for particular curriculum areas, whereas Education Studies has been concerned with more academic study of general matters of professional importance for teachers. The elements of the four courses studied, other than those concerned with practical experience, being modifications of these traditional elements, are, for convenience, being considered under these two headings.

In their concern for classroom practice, Curriculum and Methods elements can be seen to provide training for students at all three distinguishable levels (b), (c), and (d). Clearly courses differ in their concentration on work at certain of these levels and the relationships built between these and Level (a). But what any course can achieve, can be seen to depend once more on the structure, personnel and pedagogy employed. We shall therefore again examine these features of Curriculum Studies work.

Course structure

Weighting and links of Level (b) training

Of its nature, 'indirect' practical training (Level (b)) has significant limitations. Being concerned with reported or 'simulated' experience, it necessarily excludes at least some of the complications that arise in actual school situations. The basic development of students' practical knowledge and competences must therefore be through direct experience at Level (a). But if a course aims to provide in some measure, knowledge and competences that cannot be readily acquired in available schools, or aims to prepare students in the training institution *before* they are involved in practical experience, work at Level (b) must be given a major place in the programme. At Sussex, for example, because of the responsibility devolved to Teacher Tutors, University-based practical training in Curriculum Studies was frequently seen as supplementing the direct practical training students undertook in school. Because of the emphasis on practical school work and the concurrent structure of the course, students were in a position to interpret the practical implications of their Curriculum Studies work even though it took place in the University. At Leeds and RIHE a more traditional approach was taken to Curriculum Studies. College-based practical training at Level (b) was largely detached from students' own school experience and, particularly in the early stages of the courses, was seen as *preparatory* to teaching practice. Despite the thoroughness of the coverage, students on these courses may well have lacked the necessary framework to understand or to apply with any sensitivity what they had learnt. Courses which emphasize institution-based preparation in this way may, as a consequence, have to devote more attention to school supervision if they wish to train students in how to 'apply' their abstract knowledge appropriately.

Weighting and links of Level (c) training

Where attention to work at Level (c) is concerned we have already indicated that teachers in schools gave little or no explicit attention to elucidating the principles of practice. All the significant training in understanding the principles of the teaching of particular curricular areas, therefore, fell to Curriculum Studies work. In a course which is as heavily school-based as that at Sussex, the time available for Curriculum Studies work is strictly limited. If, as at Sussex too, only one school is used for practice, work on principles at Level (c) must compete for Curriculum Studies time with important work in indirect practice at Level (b). In the competition for time, we were impressed by what was done, no doubt because of the course's very firm commitment to reflective work. In the other courses, less explicit attention was paid to the underlying principles of curriculum practice. Particularly in the primary courses, the main emphasis was with practical work at Level (b).

This relative lack of explicit attention to work at Level (c) did not, of course, leave Sussex students without a body of principles for deciding on matters of classroom teaching. These they acquired implicitly in their practical work in school and in the training institution. As a consequence, however, they lacked conscious, overt critical assessment of what they were doing. Such public, comparative assessment of the guiding principles of teaching practices is not common amongst teachers, certainly not in any depth. Without clarity on these matters, however, practice is inadequately considered and tends either to get stuck or to be at the mercy of new ideas. Work on the principles of classroom teaching at Level (c) would seem necessary for responsibile developments in practices by teachers. For students not to reach this level of consideration of practice would seem to be a major weakness in training.

In work at this level it is of course crucially important how far the consideration of the principles of teaching is linked in some way to students' own experience at Level (a), and not merely 'indirect' work on practice at Level (b). Much of value can be achieved, especially in workshop sessions, even though the analysis is of 'second-hand' experience. Yet, if students are not, at some stage, helped to consider the principles of their *own* practice, they are missing out on a matter of vital consideration for their work. It is through the concurrent structure of serial practice that it becomes possible to build into Curriculum Studies some attention to the principles underlying students' own practice as that develops. Two of the four courses considered achieved significant work of this kind.

Weighting and links of Level (d) training

In only one Curriculum Studies element in a secondary PGCE course did we come across substantial work at the level of the foundation disciplines, i.e. at Level (d). All other Level (d) work took place in Education Studies. To some extent, this reflects the relative paucity of work in the foundation disciplines which has been directed to the practices of teaching in specific curriculum areas. But the place of considerations of fundamental values and theoretical assumptions behind educational practices within initial training is in any case a matter of considerable dispute.

No one, who takes training of any kind seriously, doubts the priority of practical work at Level (a). Most would also agree that practically orientated work in the training institution (Level (b)) should figure significantly. But as practice, and indeed good practice, can be conducted effectively without explicit attention to the principles behind it, Level (c) training becomes more disputable. But even if some grasp of 'the reason why' of one's practice at a pragmatic level is considered desirable, it is yet another matter to raise the difficult and usually very controversial questions the foundation disciplines seek to tackle. Yet the model of the 'reflective practitioner' we have developed from Schön, and the work of the courses we have considered, suggests that a student should at least become aware that the principles of some contemporary curriculum practices involve beliefs and values which are open to fundamental consideration and dispute. Our courses gave this form of analysis very low priority.

A further question concerns the relationship such work should have to work at other levels. Should it be detached altogether from work at other levels, being determined primarily by material from the disciplines? Should it be related to other 'indirect' forms of study at Levels (b) and (c)? Or should it be linked, somehow, to students' own practical experience at Level (a) and the principles behind that? The first of these approaches runs into serious practical difficulties in a short course as most students simply do not have the appropriate background to cope with advanced theoretical study of the teaching of their discipline. Even if such an explicitly academic approach is considered valuable, its significance for practice is likely to prove too complex for students to grasp. If linked in some way to work at Levels (b) and (c), its proper bearing on practice can be more adequately exposed. What is then required is that it be structured into Curriculum Studies to fit coherently with work on these practices. To be seen as a critique of students' own practice, it must, of course, also be linked coherently to school experience. In the one case of serious theoretical work at Level (d) we saw this was how it was used. Theoretical analysis took place in Curriculum Studies which ran in parallel with serial practice and had clear and effective links both to a consideration of principles at Level (c) and to students' own work at Level (a) in observation and practice.

Personnel

The contribution of lecturers at Levels (b), (c) and (d)

By virtue of their training and experience, Curriculum Studies or Methods lecturers have a great deal of expert knowledge, direct and indirect, of a great variety of professional practices within their curriculum specialisms. They too can, above all others, be expected to be expert in the analysis of practice in terms of the principles underlying the use of different teaching methods, materials, syllabuses and forms of assessment. In related work in foundation disciplines, they can be expected to be knowledgeable, if not expert, in the different disciplines. On this basis, they are in a position to make informed judgements about the kind of practical experience students should have at Level (a) in their subject areas, the teachers they should work with, the complementary work they should seek to provide at other levels, and the way it should be inter-related with work at Level (a).

In all three courses other than Sussex, students were provided, in Curriculum or Methods classes, with a substantial amount of detailed work in areas chosen to make sure all students had at least detached Level (b) knowledge and skill across a prescribed range of professional activities. At Sussex, with limited time for Curriculum work, what was done was chosen, above all, to link closely to Level (a) and to develop reflective skills. Systematic, wide-ranging coverage at these levels was, however, very difficult to achieve. In particular, certain students at Sussex felt the lack of knowledge of a wide range of professional practices. On the other hand, students on other courses showed a degree of scepticism of the value of some of the 'indirect' work they had undertaken. The dilemma is whether to emphasize broad and systematic preparation for class teaching within the training institution, with all the inadequacies of detached knowledge that that involves, or to opt for more realistic, but necessarily narrow, school-based preparation. We were not convinced that any of our four courses had got right the fine balance that is necessary in this area.

The relative absence of work on principles (Level (c)) in certain Curriculum courses, can readily be attributed to lecturers considering explicit attention to principles and their critical examination of much less importance than the development of students' practical competences at secondhand. With the pressure on time, this is understandable, but means that young teachers can lack significant rationale for much of what they do. If training is to produce reflective practitioners it would seem vital that attention to Level (c) work must be increased.

A major difficulty with seeking to include work at Level (d) within Curriculum Studies, arises from its anchorage in a range of sophisticated and very complex foundation disciplines. Curriculum Studies lecturers cannot be expected to be experts in areas of philosophy of education as well as psychology of education and other major disciplines. Further, those who are experts in these areas have, as yet, paid only limited attention to the practices of teaching specific curriculum subjects or topics. In none of the four courses considered did we come across lecturers in the disciplines being involved in Curriculum work. In so far as Level (d) work is judged important in relation to Curriculum Studies, the question as to who exactly can undertake it is, in present circumstances, very difficult to answer.

In choosing what particular issues of classroom teaching to consider, lecturers clearly decided on very different principles. Some were wide ranging and eclectic, using broad criteria for selecting the teaching methods and materials they introduced. Others, with decisive views on the best methods and materials, were much more restricted, and sought to prepare students to initiate certain activities in schools, and to experiment practically in ways particular schools might even oppose. If such work is very distinctive and out of keeping with the practices encountered in school experience, students can, if they are not carefully supported by teachers as well as lecturers, find themselves in situations in which they are unable to cope. On the other hand, if such support is forthcoming, students may be given a very real opportunity of introducing change into a teaching context. If carefully handled, this can be an important learning experience and help in the development of advanced professional skills.

Linking Curriculum Studies and school experience

So as to link Curriculum Studies or Methods work as tightly as possible to practical training in schools, lecturers, where knowledgeable about the classroom experiences of individual students themselves through supervision of school practice, introduced accounts of these into their classes. In this way, they were able to help individual students understand more adequately their own experience at Level (a), while extending other students' understanding at Level (b). Not infrequently, particularly at Sussex and in 'Method' seminars at North-ampton, students themselves were asked to report on their recent personal experiences during serial practice in schools. As commented earlier, though in principle these accounts can be effective in linking Curriculum Studies to Level (a) work, in practice there are real difficulties with this approach. Early in the course, students are likely to lack the necessary abilities to abstract and report from their practice in ways that can effectively communicate their under-standing of practice to other students. The areas of recent practical experience of one student may well have little or no relationship with the areas of recent experience of others. While, therefore, questioning and comments by other students might once more help to articulate what has happened more precisely, and contribute to his or her Level (a) development to some degree, student contributions are likely to be of limited value to others, particularly at the start of training. Skilful re-interpretation by an experienced lecturer can come to the rescue, but this is not easy without detailed knowledge of the schools and students' work there. Once more, the lecturers' participation in the supervision of school experience is significant. Without close collaboration with teachers or the use of structured materials, the possibility of links would seem to be limited.

A further way of linking Curriculum Studies to practical experience was to involve teachers as contributors to classes. In so far as they have worked with students in schools, teachers are in a position to help certain students in their understanding at Level (a), and to help link that work to a consideration of practice elsewhere. In general, however, their contribution appears to be to articulate with insight what currently happens in their own schools. To the extent that teachers do have the skills to contribute effectively in this way, (though this is not necessarily the case), they can, by virtue of their successful classroom professionalism, provide another very valuable extension of indirect practical training at Level (b) and an important base for other levels of work.

The contribution of teachers is, of course, all the more effective if students can observe and even, to some extent, take part in teachers' practical work in schools. When carefully selected and well planned, such single visits organized as part of Curriculum work can be used to extend students' understanding at Level (a) considerably, and can be a powerful base for work at other levels to be linked closely to practice. Another similar form of school visit that can clearly have a place is when students accompany a lecturer to observe and take part in teaching he or she is engaged in. If staged as one-off occasions when the lecturer is in that school, there is an inevitable major artificiality about a situation in which the lecturer has very limited knowledge of the class and carries only brief responsibility for what is being done. If part of regular school teaching by the lecturer, possibly with a joint appointment, such visits can be more carefully used within a curriculum course, though there are severe practical limits to the opportunities of this kind any one lecturer can provide for a large group of students when holding direct responsibility for the coherently planned and uninterrupted regular teaching of school classes. Visits with a lecturer teaching on particular visits only, but in a very familiar school, were used in one or two Curriculum courses for quite specific and well-planned purposes. They were clearly considered learning opportunities which students valued greatly.

Pedagogy

Level (b) and links to Level (a)

Central to considerations of the pedagogy of Curriculum Studies must be a clear view of the purpose of this work and the relationship it is seen to have with students' practical work in schools. In terms of practical preparation in the training institution (Level (b)), the approach can be heavily didactic and expository; students can simply be taught what are appropriate methods to use. But even in terms of understanding what is being presented to them, students are likely to find it more helpful if a more 'interactive' teaching style is adopted, so that they can explore the details of other practices in discussion, using their own developing practical experience as a base. If accounts of students' own experiences are to be used in this context, providing a closer link with Level (a) work, such an exploratory and analytical approach would seem essential.

Where the purpose of institution-based Curriculum Studies is the development of practical judgement and skills, then the closer methods of training approximate to those of actual training in classroom practice, the more effective training is likely to be. Much Curriculum Studies work in all four courses was of this character, using such activities as lesson preparation, experimentation with materials and simulation exercises. In most cases, work in the four courses was eclectic and not tightly prescriptive in its implicit principles. However, examples were encountered where lecturers concentrated on a narrow range of practices of which they particularly approved. The purpose was then clearly linked with the hope that students would seek to use such methods in serial or block practice. In one course, persistent use of skilful analytical questioning about students' own practices and their consequences by a lecturer familiar with their work, was used to great effect. Though not exclusive of all other approaches, it established firmly for students, both a repertoire of possible practices, and implicitly, a body of approved principles.

Level (c) and links to Level (a)

In explicit work on the principles of classroom practice (Level (c)), the approach was usually analytical, working from examples of practice that a group of students could take as commonly understood for the purposes of discussion. To this end, increasing use is being made of video-tapes, transcripts and materials from schools in many courses. But work on reflection at Level (c) that attends to principles and their validity, can itself be presented didactically by a lecturer in a set of examples rather than taught as a practical skill by training students to conduct the necessary analysis and argument themselves. Such work is difficult to carry out, requiring a high analytical ability and very particular group teaching skills. It is, however, a mark of the prime emphasis in school-based courses on working from practice that this approach is being developed with increasing sophistication.

Level (d) and links to Level (a)

As was noted above, only in one relatively brief course element did we encounter Curriculum work that explicitly considered, to any significant degree, matters of fundamental value and theory at Level (d). The approach in this area was largely didactic, working from a particular philosophical position to the advocacy of a range of practical principles and examples of practical teaching activities exemplifying these. The whole process was completed by certain demonstration lessons taken by the lecturer in school. In itself, the practical significance of such work for students is largely that of providing examples of what they are being urged or expected to do during school experience. It is a form of 'preparation' rather than of practical training, but can come with a formidable rationale and be followed through during practice. In seeking to develop a reflective practitioner, however, such work can form only an element in a programme that works analytically from practice through to fundamental issues.

When so little has been done that effectively uses the foundation disciplines in the analysis of classroom practice, Curriculum lecturers can hardly be expected to devote much time to such matters, or to be particularly experienced in such analysis themselves. In general, it would seem more appropriate at present for lecturers to concentrate on developing analytical work with students through to Level (c) before raising questions about the principles of practice of a more fundamental kind. The latter would illustrate what can be done in foundation work without attempting the training of students in Level (d) work as such. Anything more ambitious within Curriculum Studies work would seem premature.

Training within Education Studies

Structure

Weighting and placing of Education Studies

The importance any course attaches to Education Studies is manifestly reflected in its weighting in comparison with school experience and Curriculum Studies. Systematic work at Level (c), both on classroom and on wider professional issues, would seem important if student professionalism is not to be dangerously uncritical. What is more, work needs to be effectively linked to students' own experience of practice. With the exception of RIHE, the courses studied devoted much the same proportion of their time to this area as traditional courses, though as will be seen, the character of the work was in some cases significantly different. The prime use of Education Studies for developing students' explicit attention to matters of principle, however, is particularly important if only because in both school supervision and in Curriculum Studies so little of such work occurred. In very large measure, students on the four courses, as on more traditional courses, were dependent on Education Studies to introduce them to explicit questions of principle about practice.

In traditional courses, Education Studies has usually consisted of series of lectures and seminars in each of a number of foundation disciplines, usually selected from philosophy of education, psychology of education, sociology of education and history of education. The content of these course elements was generally chosen to teach certain results of work in each discipline as well as give some insight into the nature of the discipline and the kinds of questions it deals with. The relationship with matters of practice and practical principle was always there, but when not remote, the complex and often obscure relationship with the practices of direct concern to students was not usually explored. In three of the courses studied, the agenda of the work undertaken still arose at least as much from the disciplines and a range of their achievements, as from any questions of professional practice.

In Education Studies, as in Curriculum Studies, the importance of work in the disciplines for initial training is now in dispute. However, bearing in mind what was said above about the importance of Level (c) work in developing students' critical concern for professional practice, it would seem important that they are also at least aware that the disciplines are concerned to raise questions of fundamental significance at Level (d), even if in the day to day business of making practical judgement such considerations may seem pragmatically less pressing. Whether or not it is possible or even desirable in a short course that necessarily focuses on the practical matter of initial training to do more than instance examples of such fundamental considerations by undertaking training at Level (d) in any systematically structured way, is a matter not easily settled. But unless they are aware of certain major examples of the significance of the disciplines for professional practices they are themselves engaged in, many students are unlikely to appreciate the fundamental nature of their professional role.

Education Studies and school experience

In building links between work at both Levels (c) and (d) with work at Level (a), the four courses had developed different degrees of inter-relation. At RIHE, considerable integration of work was achieved by the presence in their school during their serial and block practice of the Education Tutor who taught them. Through very considerable direct knowledge of the school and students' experience, plus the use of structured activities by the students, the lecturer was able to explore their experience in a highly effective way, relating it to the matters of principle and theory he or she wished to cover. By involving teachers in these school-based seminars, the inter-relation of the levels of work was enhanced yet further. By occasionally combining students, teachers and lecturers from more than one school, an important element of 'indirect' practical training at Level (b) was also introduced into the programme.

At Sussex, the Personal Tutor who was responsible for education studies again worked with students from one school only, a school with which he or she had close contact. Though not based in the school while students were on school experience, there were close links with the students on supervisory visits. In addition, there was contact with the General Tutor who was both responsible for the whole group of students in the school and held a regular seminar with them on wider professional matters. At Leeds, the link between practical experience and Education Studies was built primarily through appropriately structured activities which students undertook in school. At Northampton, in the relatively brief Education Studies programme, there were links by means of examples from practical experience which both students and their Teacher Tutors contributed to discussion following more formal presentations. In the IT-INSET that complemented the Education Studies programme, activities engaged in by students during serial experience were built into work with both lecturers and teachers on matters of principle and fundamental theory. In these ways, all the courses endeavoured to make a reality of inter-relating practical training and critical reflection at other levels. To this extent, Education Studies played a crucial part in developing the kind of professional practitioner we have come to advocate.

As in the case of Curriculum Studies, the particular links a course wishes to develop are clearly in part a question of how direct a function this element of the programme is seen to fulfil in relation to students' own practical training. It is also in part a matter of the particular relations that have been established between schools and the training institution. It is also in part a matter of the availability of lecturers to work closely with schools. What a course does in this respect is, however, likely to be an issue of major importance for the overall character of the training students receive.

Personnel

The contribution of lecturers

The teaching of Education Studies has traditionally been the responsibility of specialists in the foundation disciplines of educational theory, whether or not also trained in the wider parent academic subjects of, say, philosophy or psychology. Such lecturers have thus been engaged in work related to principles of educational practice, though they may themselves have lacked direct experience of the relevant practices. Not surprisingly, as indicated earlier, traditional courses in Education Studies put a major emphasis on theoretical work at Level (d) with related attention to principles at Level (c). Links with practice at Levels (b) and (a) were incidental to dealing with matters of general principle. The range of topics covered tended to be determined by considerations within each discipline as much as any attempt to cover those matters of practice important to students. As a result, courses lacked any adequate consideration of general teaching issues and issues of wider professional practice, even at the level of practical principles let alone at the level of the details of practice. Such topics as were selected were only seen through the eyes of separate academic disciplines.

In all the four courses studies, however, the topics considered in Education Studies courses were firmly chosen because of their importance for students' professional practice, matters of practical principle were examined in their own right and serious attempts were made to link the work to students' own experience in schools. Issues of fundamental theory from the disciplines still figured prominently, and were at times systematically addressed, but were now being approached more as offering a critique of practice. In the interests of developing training in critical reflection across all the levels, Education Studies can thus be seen to have played a key role in all four courses. Granted proper links are built with students' current practice, Education Studies lecturers make possible work right across these levels, if only on a range of general and wider professional practices rather than particular teaching activities.

Linking Education Studies and school experience

In forging direct links with practice, the RIHE course not only arranged for the Education Studies lecturer to be based in school to work with students during school experience, Education Studies seminars were themselves planned and conducted in school. Joint planning and carrying out of the work by lecturers and teachers, each using their own expertise, enabled each weekly topic to be studied in a way that ranged clearly and coherently across all four levels of training. Regular contributions from teachers anchored matters in considerations of practice with which all the participants, students, teachers and lecturers were familiar.

At Sussex, the topics for Education Studies work in the Personal Tutor groups were chosen by students or were negotiated with them; moreover, students were often responsible for preparing and running the classes. By influencing the preparatory reading and by their contributions to discussion, lecturers sought to make sure that issues of principle and fundamental theory were considered. At Leeds, the results of structured activities undertaken by students using their 'Activity Booklets' were used by lecturers in work across all four levels.

Though in transition, formal Education Studies classes at Northampton had retained more of a traditional character, still being labelled under one or other of the disciplines. The focus, though, was on each occasion a particular topic of professional practice, and contributions to discussion from students and teachers on their experience were invited. In IT-INSET work, which complemented the formal classes, the starting point of each project was a specific issue of school practice, the principles behind which were investigated as appropriate, in terms of one of the disciplines. The scope of the project thus once again ranged across and inter-related considerations at the different levels. In doing this, students worked jointly with teachers and tutors, the contribution of each being to secure attention to elements within their knowledge or expertise. Thus, at Northampton as at RIHE there was a deliberate attempt in Education Studies to integrate fundamental theory with students' own practice whereas the other two were content with building various links of a more indirect sort.

Pedagogy

Didactic and analytical approaches

From what has been said, it can readily be inferred that the training students received in Education Studies varied significantly in the four courses because of the different teaching styles adopted. The most formal, didactic approach, through lectures and discussions, was found in one part of the work at Northampton. Here, a content of principles and theory (at Levels (c) and (d)) was presented to students for their consideration and use as they saw fit. The content was illustrated by contributions from individual experience at Level (a).

By contrast, the work at RIHE was, in general, based on a discussion of practical experience in the students' own school. From this, and by references to practice elsewhere (Level(b)), principles were either presented for consideration with practice seen as illustrating them, or analytically derived from practice (Level (c)) work. Elements of theory from the disciplines were then introduced in formal teaching or via readings, to illuminate these principles and raise more fundamental issues. The overall result was a concern to articulate the relationship between practice and theory. It showed how one can, in analytical terms, critically reflect on and evaluate practice in progressively more fundamental respects. But at the heart, for all its concentrated involvement of students' own experience at Level (a), it remained didactic, being dominated by presentations of reflection at Levels (c) and (d) carried out by the lecturer. Although, therefore, it was instructive in matters of reflection, it did not constitute a training of students themselves in carrying out that process; students were in this sense passive receivers of reflection.

When students necessarily lack any knowledge of relevant work in the foundation disciplines, it is certainly difficult for them to engage directly in any detailed or sustained reflection at Level (d). But, with help from knowledgeable experts students can, if required or provoked, be involved in such reflection. At Sussex, Personal Tutor group seminars were frequently conducted for this purpose. Students were expected to take the initiative in terms of topics chosen, preparation for and conduct of the seminars, with the lecturer helping as appropriate. In discussion, students were expected to form their own conclusions on matters of principle and practice, not to accept the judgements of lecturers. Lecturers were in this context concerned with training in the *process* of reflection not in any particular conclusions. Though similar work was done in some of the Curriculum Studies workshops at Sussex, it was in the Personal Tutor group seminars above all that training in analytical reflection across the levels was most prominent. It was principally through the Personal Tutor group seminars that students were expected to develop the skills of analysis and reflection that were the primary goal of the whole course. Students were then expected to demonstrate these growing skills in their individual Course Files on which they were formally assessed.

Pedagogy of IT-INSET

IT-INSET work at Northampton, which sought to serve a number of important purposes, shared with Sussex Personal Tutor group seminars an aim of direct training in reflection on matters of practice. The means, however, were very different. The work was conducted entirely in pairs, in an enquiry on one issue of practice only, which was studied in some depth with the aid of teachers and lecturers. It might be an issue of relative detail, as in the case of the study of classroom interruptions, or a matter of more general import, say in terms of syllabus reconstruction. The enquiry method used might vary too in its sophistication, bearing some close relationship to established research methods or being more direct and non-technical.

Such a study carefully planned, could, as a 'paradigm' case, serve as a training of students in reflection across all four levels. The difficulties of carrying out such a project in this way are, however, considerable. The restrictions on its practical reference, its form of reflection and its connections with foundation disciplines, are severe. The detail of the enquiry too, may be time-consuming and over-burdening in both preparation and execution for the return in training the project can offer. It is, therefore, difficult to see IT-INSET work as more than one element within Education Studies. It can contribute real insight into one form of reflection carried out in depth. That can be of great value to a student in itself. But it leaves untouched sustained training in many of the forms of reflection that teachers must engage in daily. It remains, however, an example of teachers and lecturers combining to provide an element of training in a joint enterprise with students that can with integrity span the levels of thoroughgoing critical reflection.

Conclusion

In this chapter we have endeavoured to set out the central significance of school-based work for professional training as revealed in our analysis of the four courses we studied. In particular we have sought to show how decisions about course structure, personnel and pedagogy can determine the nature of direct practical training itself and how that can be linked to other levels of training to develop a reflective practitioner. The complexity of the issues we have touched on is obvious and this attempt to extract a number of defensible principles for course development, even at a very general level, has mapped only some of the considerations at stake. Clarification of the character of professional training and how different course elements can contribute to that is as yet at a relatively undeveloped stage. Our conclusions are therefore inevitably somewhat tentative. But the matters we have stressed we have come to see as of fundamental importance and have therefore concentrated on these rather than enter into more detailed and yet more controversial considerations. The analytical framework we have devised in 'critical reflection' on the four courses we studied and the 'principles' we have sought to make explicit, we see as a contribution to the development of 'reflective practice' by all those engaged in PGCE training. They are offered not for crude 'application' in course development but as important elements in the framing that course developers might experimentally and sensitively use in the exercise of their own professional practice.

7 Implications for Schools and Training Institutions

In setting out the implications for training of many decisions in course planning we have only incidentally commented on the logistical and resource implications of different course arrangements. It has become apparent, however, that courses similar to those we have considered, which move away from the traditional model of training to more school-based arrangements, make particular new demands on schools and training institutions if they are to be effectively implemented. We have, therefore, sought to draw these out for consideration by those concerned with school-based developments.

Schools

Teacher Tutors

The traditional role of the Teacher Tutor has been primarily one of organizing opportunities for the students first to observe classes being taught and then to undertake progressively more teaching, giving advice and help to the students as seemed necessary. The assumption was that the training institution *prepared* students for this work which they could be increasingly entrusted with carrying out as they became familiar with the particular circumstances of the school. Practical teaching skills were seen as largely the product of trial and error experience once what was to be done was clear. As we have seen, however, moving to more school-based forms of training can involve radical changes in this approach. Where the move is related to a belief that students need direct and positive training in developing practical understanding, judgement and skills (at Level (a)), the demands are very specific for detailed, systematic training which can only be provided by teachers familiar with their own school context.

If taken seriously, this amounts to asking the teacher to devise a structured programme of training appropriate to the student and the school, to introduce the student progressively to the work of the programme, to analytically and critically observe the student's activities, to tutor the student effectively as the programme proceeds and to assess his or her competence in many different respects. If, in addition, teachers are being asked to undertake work at other levels of training, clearly the demands on them increase further. For example, if teachers are responsible for introducing students to a broad range of methods, syllabuses, materials and forms of assessment used in other schools so as to give them a wide and systematic range of practical understanding and skills, that is to ask teachers to undertake a quite new tutorial and training job; it involves work we have characterized as Level (b). Handing over to teachers progressively more of the responsibilities usually associated with the role of Curriculum Studies lecturers also, in effect, implies that they should engage in explicit concern for general principles of classroom teaching and critical examination of these at Levels (c) and (d). That task demands both *skills in the sophisticated analysis of teaching and skills in the training of students which are widely considered to form quite distinct areas of professional expertise*. The move, step by step, to making teachers progressively more responsible for the training in classroom teaching of critically reflective professionals, thus makes progressively more demands on them which, by virtue of their own professional training and experience as classroom teachers, they cannot be expected to fulfil.

It is clear from our investigation that, whatever the training institution may expect, Teacher Tutors are, in general, currently undertaking little more than supervision of a traditional kind. When asked to undertake more systematic practical training at Level (a) as appropriate to their own school circumstances, though many are very interested to do this, they are unlikely to embark on it in any detailed way without much joint work with lecturers on developing and implementing a training programme. In addition, teachers need to be given appropriate opportunities for professional development. That development needs to cover both the skills of the systematic and explicit analysis of practice, their own and others, and those of working with postgraduate students to extend their understanding, judgement and skills. With jointly planned programmes and with teachers with appropriate skills, the potential for the systematic training of students in their direct practical experience (Level (a)) by teachers is considerable.

Nevertheless, even with such training, we saw little indication that teachers, either working in schools as Teacher Tutors or taking part in Curriculum Studies seminars, are at present generally confident to engage in training at levels other than Level (a), unless they have undertaken relevant advanced study. As the overt analysis of practice in terms of principles and fundamental theory is not a regular activity of teachers in fulfilling their daily responsibilities, they are unlikely to be in a position to engage in analysing practice in terms of principles and theory (Levels (c) and (d)) without opportunities for quite substantial advanced study and training. It remains, however, the case that because they work so closely with students, Teacher Tutors alone are in a position to pursue regularly these higher levels of critical work directly in relation to students' own practice. If ways were found to engage them in Level (c) work in particular, a quite new sophistication of training could be opened up.

But, granted all the necessary professional development, Teacher Tutor responsibilities can only be satisfactorily carried out in close collaboration with training institution lecturers. If inter-related and over-lapping levels of training are to be carried out by both teachers and lecturers, sometimes working together in school or training institution, sometimes working quite separately, no coherent course can be developed or implemented without considerable and sustained collaboration between those directly involved in the work. The more complex the inter-relation of the elements of training in the course, the greater the importance of regular and detailed collaboration. Across all the courses we considered, the extent and detail of that collaboration between Teacher Tutors and lecturers was, at its best, adequate for that course's training pattern; more often, it was a cause for critical comment. For many complex, practical reasons, communication between the two parties can be difficult and the course pattern may really be too complex in its demands on collaboration for what is feasible in the circumstances. A lack of clarity in the precise definition of roles is also a recurring element in the picture we have formed. Somewhere, a balance has to be struck between an ideal of joint training and a practically effective structure. What that is, needs to be jointly agreed and worked out in detail.

The professional development for teachers required by their increasing involvement in school-based training is, of course, only possible if their school responsibilities allow them the necessary time. Once given these increased responsibilities, they also need the time to do the work with students. In addition, whatever those responsibilities are, there must be time for the proper collaboration between the teachers and lecturers which course planning and implementation demands. In the courses we considered, schools were given by the LEAs staffing allowances to help cover the demands on Teacher Tutors and other teachers for contact time with students in contributing to a school-based course. These varied from the equivalent of 0.015 to 0.2 teachers per student, but were not based on any detailed calculations of the time taken by teachers for their work with students. Even more significantly, resourcing in no way reflected the differing ranges of responsibility that teachers were given. As within any one pattern, the time devoted to training by Teacher Tutors and others was frequently left very much to individual teachers and frequently reflected their varying assessment as to what exactly was expected of them.

Given the variability of demands and commitments shown by individual Teacher Tutors, we were unable to form any valid, quantifiable measure of the time required for the execution of their role. However, we can report that only in the course where the funding was most generous (i.e. in Leeds with 0.2 teachers per student) was the degree of resourcing considered adequate by teachers, heads and college personnel. Perhaps, significantly, the most complaints about the difficulties imposed by limited resources were heard at Sussex where the demands on Teacher Tutors were greatest. *If Teacher Tutors and others in school are to carry out the new and increased responsibilities that such courses demand, then it is difficult to see how that can be achieved without adequate resourcing at this level.* This has implications both for LEAs and for individual schools in the distribution of any additional resourcing made available.

General Teacher Tutors

With the increased school basing of courses, and the development of more structured forms of training, has gone an increasing recognition of the need to train students in many matters of professional practice apart from those of classroom teaching. Certain courses, like Sussex, have, therefore, sought to include explicit attention to wider professional practice during students' school experience. As a result, an appropriate senior member of the school staff has planned the progressive involvement of students in all the relevant aspects of school life and has undertaken or organized their training in these areas, in tutorials and seminars. Clearly, such a training, as training in classroom practice, can be carried out at Level (a) or at more critical and reflective levels. But to undertake this work at whatever level involves a senior person accepting a training role not expected of schools in most traditional courses.

The more developed and structured the work, the more it requires capacities parallel to those outlined for Teacher Tutors. These range from the skills of analysing practice in terms of critical reflection on principles, to the skills of working with students. With the absence in many schools of people with these professional abilities, there is once more the need for professional development in this area to the extent that schools are to take on the responsibility. Moves in this direction also require the establishment of collaboration in planning and implementation with lecturers who undertake inter-related work in the training institution. Once more, all of this makes demands on time which needs to be realistically catered for if teachers are to be expected to undertake these responsibilities effectively.

Increased involvement of teachers in training activities has inevitably involved schools in the need for more careful consideration of policy and more management and control at a senior level. The forms of involvement of teachers with a course, the consequent deployment of staffing and resources, the impact of students and work with them both in the school as a whole and, in particular, on the education of pupils, all these are major matters of school policy. In schools where large numbers of students and often staff are regularly and irregularly in and out of the institution there are clearly not only policy but management matters to be handled. In addition, collaboration and liaison with a training institution on any scale clearly needs a senior member of staff who can act on the school's behalf. Many schools have, therefore, moved to designating a member of staff at deputy head level to take on the responsibility of overseeing this whole area of its work. In those schools in our study where these matters were not clearly in the hands of a specific senior teacher, problems of organization and collaboration constantly arose. Yet again the responsible teacher needs appropriate skills and time for the job.

The school and collaboration

In these major considerations for schools embarking on increased responsibilities in school-based training, we would finally stress the importance of considering the significance for the school as a whole of the extent of collaboration involved. For the work to be successful, there needs to be an appropriate level of collaboration with the training institution in the planning and implementation of the course. But the more elaborate the mutual involvement is to be and the greater the number of students, the more complex the organization required. For a small school, the demands of the necessary machinery for extensive collaboration can be very considerable. In a small primary school, it would seem only reasonable to limit the level of responsibility and to have only a small number of students. In a small school it may also prove too demanding to have students every year, even if the staff have developed all the necessary training skills. On the larger scale of a secondary school where, for major parts of their work, students are dispersed to different subject departments, the demands of greater responsibility and closer collaboration may be more readily justified. Within any one department, however, the significance of numbers obviously needs careful consideration. In coming to an agreement on the work to be undertaken it is surely necessary to remember that to pursue an ideal model that cannot be adequately realized may well not be to pursue the best in the given circumstances.

Training institutions

Curriculum lecturers

In this study we have sought to show that, in the PGCE courses considered, the increased school basing of training has opened up a number of important moves away from a traditional approach. Certain of these moves have important consequences for the work of lecturers in Curriculum Studies. First, the traditional aim of the 'preparation' of students in the training institution and the 'application' in school of what they have learnt has been replaced by seeking to develop a reflective practitioner capable of informed and critical judgements of some sophistication. With that, Curriculum lecturers have begun to move from the didactic presentation of teaching practices to analytical and reflective work on practice involving direct training in the processes of reflection. Secondly, the

consecutive pattern of courses, with students training first in the training institution and then engaging in practice in schools has given way to a more complex
pattern of block and serial school experiences, the latter permitting concurrent
training in the two institutions. With that, lecturers have increasingly begun to
structure their work more developmentally, linking course work with forms of
practical training. Thirdly, the separation of work taught in the training institution by lecturers and work taught in schools by teachers has given way to the
planned inter-relation of teaching by both groups, including, at times, joint
work with students. With that, lecturers have increasingly come to work in closer
collaboration with teachers in both planning and in carrying out their particular
contribution to the course.

But these changes have been seen to demand of lecturers the development of
new professional skills. Analytical training requires expertise in detailed and
systematic ways of analysing practice and of clarifying the principles on which it
is based. At a more abstract level, there is the need to undertake the thoroughgoing critical assessment of principles and the examination of these in the light
of work in foundation disciplines. Developmental training that concurrently
links work in schools and the training institution is a complex and difficult
matter which requires experiment in new forms of training and their evaluation.
Planning and implementing work jointly with teachers in a systematic and
sustained way involves quite new and demanding working relationships. What
exactly is being asked of lecturers depends on the particular way in which their
contribution and that of teachers fit together in any given course.

It is clear, however, that unless teachers are to have extensive in-service training and then considerable time to work with students, lecturers are likely to be
expected to retain full responsibility for student training at Levels (b), (c) and (d),
but using more analytical and reflective teaching styles. Their expertise has always
been at these levels, though the changes outlined make important new demands
on them. What is crucially important, however, in moving towards training a
reflective practitioner, is that the distinctive contribution to be made by lecturers
working at these levels be linked effectively with work at Level (a) which can, in
general, only be undertaken by teachers. If it is recognized, as our study indicates,
that only someone working in daily contact with a class is in a position to analyse
work there in the detail required for the systematic practical training of a student,
then that role at least must, in general, be accorded to teachers. It follows, too,
that the role of lecturers when working with students in school supervision, if it is
to be profitable, must have a related, yet different, function. That function we
suggest is to analyse students' own practice in more general terms that link it to
other forms of practice, considered at Level (b), thus illuminating students' work
from a wider context, and preparing the ground for considerations of principle at
Level (c) and fundamental theoretical analysis at Level (d). In this way the roles of
teachers and lecturers in supervision can be seen to be complementary, each bringing to the joint enterprise of training their own expertise.

Under very particular circumstances the work teachers do at Level (a) may, to some extent, be undertaken by lecturers, but that requires conditions that, in general, cannot be expected. It is normally quite impossible for them to have the detailed day to day knowledge and experience of classes required for Level (a) work by their students. For their supervision and other work, what lecturers require then is not current experience of teaching particular classes as if they were being equipped to do Level (a) work, but wide-ranging analytical experience of practice that is directed to elucidating matters of principle. Such analysis, if not to become detached from the terms of actual practice, needs, of course, to be developed from within practice itself by teachers and lecturers. *But that requires lecturers to be involved with practice not for the sake of the experience of teaching itself, but for quite specific analytical and reflective purposes.*

But if it is through their engaging in such analytical and critically reflective work that lecturers can be equipped for their distinctive contributions to training, it is also by these means that a body of research and enquiry directly concerned with practice can be built up. Sophisticated training at Levels (c) and (d) in Curriculum Studies requires what high quality classroom teaching itself requires – much more elucidation and critical examination of the principles of classroom teaching. At present there is a dearth of such well-founded work in most curriculum areas and it is to Curriculum lecturers we must look, working on the one hand with teachers and on the other with specialists in the foundation disciplines. If lecturers are to endeavour to produce much of this work, basic to developing more considered teaching in schools and to develop the new skills of employing this work in training students, very great demands are being placed on them.

If, with their distinctive contributions, work by lecturers and teachers is to be linked together so that students are trained in reflection on their own practices across the levels, then lecturers themselves must be able to tie in what they do at other levels with analysis of students' own practice at Level (a). It is, above all, the need for training in this form of reflection that makes it critical for a course to establish well-thought-out forms of collaboration between teachers and lecturers. As can be seen in the courses we studied, these arrangements can seek close integration of work at other levels with that at Level (a) by involving both teachers and lecturers in the joint or co-ordinated supervision of practice. The less lecturers are directly aware of students' experiences in schools, however, the more they are dependent on teachers and students for the links. Simply reporting school experience in workshops and classes provides a minimum link, but this demands the capacity to report adequately and in terms that can be used in analysis by the lecturer. More structured forms of analytical reporting can give focus to the work and can help co-ordinate the experiences of students in school with Curriculum Studies work in an ordered and developmental way. Detailed planning and co-ordination of the work of lecturers with that of teachers can, of course, go a considerable way to making the links effective.

But it would seem important here that lecturers recognize the demands of effectively obtaining and maintaining the collaboration that a particular pattern of training requires. For lecturers to seek to undertake regular school supervision of students may be quite unrealistic, and other forms of co-ordination or collaboration with teachers may produce more effective links. Competing claims on lecturers' time must once more be considered in moving towards any particular form of more school-based training.

In considering the consequences for Curriculum lecturers of moving away from a traditional form of training to more school-based forms, the implications for primary training are different in one major respect. In many primary courses one lecturer has the central role of drawing together the contribution to training of a range of distinct Curriculum Studies elements and relating this work with practice in schools. At Northampton, for example, the Course Director, in a regular 'Method' seminar, forged the links required in that course pattern. The relative brevity of particular Curriculum Studies elements within a primary course, and the large number of lecturers involved, make direct linkage with practice in each of these elements individually an extremely complex matter.

It would, however, seem important, if analytical and reflective training is to be developed, that the precise character of work in these elements be planned to contribute coherently to this end. Effective links between the different levels of training need establishing for these curriculum areas collectively, if not individually. In the absence of a lecturer with the responsibility for drawing together discrete Curriculum Studies contributions to primary training, it is difficult to see how effective links with students' own experience can be made. The problem of moving to analytical and reflective training overall becomes acute if, in addition, as in some institutions, contributing Curriculum lecturers have little or no direct knowledge of practice and its analysis at different levels. Didactic teaching of methods and principles of practice can, to some extent, be based on indirect knowledge. But to try to didactically train students to carry out analysis and reflect critically in ways that link to their own practice would seem likely to prove impossible. In these circumstances, moving to reflective training can be seen to make very considerable demands on the re-training of certain lecturers; re-training they may not be prepared to undertake if they have no substantial commitment to teacher training work.

Education lecturers

The move of courses to more school-based work can be seen to have certain implications for Education lecturers similar in part to those for Curriculum lecturers. In so far as school basing has led to the development of training for students in their professional responsibilities beyond the teaching of particular curriculum areas, Education lecturers have, for reasons in part historical, often found this work their responsibility. In traditional courses, Education lecturers have been responsible for work in the foundation disciplines. As developments in these disciplines have been largely on non-subject-specific topics, Education lecturers have usually seen themselves as contributing to students' training on general and wider professional matters, rather than on those distinctive of teaching particular curriculum areas. With no one else concerned explicitly with this wider area of training, they have progressively come to be seen as the focus for all work in this area.

By their training, however, Education lecturers are usually specialists in only one foundation discipline and, though thoroughly equipped to undertake training at Level (d) and related issues at Level (c) from this one perspective, they are not usually in a position to undertake this training from the point of view of other disciplines, nor are they likely to be knowledgeable enough about practice to be able to undertake 'indirect' practical training at Level (b). If in addition, training at these levels is to be linked to direct practical training at Level (a), then they are usually not in a position to contribute effectively in that way. If, then, students are to be trained across the inter-related levels in the areas of general and wider professional practices, many Education lecturers are unlikely, by virtue of their training and experience, to be able to do more than contribute to this in a limited way.

In most training institutions, including all four in our study, certain Education lecturers have progressively, and often of necessity, adapted to a new role provoked by this situation. They have, in effect, moved from traditional Education Studies work rooted in a single foundation discipline, to work paralleling that of a Curriculum Studies lecturer but concerned with areas of general and wider professional practice. If work in these areas is to be effective, however, this move needs to be undertaken thoroughly and sufficient time allocated to the task. The precise form of the work undertaken will, as in the case of Curriculum Studies, depend on the work in these areas undertaken at Level (a) by teachers. Clearly, lecturers moving over to this work need opportunities to acquire the knowledge and skill which reflective analysis across the levels requires. If the work is to be taught analytically and reflectively rather than didactically, they need to acquire new training skills. They need time to engage in relevant visits to schools for the supervision responsibilities it may require. They need time for the collaboration with teachers that is involved.

The re-casting of Education Studies in this way, however, raises a more fundamental question of course organization. If there are merely contingent reasons why the professional preparation of students in areas of general and wider practice has fallen to Education lecturers, other ways of organizing this work might be advantageous. Curriculum Studies could embrace more, if not all, of the work, with Curriculum lecturers extending the range of their professional concerns. Perhaps more adequately, a new cadre of lecturers could be recognized as having professional specialisms in areas of practice parallel to those of Curriculum lecturers but without links in any particular foundation discipline. Such lecturers, who might move over from either Curriculum or Education Studies, might then promote very directly research and enquiry into practice within their areas of specialism. They might be responsible for training students in wider professional studies, complementing Curriculum Studies work.

Any development of this kind, however, needs to face squarely the place in initial training that is seen for the foundation disciplines. In the four courses investigated, Education Studies, though accepting to some extent a training role across all levels in these wider professional areas, retained firm links with the foundation disciplines. In the absence of fundamental theoretical work in Curriculum Studies and limited work at Level (c) on principles, Education Studies provided the only significant work students undertook that involved sustained critical reflection. If, therefore, a course element of 'wider professional studies' is developed, it is important that its links with Level (a) through to work at Level (d) be planned with care. Without this, the present deficiencies of much Curriculum and Methods work might come to infect the whole training programme. Surely no course could claim to adequately prepare reflective practitioners which failed to develop a clear grasp of the critical importance for professional practice of work in the foundation disciplines.

The training institution and collaboration

In considering the implications for training institutions of more school-based work, we finally wish to comment on the question as to who should take responsibility for the design of the course and its implementation. In most traditional models, both the design and the implementation of the course were seen as finally the responsibility of the training institution. Not only was the course usually planned without consultation with co-operating schools, the approach of the course was essentially that the training institution 'prepared' students who then 'practised' what they had been prepared to do under the general supervision rather than training of the teachers involved.

The move to more school-based work, however, can be seen as in part a move to giving teachers much more responsibility in both the planning and implementation of the course. In so far as courses seek to be more firmly anchored in preparing students for contemporary practice in schools, teachers may be seen as more immediately up to date in their knowledge of what schools actually do. In so far as they alone can undertake detailed and systematic practical training of students at Level (a), teachers can be seen as necessarily having to take on responsibility for the implementation of that element of the course. But if practical training in schools is to involve lecturers as well as teachers and if school work is to be inter-related with what lecturers undertake elsewhere at other levels, then there must be shared responsibility, at least for close collaboration over relating what would otherwise become unco-ordinated training responsibilities.

All of the four courses studied, whatever the consultation procedures undertaken in the planning stages, were, in design, clearly the product of the training institution. That that should be so is in one sense only to be expected as they carried the formal responsibility for the course. Nevertheless, as courses are now developing, teachers are involved increasingly not only in consultative but also in decision taking processes. As most courses involve work with many schools and many teachers in general, overall planning can only involve them in a representative way in an appropriate professional committee. But by these means, they can play an important part in deciding the character, form and pattern of school involvememt in the total programme. Local Education Authorities and others whose schools will help to train students are now also included in such committees as they too have a proper role in these decisions. If, for instance, teachers are to be involved in extensive direct practical training of students at Level (a), particularly if this will involve them in prior in-service preparation and in detailed collaboration with lecturers during the course, the staffing implications can be considerable and LEAs need to be party to the decisions taken. In all four courses considered, the LEAs were so involved and agreed to resourcing arrangements for the schools.

At the level of the detail of the courses, those who are responsible for carrying out the training may or may not be given the responsibility for deciding what exactly shall be done. At Sussex teachers were fully entrusted with the decisions for determining all the extensive work undertaken by students in schools. For that arrangement to work effectively, if the practical training of the course at Level (a) is not to be dissociated from work at other levels undertaken by lecturers, important forms of collaboration between teachers and lecturers need to be established. Prior agreement about certain major features of the work by both parties needs to be reached and deliberate steps also need to be taken during the course to link together in a regular way what each party is doing when. Indeed, unless a lecturer can work with students in very few schools and with very few teachers, the degree of real linkage that can be effected is bound to be small.

Whatever the potential advantages there may be in devolving responsibility to teachers for areas of work they conduct, these must be balanced with the potential disadvantages of the separation in levels of work that is liable to result. In the three courses other than Sussex that we studied, the training institution retained a very much greater degree of control over the work students undertook in schools. As a result, in at least some areas of professional preparation they were able to relate very effectively work at different levels. At RIHE an Education lecturer based in each school could engage in the practical work of students alongside teachers and could integrate this directly with work in Education seminars. At Northampton lecturers were involved in constant visits and discussion with teachers, helping to determine students' practical training. They could then use their considerable knowledge of work done in schools within Method seminars in the training institution. At Leeds, accounts of structured activities in schools were used in Education Studies.

Full integration of work from Level (a) to Levels (c) and (d) is at present only possible by lecturers. To the extent that that is considered important, lecturers must themselves be directly involved in some way in the practical training of students in schools. In so far as linkage rather than integration of levels of work is important, the more lecturers retain responsibility and control in detail of some of the work in schools the easier that linkage is. The less they have responsibility and control of such work, the greater the importance of real collaboration in planning and implementation if the linkages are to mean anything. With so many students, schools and teachers for any one lecturer to work with, it is not surprising that in general full integration of levels of training is almost impossible to achieve. Nor is it surprising that lecturers' control of at least some areas of training in schools has strong attractions, particularly if it is done indirectly through structured activities.

If the detailed, regular and systematic practical training which can only be done by teachers is to be realized, and other levels of training are to be effectively linked to this, there would at present seem no way round the following forms of detailed collaboration between the lecturers and teachers who actually do the training. Collaboration:

in planning, so as to co-ordinate who intends to do what form of training and when

in establishing in that planning the precise links between students' individual practical training in school and other levels of work

in regular meetings to review what is actually being done and achieved by individual students as they proceed through the course.

Conclusion

The four courses we have studied have led to no simple conclusions about the precise place and form of school-based work a PGCE course should contain. What each course did in its own way was in fact to re-order the relationship that traditionally existed between teachers and lecturers, schools and training institutions. The introduction of serial alongside block experience had made possible concurrent or parallel as well as sequential training. In new roles, teachers and lecturers had begun to inter-relate their contributions to professional preparation as never before. But behind these practical changes were more fundamental changes in the very notion as to what professional training is all about.

By our analysis in terms of levels of work, we have endeavoured to illuminate the training process as it occurred in the various elements of each course, bringing out at each stage the significance of practical training and experience. In the light of what we have seen of work at these levels and of links established between them, we have become convinced of the value of a course that anchors all it does to students' own school experience. By that is meant, in part, that students should have substantial and systematic developmental training in practice itself. But they must also be directly trained to professionally analyse their own practice in critical reflection at each of a number of different levels. Not that all non-practical work must necessarily always be approached from personal experience. But whatever level of work is undertaken, students must be trained to use it in reflection on their own practice. *Whenever we came across elements of courses that forged such relations with practice we were impressed by their potential* even when they were not particularly well handled.

There are clearly many ways in which courses can be developed in terms of structure, personnel and pedagogy to move more toward this ideal. What we have sought to do is to highlight from our investigations the considerations that must be taken into account in bringing about these changes. What must surely be apparent is that changes towards this ideal are enormously demanding on all concerned. Above all, work of an inter-related, reflective kind, demands far more time than the more formal traditional approach. Time for students that a pressurized 36-week course cannot provide. Time for teachers and lecturers to work with students in practical, analytical and reflective modes and to work with each other in effective collaboration. Time, in the interim, for course development and the acquisition of new professional skills. But the benefits of every realistically planned step in this direction are hard to doubt. From the four courses we investigated, PGCE training appears on its way towards a fundamental transformation. With these and other experimental programmes behind us, what is needed now is the will and the resources to carry that transformation through.

8 Summary and Recommendations

Analysis

In our analysis of the principles of school-based training we found it of central importance to distinguish four distinct 'levels' or forms of training that these and all other such courses can be seen to employ. They were:

Level (a) Direct practice
Practical training through direct experience in schools and classrooms
Level (b) Indirect practice
'Detached' training in practical matters usually conducted in classes or workshops within training institutions
Level (c) Practical principles
Critical study of the principles of practice and their use
Level (d) Disciplinary theory
Critical study of practice and its principles in the light of fundamental theory and research.

In these terms the main differences between PGCE courses can be seen first in the *structure* of any given course which gives particular weighting to each of these levels of work and establishes a framework for relating them to each other. Secondly, it can be seen in the allocation of training at these levels to different *personnel*, teachers and lecturers who have different forms of expertise to contribute. Thirdly, it can be seen in the character of the *pedagogy* or style of the training that students actually receive.

Traditionally PGCE courses were designed in these three respects to prepare students in the training institutions with a 'detached' understanding of how best to work in schools, to give them practical experience in the skills of applying this understanding and then the oppportunity finally to reflect on the experience prior to their taking on the full responsibilities of a teaching job. To this end the most common course *structure* started with a term in the training institution devoted to work on 'indirect' practice, principles and theory at Levels (b), (c) and (d). There followed a term on block teaching practice in school devoted to work at Level (a) and finally a term back at the training institution working again at Levels (b), (c) and (d). As regards *personnel*, in the training institution, 'Methods', 'Curriculum' or 'Professional Studies' lecturers provided training at Levels (b) and (c), whilst Education lecturers coped with the fundamental theoretical matters of Level (d). In schools, teachers had a general supervisory rather than a training role, 'Methods', 'Curriculum' or 'Professional studies' lecturers doing all they could on regular visits to train students in applying what they had previously been taught. Thus, practical training at Level (a) was linked to work at Levels (b) and (c) as far as practically possible, while theoretical work at Level (d) remained a separate element. In keeping with this approach, the style of *pedagogy* of the training provided was largely didactic with lecturers presenting knowledge and understanding for students to master in traditional ways, followed by advice on its application in practice.

Using this analytical framework, the development of increased school basing of training can be seen as a progressive rejection of this traditional model. Instead of students being first independently prepared and then asked to apply their knowledge and understanding in schools, they are now increasingly being trained by direct involvement in the practical business of teaching, their understanding and skills being developed in structured analytical and critical reflection on their own and other people's practice. Behind this move has been a growing rejection, on both theoretical and practical grounds, of the idea that professional practice is to be understood as 'the application of theory' in favour of the view that it is a form of 'reflection-in-action'. If intelligent practice is not and cannot be adequately seen as a matter of 'application', training on that model is simply misconceived and can never develop first class practice. The four courses studied all showed in varying ways moves towards the training of reflective practitioners rather than of those seeking to apply theory. *In such a reflective approach students' direct practical training at Level (a) in the classroom and school is the heart of the matter. Other levels of training are used to develop increasingly more informed critical reflection and through that, progressively more effective professional practice.*

By an examination of the four levels of training outlined above and the relationships built between these in course structure, use of personnel and forms of pedagogy, we were able to analyse the character and significance of the school-based elements in the four courses. In particular those ways in which it was used to develop 'reflective practice' rather than 'the application of theory' became the object of attention. It was in these particular elements that we repeatedly saw the students' own very strong concern for direct practical help and training being used to develop not only basic classroom survival skills, but more considered and professionally well-grounded forms of practice. We came to appreciate how elements of training based on the inadequate traditional notion of practice as the 'application of theory' inevitably creates a psychological gap between theory and practice which no amount of practice can bridge. In contrast, elements of training based on the analysis of actual practice established no such gap and give theoretical work at Levels (b), (c) and (d) its proper professional significance. Students not surprisingly responded well to theoretical work encountered in this context, voicing their conviction of its importance. In terms of their performance in school as probationary teachers, students from all four experimental courses were generally considered by head teachers to be more professional than most of those entering teaching from other courses. Though students on all four courses had more extensive school experience than those on many other courses and this no doubt contributed to the confidence they showed, it is of note that it was in areas of work where they had had more reflective preparation that they felt themselves able to operate most successfully. Wherever we came across elements of the courses that trained students to critically reflect on their own practice we were impressed by their potential even when they were not particularly well handled and we therefore became convinced of the value of a course that anchors all it does to students' own school experience.

Implications for course structure, personnel and pedagogy

From our analysis of the four courses it is apparent that the approach to professional preparation set out above requires a course *structure* in which periods of regular practical experience and training at Level (a) are accompanied by periods of reflection at Levels (b), (c) and (d), with these so organized that work in these periods is both tightly interrelated and developmentally effective. The result in the four courses studied was an alternation of periods of 'serial practice', when students spent between one and three days a week in schools with the rest of the week in the training institutions, and periods of 'block practice' spent entirely in schools.

Within such a framework, this form of training demands that from the start students be involved in the practical details of teaching which they learn to analyse and assess. To this end the experienced teachers of those classes with which students are involved are at least in principle in the very best position to train them in the immediate practicalities and understanding of teaching those particular classes at Level (a). For the analytical and reflective work of students to progress beyond the severe limitations of Level (a) work in one context, however, they need to acquire a knowledge of other ways of teaching (at Level (b)) an understanding of general principles (at Level (c)) and their justification (at Level (d)). What is more, these other levels of training must be so linked to work at Level (a) that students are *trained to employ them in critical reflection on their own and other people's teaching and in the development of their own professional skills*. How far it is reasonable to expect practising teachers in schools to engage in these other levels of training is at present uncertain. Lecturers, by virtue of their appointments, can be expected to be expert in work at Levels (b), (c) and (d). The critical question for the management of the *personnel* in reflective teaching is how practical training at Level (a), which only teachers can effectively do in detail, is to be integrated with or tightly linked to training at Levels (b), (c) and (d) in which only lecturers can be expected to have sophisticated expertise. In the four courses studied the particular training roles undertaken by teachers and lecturers and their inter-relation in developing reflective practice by the students emerged as central to understanding both the kind of training offered and its effectiveness.

But granted an appropriate framework for the course and appropriate roles for teachers and lecturers according to their expertise, the character of the training students receive is also influenced by the forms of *pedagogy* they experience. If they are to develop practical judgement and skills they must do this through experiential learning – 'trial and error'. But if this process is to be seen as depending on the students' own developing 'critical reflection' rather than the direct 'application' of pre-determined ideas, students must be trained to analyse and reflect on specific practical situations themselves. While there might be some place for elements of didactic teaching about practice and principles at Levels (b), (c) and (d) within such a training, critical reflection itself being a skill or art must be developed by students' own activities of analysis and judgement. Students must thus be trained in the way they work at Levels (b), (c) and (d) in making their own informed and sensitive judgements about practice at Level (a) and in the light of that in developing their own practical professional skills. Even the didactic teaching of what 'reflective practice' requires and its 'application' is not to be confused with the development of students' own reflective practice. The four courses studied differed considerably in the ways in which they sought to develop directly both the analytical and reflective capacities of students across the different levels of work and their use of those capacities in the development of their own practical skills. Forms of direct analytical and reflective training must at present be seen as experimental. Yet the attention to such training and the forms it takes can be seen to determine very significantly the type and quality of professionalism that students develop.

Recommendations

We therefore recommend that those responsible for PGCE courses review them in the light of the analytical framework we have developed so that through course structure, personnel and pedagogy, training in reflective practice may be more consistently and effectively carried out. In particular we offer the following suggestions.

(i)   To provide the basic experience for reflective training, students should have school experience in which they observe and participate in all the central professional activities for which they are being prepared, both in the classroom and more widely in and out of school.

(ii) Such school experience should include at least observation and reflection on as wide a range of different forms of successful practice as is compatible with the sustained practice necessary for developing basic professional skills.

(iii) A pattern of 'serial' and 'block' practices should be devised for the progressive involvement of students in practice from the very start of the course. This should be supported by the concurrent development of analytical and reflective work on that practice until students are in a position to benefit from the intensive demands of 'block' practice. A minimum of two serial practices and one block practice using a total of at least two different schools is desirable.

(iv) As, in general, practising school teachers, not lecturers, are in the position to have the direct knowledge and experience of the classes with which students will be involved and alone are practically able to undertake the day to day training of students in this context, they should be given responsibility for the training of students in the immediate practicalities of reflective practice at Level (a). However, at present teachers' abilities to take responsibility for such training varies greatly. Where necessary, appropriate forms of in-service training should be established so that teachers have the necessary expertise to carry out such training in a systematic professional manner. Moreover, given that effective training at this level is demanding in terms of time, it is difficult to see how teachers' increased involvement can be achieved without adequate resourcing at this level. This has implications both for LEAs and for individual schools.

(v) Alongside such Level (a) training, students need an introduction to alternative forms of good practice presented in as concrete and practical a form as possible (e.g. using video and other materials) at Level (b). How far teachers are in a position to undertake such 'indirect' practical training at Level (b) is uncertain unless they are given special opportunities to acquire the necessary extensive knowledge of professional practice. Lecturers are more readily able to acquire that 'detached' knowledge of practice and to have the facilities to work with students at this level of training in training institutions. In most cases it would therefore seem sensible for lecturers to retain prime responsibility for training at this level.

(vi) To develop critical reflection, students need to be introduced to the analysis of the professional activities of the teachers with whom they work, of other forms of practice they encounter and of their own attempts at practice. This involves the elucidation of practical principles and the critical assessment of practice, i.e. training at Level (c). How far teachers are equipped to undertake explicit analytical and critical work in the light of practical principles and to train students in these matters at Level (c) varies greatly. Without such expertise the practical Level (a) work which teachers undertake with students will be limited in character and concerned only with immediate practicalities. We suggest therefore that all teachers working with students should have the opportunity, through some form of in-service training, to develop the explicit use of the necessary analytical and critical skills of working with students at Level (c), at least in relation to their own practice and that of the student.

(vii) In so far as teachers do not undertake Level (c) work in relation to students' own practice, then lecturers must take on that responsibility. To do this in detail is practically almost unworkable as it would demand that lecturers spend very considerable time in schools working with individual students. The more teachers can undertake this responsibility the more readily lecturers can undertake more wide-ranging Level (c) work while linking this in appropriate ways to students' own experience at Level (a). To this end lecturers must undertake some work with students in schools at Level (a) and that in conjunction with the teachers having similar responsibility. Without this involvement and the closest collaboration between teachers and lecturers in relating their distinctive contributions to critical reflection on students' own practice, coherent training is not possible.

(viii) Training at Level (d), concerned with the critical study of practice and principles in the light of fundamental theory and research, can in general only be carried out by lecturers. To develop this work in appropriate relation to the other levels of training requires its incorporation in the analysis and critical assessment of practice undertaken by lecturers familiar with students' school experience.

(ix) Developing adequate links between the practical training of students at Level (a) and their training at other levels demands the detailed definition of the interlocking roles of teachers and lecturers in promoting students' reflection on their own practice. As lecturers can spend only limited time in school with any one student, explicit means must be adopted for lecturers to be able to relate their work to students' experience in schools. We suggest much fuller experiment with the following initiatives we encountered: IT-INSET activities, teaching in schools and seminars undertaken jointly by students, lecturers and teachers working together, the attachment of lecturers to larger schools for regular work with teachers and students.

(x) Training in reflective practice requires that students be introduced in a developmental way to the compexities of teaching situations, starting with those simple situations which they can more readily be expected to deal with adequately. Progression in the handling of ever more difficult content, in using different teaching styles, from work with individuals, to groups, to whole classes, from joint teaching and part-lesson teaching to full-lesson responsibility over a period, enables students both to understand more clearly the demands of teaching and to develop systematically the more difficult practical skills required. Courses therefore need to be planned so as to co-ordinate work in schools and in the training institutions within an agreed developmental structure.

(xi)   Work of the character here advocated demands detailed collaboration at the level of individual teachers and lecturers. It demands considerable professional expertise in training on the part of the teachers involved and time for the job. For the central activities of training, institutions will therefore need to work very closely with a relatively small number of schools where appropriate staffing and facilities exist.

(xii)   Within such collaboration new elements of course structure, use of personel and styles of pedagogy need developing. The four courses studied have shown, in various initiatives, ways in which training can become much more professionally adequate. What is now required is the will and the resourcing for both training institutions and their associated schools to develop their work systematically along the lines here proposed.

Appendix: Research Design and Methodology

The research paradigm

Educational evaluations are frequently located in one of two competing paradigms: the psycho-statistical approach with its origins in the natural sciences, and the case study approach with its roots in certain of the human sciences. Historically, the psycho-statistical paradigm, with an emphasis on the 'products' of educational innovations, has predominated. Having first identified teaching intentions in terms of measurable end products, the evaluator in this tradition is concerned to determine how effectively these products have been realized. In the context of this research task this might therefore have involved first defining, in some measurable way, the characteristics of a well-trained teacher (e.g. ability in classroom control, effectiveness in the teaching of reading) and then comparing the four experimental courses on their achievement in relation to these objectives. The measured outcomes of the four school-based courses could then have been compared with the outcomes of more traditional courses used as a 'control'.

However, such a model of evaluation seemed inappropriate in relation to the research brief for a number of reasons:

(i)   Direct comparison between the four courses would have been difficult. Two of the courses were secondary and two primary; the primary courses addressed different age ranges while the two secondary courses prepared students in different subject areas. In addition, each course varied considerably in its approach to school-based work. For example, the amount of time students spent in school varied from one to three days and quite different arrangements for the involvement of teachers and lecturers were made.

(ii) The research brief from the DES suggested that the team should document the experience of no more than 20 students from each course. Such small numbers from radically different courses would have made statistical analysis quite inappropriate.

(iii) Whatever the size of the sample, a more fundamental problem was that there is little agreement within the profession as to the precise characteristics of a good teacher except at the level of simple identifiable skills. Given that the graduates from these four courses would each be working in a different school, measuring such characteristics in any meaningful way would present even more intractable problem.

(iv) Even if certain characteristics could be isolated for measurement, research experience indicates clearly that it would have been almost impossible to disentangle, in a statistical way, specific factors critical to their development. In particular, it would have been impossible to distinguish the detailed significance of work that was school-based as opposed to learning that took place elsewhere.

Any complex educational innovation suffers similar problems of definition and measurement and it is therefore not surprising that despite its initial appeal, the psycho-statistical model of evaluation has been subject to considerable criticism in recent years. Our purpose, however, is not to enter into such a debate here, simply to suggest that as a research approach, it was inappropriate to the nature of the subject matter and the research brief. Exploring the nature and significance of school-based elements of training in the four courses, and their implications for the work of a small group of probationers who graduated from each of them, seemed to demand a different methodology.

The approach to evaluation adopted was more in keeping with the case study model and as such had a number of distinguishing features in common with evaluations of this character:

Multiple-perspectives   Central to an evaluation of this kind are the perspectives of participants on intentions, practices and outcomes. The intentions of teachers, lecturers, LEA administrators, advisers and students were therefore systematically investigated and related to what actually happened within any one programme. The notion of 'outcomes' was broadly conceived and while students' learning achievements were clearly central, other consequences for all those involved were also of major importance. These included issues such as the impact of a programme on a school or training institution as a whole, the demand for resources, the need for training both for teachers and lecturers.

Multiple-audiences   In carrying out a study of this nature it is essential that the work should be focused on the interests of the target groups for whom the evaluation is being conducted. In our case these were primarily: staff of training institutions charged wih translating such policies into practice; school personnel who might perhaps in the future become increasingly involved in the professional preparation of students teachers; students themselves; LEA officials on whom it falls to build upon initial training by means of induction and in-service programmes; policy makers at national and local level with responsibility for shaping PGCE training in the future. Such diverse audiences brought different lists of priorities with regard to questions to be considered. These different questions were used to help structure the agenda of issues to be pursued within the evaluation.

Progressive focusing and contextualizing   Although deliberately starting in an open-ended, consultative fashion, it is intended that in research of this character, questioning becomes progressively more focused throughout the fieldwork and this is the procedure that was adopted. By working in this way, critical objectives, processes and achievements were clarified and refined. At the same time there was a continuing exploration and documentation of the personal and institutional contexts in which the four courses operated.

Research design and procedure

The research brief necessitated the establishment of two separate, but interrelated studies; in 1983/84 case study evaluations of the four experimental courses, in 1984/85 the 'probationary year' study. Although pursued within a common research paradigm, these two sub-studies necessitated different research designs and data gathering procedures. Each will be summarized in turn.

Studying the four courses

As was noted in Chapter 1, the four PGCE courses to be investigated were identified by the DES prior to the involvement of the research team. The brief for the team during the academic year 1983/84 was to make a study of these four training courses and monitor the experiences of 15 to 20 students from each. However, in developing a research design the first important decisions to be made in each institution concerned the schools and students selected to participate in the experimental programme. In two of the institutions (Northampton and Leeds) the designated courses had an intake of 22 and 14 students respectively. In each case the team were therefore able to work with the full course. The Northampton course worked closely with five lower primary and first schools. In Leeds, six primary and middle schools were involved. In both cases, significant changes were established in the courses prior to and during the year of the evaluation in order to increase the school-based nature of the training.

The situation in the two secondary courses was different as the courses were much larger. At RIHE course leaders decided to establish an 'experimental' school-based course for a group of 23 of their 100 secondary PGCE students. The course was based upon three local schools. Although RIHE had worked closely with these and other schools in the past, the experimental course was new in certain important respects. The training received by the 23 students on this experimental course which became the focus of the research therefore differed significantly from that which the main body of students followed.

The situation at Sussex was different yet again. Here a school-based course had been established some 18 years. The secondary PGCE intake was allocated throughout 10–12 schools in East and West Sussex and selection on some basis was necessary. As was noted above, an essential element for all four courses was that additional funding would be made available by the LEA to assist schools in collaborating with the training institutions. In the event only East Sussex felt able to provide additional funding. This removed schools in West Sussex – which the University continued to use – from the research team's consideration. Representatives of East Sussex and the University agreed that resourcing should be channelled into two schools nominated by the University. These subsequently became the schools which the research team worked in. Between them these two schools accepted 18 students. The training offered to these 18 students was, in principle, the same as that experienced by the remainder of the Sussex Secondary PGCE students. For the purposes of the evaluation the pattern of the course changed very little from that which had been established for several years.

The 'population' to be researched in the first half of the project, therefore, included the four training institutions, a total of 16 schools with which these courses were closely associated (in one course, Northampton, 40 additional schools were used for teaching practice purposes) and a total of 75 students.

The training institutions, their associated schools and the number of students attached to them in 1983/84 are set out in Table I.

Methods

While it was essential for the research team to gain an overview of the four training courses as put into practice in 16 schools and across a range of subjects, it was also clear from the start that a more detailed analysis would be necessary if the requirements of the case study approach were to be fulfilled. As a result, two distinct but interrelated methods were used in data gathering. These were (i) a survey of the whole cohort of students using questionnaires, logs and written reports and (ii) a more in-depth study based on interviews, observations and diaries of the experiences of a sub-sample of students and the professionals with whom they worked.

(i) The survey

During the first year of the study all 75 students were asked to complete two major questionnaires – one at the beginning and one at the end of their training. The purpose of these questionnaires was to assemble background data on each student (educational qualifications, reasons for choosing a school-based course

Table I
The training institutions, their associated schools and the number of students attached to them in 1983/84.

Northampton	
Schools	No. of Students
A (Lower)	6 (one withdrew)
B (Primary)	6 (one withdrew)
C (Lower)	6
D (Lower)	2
E (Lower)	2
	22

Leeds	
Schools	No. of Students
F (Middle)	3
G (Primary)	2
H (Primary)	2
I (Primary)	2
J (Middle)	2
K (Middle)	3
	14

Sussex	
Schools	No. of Students
L	12
M	6
	18

RIHE	
Schools	No. of Students
N	8 (one withdrew)
O	8 (one withdrew)
P	5 (one withdrew)
	21

Overall total – 75 students of whom 5 subsequently withdrew.

etc.) and to document their assessments of specific aspects of the training they were offered. A critical feature of the questionnaire at the end of the course was a series of self-assessment items covering basic and more advanced teaching skills similar to that used in the HMI survey *The New Teacher in School* (DES 1982) The response rates for the first and second questionnaires were 97 per cent and 96 per cent respectively.

In addition to these questionnaires, all students, lecturers and teachers associated with the courses completed 'time logs' which covered selected days of school-based practice in the Autumn term. The objective here was to provide a review of the activities undertaken by each participant. Finally termly written reports on the progress of each student were made out by both teachers and lecturers.

The limited data developed by the above means in relation to the whole research population was essentially 'secondary'; it formed a background for a much more detailed examination that was made of the training experiences of a sub-sample of 38 students. This sub-sample of students and the teachers and lecturers with whom they worked became the main focus of the second part of the research – the in-depth study.

(ii) The in-depth study

Selecting the sub-sample   The decision as to how many students, schools and subject areas would be studied in depth was determined by the degree of detail required if the training of students was to be adequately explored and by the resources available to the research team. Within the staffing and budgetary constraints of the project it was decided that only two schools and approximately eight students from each course could be investigated in the fullest detail. The sampling frame for the selection of students per course was a complex one for it was considered that the critical variables to be investigated were not the characteristics of the students (age, sex, qualifications) but rather the type of training provided. The structure and organization of each course demanded that different decisions be made in each case. In some cases, systematic selection on a variety of inter-related criteria was possible (e.g. matched subject specialisms for secondary students; urban and rural schools); in others choices were more tightly constrained.

In the event 38 students were selected. Each of the students chosen worked closely with a network of teachers and tutors and these professionals formed the basis for the in-depth study. The student sub-samples in each of the four courses are set out in Table II.

Fieldwork procedures in the in-depth study   The primary strategy for exploring the four courses was to take the sub-sample of students from each as a focus and explore their work within the training institution and the school. The main techniques of data gathering were semi-structured interviews coupled with observation in selected key sites within schools and colleges. Throughout the year, interviews were conducted with four principal groups of respondents; teachers, lecturers, students and LEA officials. Some observation, both in the classroom and in tutorials and seminars, was also conducted. It was not, however, always possible to time visits to coincide with particular topics. Observation was therefore seen as illustrative of parts of a process rather than a study of the substantive content of each course. As such it provided a basis for focused discussion about certain of the objectives held by tutors and teachers – as well as some degrees of validation of their stated claims.

During the first term, a great deal of research time was necessarily devoted to introducing the project and establishing sound relations with respondents. Towards the end of the first term, however, a tentative model for analysing the four courses was proposed. (This model was later substantially revised and extended and is presented in Chapter 4.) Nevertheless, as a result of our initial analysis it was decided that a more detailed review of the way in which the different professionals associated with each training programme actually operated was essential. [1]

Of particular interest was the nature of the work they undertook directly with students while in school. Consequently during the second term, in addition to the detailed descriptive work, the team opted to focus on specific interactions involving teachers, lecturers and students. A number of 'triangulations' were conducted whereby the researcher first observed a student teach, then observed a teacher or lecturer discussing that teaching with the student and subsequently explored with the respective parties what they perceived the intentions behind this discussion were, and what they considered had been achieved. In this way it was not only possible to record the trainer's objectives, but also to have an independent record of the nature of the interaction as well as comments from students as to what they considered they had learnt. Predictably timetabling such triangulations proved extremely difficult given the other demands on the research workers and on school and college personnel. A more or less full record was achieved on 25 occasions however, thereby providing examples of the working process of both teachers and lecturers in each course.

In all a total of 89 formal interviews were conducted with College and University staff, 123 with school teachers and head teachers, 91 with students and 8 with LEA officials. On average these interviews lasted from 45-60 minutes each. Sixty-one school-based and 39 College or University-based 'training sessions' were formally observed. These sessions varied substantially in length from 20 minutes to three hours.

Table II
Student sub-samples in each of the four courses

	Student	Sex	Age at 1/10/83	First Degree
Northampton				
School B	1	f	21	Music
	2	f	29	English, Art, Drama
	3	f	21	Geography
	4	f	22	Music, English, Social Studies
School C	5	f	22	Politics and History
	6	f	36	Mathematics and Biology
	7	f	32	Earth Science, Env. Biology and Mathematics
	8	m	24	Politics and Economics
Leeds				
School H	20	f	21	History
	21	f	22	English
	22	f	21	English
	23	f	21	English
School J	24	f	22	Home Economics
	25	f	24	Social Science and R.E.
	26	m	21	Land Management
	27	f	22	Psychology
Sussex				
School L	40	f	23	English
	41	m	25	English
	42	m	31	History
	43	m	22	Mathematics
	44	f	22	Mathematics
	45	f	22	History
School M	46	m	21	Mathematics
	47	m	21	Geography
	48	m	23	Geography
	49	f	20	Mathematics
	50	f	40	English
	51	f	43	English

Table II—*continued*

	Student	Sex	Age at 1/10/83	First Degree
RIHE				
School N	60	f	24	English
	61	m	27	Music
	62	f	21	Biology
	63	m	27	Chemistry
	64	m	22	English
School O	65	f	21	English
	66	f	21	Biology
	67	f	40	Chemistry
	68	f	23	English
	69	f	22	Music

The probationary year study

In the second part of the project, the probationary year study, the brief was to follow up those students from the original cohort who had obtained posts. Of the 75 students commencing training in the 4 courses, a total of 67 successfully completed their PGCE of which 60 took up teaching posts in the UK in September 1984 (one subsequently resigned). This group of 59 probationers and the schools in which they worked, formed the basis of the probationary year study. (Further details of the 'destination' of the students from the four courses are provided in Table III.)

The objective of the probationary year study was to explore, as far as was possible, links between school-based aspects of probationers' training and their current teaching competence. Given that these probationers had graduated from four very different courses and were now teaching in 59 different schools, this was a complex task. Most of the probationers' new colleagues (heads, other teachers, LEA officials), had little or no knowledge about the nature of the training the probationers had undergone. Their ability to disentangle the strengths and weaknesses of a particular probationer's performance and relate this to the specific nature of that young teacher's training was therefore limited. They could, however, comment on the probationer's general performance, highlighting specific strengths and weaknesses. However, even here there were difficulties in that it was not possible to assess the basis of their judgements. Moreover, many heads and teachers, particularly those in primary schools, had only limited experience of probationers on which to draw in making their comparative judgements. Nevertheless, the opinions of fellow professionals on the probationers' competence remained one important source of data.

Table III
Destination of students

Training Institution	N. students commencing course	N. students completing course	N. students obtaining teaching posts 1/9/84	N. students working outside age range trained for
Northampton	22	18	18	–
Leeds	14	14	13 (one had post from 1/1/86)	2 (in comprehensives)
Sussex	18	18	16	2 (in F.E.)
RIHE	21	17	13 (one resigned after one week)	–
TOTAL	75	67	60	4

The second source of information was the students themselves. They too were able to comment on their development throughout the year and their strengths and weaknesses in relation to the tasks that faced them. Moreover, they, more than anyone else, were in a position to assess the links between their current competence and specific aspects of their training. The opinions and self-assessments of students as they developed throughout the year were therefore of major importance. However, it must be accepted that such data is also problematic; self-assessments are not necessarily reliable. Moreover, participants in a training scheme are not always fully aware of what specific aspects of their training were critical. Probationers, with their limited professional experience, may have only a partial grasp of their current performance and its relationship with the training they received.

In view of these difficulties, the data in relation to the probationary year study linking probationers' performance to training can only be seen as suggestive. Assessments of individual performances were made by probationers themselves, and by their new colleagues. In addition, probationers pointed to links between their performance and their training. From what was discovered about their training, it was also possible for the research team to highlight other links of which the probationers were not necessarily aware. However, it must be accepted that any such links can only be tentatively made.

Research design

In keeping with the mode of inquiry adopted in the first year of the study, a two-pronged methodology was adopted including: (i) a general survey of the whole cohort by means of questionnaires and reports and (ii) an in-depth investigation of a sub-sample of probationers based on interviews, observations and diaries.

(i) Survey of the whole cohort

All 59 probationers who were teaching in the United Kingdom were asked to complete two questionnaires during the year; the first after six weeks of teaching and the second at the end of the year.[2] The purpose of these questionnaires was to obtain basic factual information concerning the schools probationers were working in, the nature of their teaching and what induction was being provided in school and by the LEA. In addition, the questionnaires sought to explore specific aspects of their teaching role in more detail and to assess their present experience in the light of their training. Once again a battery of self-assessments on basic and advanced teaching skills similar to those completed at the end of the training course was included. A response rate of 83 per cent was achieved for the first questionnaire and 73 per cent for the second.

In addition to the questionnaires, probationers were asked to keep a diary of the first four weeks of their teaching. The diary was primarily unstructured although a list of topics on which comment might be made was included. At the end of the year all LEAs were asked to submit copies of their assessments of the probationers to the research team. The response rate to this request was 77 per cent. However, in a number of cases, only very brief statements were returned.

(ii) In-depth case studies

Seventeen out of the 59 probationers teaching in the United Kingdom were followed up in detail. Four representatives from each course were chosen, together with a fifth probationer from one of the secondary courses in order to provide a representative in Science. Once again, in determining the sample of probationers, a range of criteria were applied so as to select an adequate cross-section of the population. Full details of the sub-sample of probationers selected for the in-depth study are set out in Table IV.

Fieldwork Each of the 17 probationers within the sub-sample was visited termly during the academic year. The first visits were undertaken during the period late October/early November. Subsequent visits took place in February/March and May/June. The initial visits served two main purposes. First, to introduce the project to the schools involved and to establish relationships with

Table IV
The sub-sample of probationers 1984/85

	Student	Sex	Age at 1/10/83	First Degree	School type
Northampton	5	f	22	Politics and History	Nursery
	9	f	26	Social Science	Lower School
	10	m	24	Land Management	Infant
	11	f	22	Dance & Drama	Nursery
Leeds	20	f	21	History	Infant
	21	f	21	English	First
	27	f	22	Psychology	Comprehensive
	28	m	22	Geography	Primary
Sussex	43	m	22	Mathematics	Comprehensive
	45	f	22	History	Comprehensive
	47	m	21	Geography	Comprehensive
	51	f	43	English	Comprehensive
	52	m	24	Physics	Comprehensive
RIHE	70	m	26	Mathematics (resigned, replaced by 74)	Comprehensive
	71	f	23	English	Comprehensive
	72	f	48	Music	Comprehensive (part time)
	73	f	21	R.E.	Comprehensive
	74	m	23	Mathematics	Comprehensive

key personnel. Secondly, to commence actual data gathering focusing specifically on the probationers' experiences over the first half of the Autumn term. During the one day visits, the research worker interviewed the probationer, the Head of the school and at least one other teacher with formal responsibility for the new-comer (Head of Department, Staff Tutor etc.). On subsequent visits, the researchers interviewed the probationers, members of staff responsible for them and any LEA officials who had had personal contact with the probationers. (In fact not all probationers were visited by someone representing the LEA, 5 of the 17 having had no contact of this sort.) In total 160 interviews were conducted in connection with the follow up of the 17 probationers.

Notes

1. Our objective was to disentangle the variety of different 'levels' of training (see Chapter 4) which different professionals provided.
2. In developing the first questionnaire the team drew extensively on information derived from topics and issues which had been explored with students during their training. In addition, reference was made to instruments developed by other researchers who had studied probationary teachers, notably Taylor and Dale (1971), SPITE Report (1982) and DES (1982).

References

Alexander, R. (1984), 'Innovation and Continuity in the Initial Teacher Education Curriculum' in R. Alexander, M. Craft and J. Lynch (eds), *Change in Teacher Education; Context and Provision Since Robbins*. Holt, Rinehart and Winston.

Alexander, R. and Whittaker, J. (eds) (1980), *Developments in PGCE Courses*. Society for Research in Higher Education.

Alexander, R. and Wormald, E. (eds) (1979), *Professional Studies in Teaching*. Society for Research in Higher Education.

Ashton, P.M.E. (1983), 'Teacher Education for Cooperative Curriculum Review'. *Forum*, Vol. 26 No. 1.

Ashton, P.M.E., Henderson E.S., Merritt, J.E. and Mortimer D.J. (1982), *Teacher Education in the Classroom*. Croom Helm.

Bell, A. (1981), 'Structure, Knowledge and Social Relationships in Teacher Education', *British Journal of Sociology of Education*, Vol. 2 No. 1.

Bernstein, B. (1971), 'On the Classification and Framing of Educational Knowledge' in M.F.D. Young, (ed.), *Knowledge and Control*. Macmillan.

Carr, W. and Kemmis, S. (1983), *Becoming Critical: Knowing through Action Research*. Deakin University Press.

Cockcroft (1982), *Report of the Committee of Inquiry into the Teaching of Mathematics in School (The Cockcroft Report)*. H.M.S.O.

Council for National Academic Awards (1982), *The Content of Initial Training Courses for Teachers: C.N.A.A. Response*. C.N.A.A.

Council for National Academic Awards (1983), *Teaching in Schools; The Content of Initial Training. Council's Response to H.M.I. Discussion Paper*. C.N.A.A.

Crompton, J. (1977), 'Student Expectations and the PGCE.', *British Journal of Teacher Education*, Vol. 3. No. 1.

Dearden, R.F. (1980), 'Theory and Practice in Education' in *Journal of Philosophy of Education*, Vol. 14 No. 1

Densmore, K. (1987), 'Professionalism, Proletarianisation and Teacher Work' in Popkewitz (1987a).

Department of Education and Science (1973), *Circular 7/73; The Development of Higher Education in the Non-University Sector.* D.E.S.

Department of Education and Science (1979), *Development of B.Ed Degree Courses; A Study Based on 15 Institutions.* D.E.S.

Department of Education and Science (1980), *PGCE in the Public Sector.* D.E.S./H.M.S.O.

Department of Education and Science (1981), *Teacher Training and the Secondary School.* D.E.S./H.M.S.O.

Department of Education and Science (1982), *The New Teacher in School.* D.E.S./H.M.S.O.

Department of Education and Science (1983), *White Paper; Teaching Quality.* Cmnd 8836. H.M.S.O.

Department of Education and Science (1984), *Circular 3/84; Initial Teacher Training: Approval of Courses.* D.E.S.

Department of Education and Science (1987), *Quality in Schools: The Initial Training of Teachers.* D.E.S./H.M.S.O.

Elliott, J. (1985), 'Educational Action Research' in J. Nisbet (ed.), *World Yearbook of Education Research 1985: Research Policy and Practice.* Kegan Page.

Elliott, J. (1987), 'Educational Theory, Practical Philosophy and Action Research' *British Journal of Educational Studies*, Vol. XXXV No. 2.

Ginsberg, M. (1987), 'Reproduction, Contradiction and Conceptions of Professionalism; The Case of Pre-service Teachers' in Popkewitz (1987a).

Glaser, B. and Strauss, A. (1967), *The Discovery of Grounded Theory.* Aldine.

Handal G. and Lauvas, P. (1987), *Promoting Reflective Teaching.* Society for Research in Higher Education.

Hartnett, A, and Naish, M. (1986), *Education and Society Today.* Falmer Press.

Hirst, P.H. (1966), 'Educational Theory' in J. Tibble (ed.), *The Study of Education.* Routledge and Kegan Paul.

Hirst, P.H. (1979), 'Professional Studies in Initial Teacher Education: Some Conceptual Issues' in Alexander and Wormald (1979).

Hirst, P.H. (1983), 'Educational Theory' in P.H. Hirst (ed.), *Educational Theory and its Foundation Disciplines.* Routledge and Kegan Paul.

James (1972), *Teacher Education and Training (The James Report).* H.M.S.O.

Jonathan, R. (1986), 'Education and "The Needs of Society" ' in Hartnett and Naish (1986).

Kerr, E. (1985), 'Principles and Practice of Validation' in M. Raggett and M. Clarkson (eds), *Changing Patterns of Teacher Education.* Falmer Press.

Lacey, C., Hoard, P. and Horton, M. (1973), *The Tutorial Schools Research Project 1964–73.* S.S.R.C.

McCulloch, M. (1979), *School Experience in Initial BEd/BEd Honours Degrees Validated by the Council for National Academic Awards.* C.N.A.A.

McNair, A. (1944), *Teachers and Youth Leaders (The McNair Report)*. H.M.S.O.

McNamara, D.R. and Ross, A.M. (1982), *The BEd Degree and its Future*. University of Lancaster.

Mills, C.W. (1959), *The Sociological Imagination*. O.U.P.

Mitchell, P. (1985), *Education Theory and the Training of Teachers*. Unpublished U.C.E.T. Conference Paper.

National Union of Teachers (1969), *The Future of Teacher Education*. N.U.T.

National Union of Teachers (1971), *The Reform of Teacher Education; A Policy Statement*. N.U.T.

Patrick H., Bernbaum, G. and Reid, K. (1982), *The Structure and Process of Initial Teacher Education Within Universities in England and Wales (The SPITE Report)*. University of Leicester School of Education.

Peters, R.S. (1976), *Education and the Education of Teachers*. Routledge and Kegan Paul.

Pollard, A. and Tann, S. (1987), *Reflective Teaching in the Primary School*. Cassell.

Popkewitz, T.S. (1987a) (ed.), *Critical Studies in Teacher Education; Its Folklore, Theory and Practice*. Falmer Press.

Popkewitz, T.S. (1987b), 'Ideology and Social Formation in Teacher Education', in Popkewitz (1987a).

Robbins (1963), *Higher Education (The Robbins Report)*. H.M.S.O.

SPITE Report (1982). See Patrick *et al.* (1982).

Schön, D. (1983), *The Reflective Practitioner*. Temple Smith.

Taylor, J.K. and Dale, I.R. (1971), *A Survey of Teachers in their First Years in Service*. Bristol University.

Universities Council for the Education of Teachers (1979), *The P.G.C.E. and the Training of Specialist Teachers for Secondary Schools*. U.C.E.T.

Universities Council for the Education of Teachers (1982), *Post Graduate Certificate in Education Courses for Teachers in Primary and Middle Schools*. U.C.E.T.

University Grants Committee/Council for National Academic Awards (1973), *A New B.Ed Degree*. C.N.A.A.

Weber, M. (1948), *From Max Weber, Essays in Sociology*. Translated and Edited by H.H. Gerth and C.W. Mills. Routledge and Kegan Paul.

Whitty, G., Barton, L. and Pollard A. (1987), 'Ideology and Control in Teacher Education' in Popkewitz (1987a).

Wilkin, M. (1987), 'The Sociology of Education and the Theory – Practice Relationship in Teacher Training' in P. Woods and A. Pollard (eds), *Sociology and the Teacher*. Croom Helm.

Wilson, J. (1975), *Educational Theory and the Preparation of Teachers*. N.F.E.R.

Zeichner, K. (1981/2), 'Reflective Teaching and Field-based Experience in Teacher Education', *Interchange* Vol. 12, No. 4.

Index